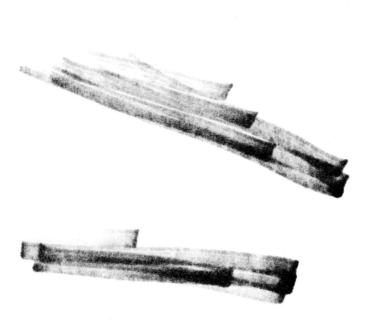

Beyond TQM

'There are so many right answers.'
Corporate Training Manager, Malaysian Airline System,
in conversation with the author

Beyond TQM

ROBERT LOUIS FLOOD
Department of Management Systems and Sciences,
University of Hull, UK

JOHN WILEY & SONS
Chichester · New York · Brisbane · Toronto · Singapore

Other Wiley Editorial Offices

John Wiley & Sons, Inc., 605 Third Avenue,
New York, NY 10158-0012, USA

Jacaranda Wiley Ltd, G.P.O. Box 859, Brisbane,
Queensland 4001, Australia

John Wiley & Sons (Canada) Ltd, 22 Worcester Road,
Rexdale, Ontario M9W 1L1, Canada

John Wiley & Sons (SEA) Pte Ltd, 37 Jalan Pemimpin #05-04,
Block B, Union Industrial Building, Singapore 2057

Library of Congress Cataloging-in-Publication Data

Flood, Robert L.
    Beyond TQM / Robert Louis Flood.
      p. cm.
    Includes bibliographical references and index.
    ISBN 0-471-93967-6 (cased)
    1. Total quality management. 2. Total quality management—Case
studies. I. Title.
HD62.15.F58   1993   93–12004
658.5′62—dc20   CIP

British Library Cataloguing in Publication Data

A catalogue record for this book is available from the British Library

ISBN 0-471-93967-6

Typeset in 11/13 pt Palatino from author's disks by
Dobbie Typesetting Limited, Tavistock, Devon.
Printed and bound in Great Britain by Bookcraft (Bath) Ltd.

*This book is dedicated to my father, Louis,
and to my mother, Marjorie*

Contents

PART 2. A NEW UNDERSTANDING OF MANAGEMENT TODAY

PART 3. A NEW UNDERSTANDING OF TQM

SECTION II. CASE STUDIES

SECTION III. EXERCISES AND GAMES

Cyber Engineering—Autonomous Parts Inc.—
Fundamental Causes of Quality Failure—
Departmental or Organisational Mindedness?—
Structure and Organisation—Finding Variability—
Does Empowerment Work?—Consolidation—
Further Reading

Preface

AIM OF THE BOOK

This book offers a critical analysis of Total Quality Management (TQM). It is not another fanfare welcoming this popularised management philosophy, nor is it an instrument to dismantle and dispose of it. This book offers a thorough analysis of the strengths and weaknesses of TQM and explores the opportunities and threats that come with it. *The aim is to advance a new understanding of TQM and to explain its value to practitioners.*

INTRODUCTION

TQM is sweeping the industrialised world, with good reason. TQM is helping to remove unnecessary and costly waste, to locate and eradicate sources of error, and to provide the consumer with reliable products that they actually want. It also makes people's jobs more meaningful. TQM makes common sense.

Unfortunately, many organisations have experienced unexpected difficulties when implementing TQM. Some of these are summarised below:

1 TQM wants to change the traditional management style. Handing down responsibility, allowing for autonomy, and promoting local decision making are all part of the new approach that TQM calls for. Greater motivation and creativity are expected. This makes sense on paper, but in practice devolving power turns out to be extremely difficult for

managers to swallow. Organisational politics do not support anything more than a 'lip-service' adoption of TQM. TQM then fails.

2 TQM advances the idea that colleagues must be thought of as internal customers. They therefore have expectations and rights, usually reserved for consumers, that must be respected. Work in the organisation should subsequently become more efficient and enjoyable. In some cases, such as in grand bureaucracies, this is taken too far. Organisations become full of internal groups and committees, serving other internal groups and committees, with no connection to the external consumers. TQM then achieves nothing more than reinforcing the bureaucracy.

3 Many advocates of TQM stress the need for hard, quantitative measures to enable sophisticated mathematical and statistical control procedures to be implemented. The organisation can be brought under tighter control in this way. Many managers, however, find that a significant number of issues in organisations do not lend themselves to hard measurement. Quantitative measures are not relevant. Managers are lost because they are given very little guidance on what to do when soft, qualitative measures are the best that can be achieved. TQM then loses direction and fizzles out.

4 TQM strongly promotes continuous improvement. This encourages slow, steady improvement of the processes in operation. Meanwhile a competitor progressing in a discontinuous fashion can improve their products in leaps and bounds. TQM then provides competitors with the opportunity to get ahead and take the advantage.

5 TQM is not a single philosophy with a clear line of argument. There is much competition over the claim of ownership over the right approach to quality management. Organisations have their Crosby advocates up in arms with Deming advocates. This serves only to confuse all concerned. TQM then is confusing.

These difficulties are caused by some very basic misconceptions about quality, management and organisations. Quality is promoted as a relatively simple, straightforward approach that will quickly get to the root of all difficulties. Splashed across management journals are tempting slogans like 'Quality is free', 'Quality without tears', 'Quality, the no nonsense approach', 'Five easy steps to improving quality', 'Improving quality improves profitability', and 'Exceed expectations with a quality approach'. In reality TQM can bring significant benefits for everybody, but there are costs on individuals and the organisation, and quality involves much blood, sweat and tears for all.

There are also misconceptions about management. Management's role in TQM is crucial. Top management's commitment is stressed in the literature, but all too often this is read as follows. Management must show commitment at the start, show others that they are committed by doing it, and pass on quality so that it spills down the organisation. Soon management is liberated of their burden. Quality is passed down and management feel that they have done their bit. Management can now get on with managing. Responsibility for quality, it seems, lies with the workers. This is not so. In reality TQM means a long term, deep involvement of management in partnership with the workforce.

The worst misconception held about organisations in quality management is that the organisational tree, without question, provides the organisational structure through which TQM must be implemented. A question that jumps off the page when I read this is, 'Why?' An organisational tree expresses the power structure of an organisation, but it does not capture in any sense how the organisation operates and functions. It therefore seems to be inadequate for the job. The proposed power structure works counter to the drive in TQM for autonomy and responsibility. The power structure obscures the operations and functions of the organisation, which is where all the action will have to take place. In reality TQM can only effectively be implemented through a new style organisation which emphasises operations and functions rather than positions of power.

In summary, TQM involves a lot of hard work for all, in a long-term partnership between management and the workforce (and the suppliers and consumers), in a wholly new style organisation that devolves responsibility for local decisions away from management to the workforce, and emphasises operations and functions rather than positions of power.

The difficulties discussed above present you with a challenge. This book tells you how to meet this challenge. In Chapter 9, a method for implementing TQM is offered. A set of practical tools to aid the process is described. Chapter 9 will become the main source of reference for most *practitioners*. In addition to this, Chapters 11 to 15 inclusive document case studies that support Chapter 9, showing how the methods have been used during TQM intervention in organisations. Earlier chapters develop an understanding of TQM that overcomes the misconceptions about quality, management and organisations just discussed. These will be of greatest interest to *researchers*. They prepare the way for a sound method to implement TQM which, as just stated, can be found in Chapter 9. Chapter 16 contains a range of games and exercises that encourage the reader to try out their new understanding of TQM. *Masters students* will find the whole text useful. We will now look at the main features, structure and content of this book in detail.

MAIN FEATURES, STRUCTURE AND CONTENT

The structure of the book divides the content into three sections. Section I sorts out and matures an understanding of the main philosophies, principles and methods of quality management. Section II underlines the main ideas set out in Section I, and introduces important additional material in four case studies reporting on organisational intervention employing quality techniques and methods. Section III provides the opportunity to seal the lessons of the previous two sections. It offers a number of exercises and games that invite participants to exercise their knowledge about TQM. Participants find out for themselves the sorts of hurdle that need to be negotiated in a genuine attempt to implement TQM. The content of the book is summarised below.

SECTION I: PHILOSOPHY, PRINCIPLES AND METHODS

There are three parts to Section I. Part 1 puts in place an understanding of quality management as it stands today. Part 2 argues that if we are to harness the true worth of quality management, we need to make fundamental changes to modern-day management assertions that underpin most of the ideas presented in Part 1. A new set of assertions are put forward. The third part of Section I applies the new assertions to construct a theory for TQM. This theory is then employed to prepare a theory for the practice of TQM. Building on this, a method for the practice of TQM is described.

Part 1: TQM as it Stands Today

Chapter 1: A Brief History of Quality Thinking

Our first feel for the theme of this book is had in Chapter 1, that pieces together a brief history of quality thinking. This places the remainder of the text into an historical context. The roots of quality management are traced. Main events in the emergence of quality ideas are then identified. The Japanese phenomenon and how the West has not won and still lags behind are also covered.

Chapter 2: Quality Gurus: Their Philosophies,
Principles and Methods

An historical background to quality ideas such as that given in Chapter 1 is essential reading. But most people who hold an interest in quality management have heard of many famous names, some of which crop up in Chapter 1, and wish for further insight into their works. Chapter 2 provides this insight with a closer look at the contributions of the gurus of quality management who have enjoyed widest recognition. The main ideas of Deming, Juran, Crosby, Shingo, Taguchi, Ishikawa and Feigenbaum are carefully reviewed. Their contributions are analysed, studying their philosophies, principles and methods. A critique of each one is offered. Their strongest ideas are organised in a simple complementarist framework at the end of the chapter, which is developed further as the book unfolds.

Chapter 3: TQM: Philosophy and Principles

Chapters 1 and 2 deal with the history and main figureheads of quality management and provide a framework through which their contributions can be understood. This information is synthesised within a whole system, or holistic, perspective labelled TQM. Chapter 3 captures the main concepts and ideas of quality management within a definition of TQM. The definition of TQM is systematically worked out by analysing its parts; 'total', 'quality', and 'management'. This analysis uncovers further concepts to be explored. These include 'customer', '(agreed) requirements', 'first time, every time', and 'at lowest cost'.

Chapter 4: International Standards: Philosophy, Principles and Model

TQM as explained in Chapter 3 has emerged as the latest and most comprehensive vision of quality management. Of growing interest and importance to modern day managers wanting to implement TQM, however, is to win accreditation, to be awarded the seal of the international standard ISO 9000 (or one of its equivalents). These standards are general models that propose a set of clauses to follow. The clauses are guidelines pointing out what needs to be done to win accreditation. They say little about how to do it. ISO 9000, then, directs attention to the main quality fault areas whilst TQM provides the techniques and methods to tackle the faults. In Chapter 4 the philosophy, principles and the model that ISO 9000 offers are analysed. A critique is provided.

Part 2: A New Understanding of Management Today

Chapter 5: Changing Assertions of Management Today

A comprehensive introduction to TQM as it stands today is established in Section I. To harness the true worth of TQM, however, necessitates challenging and overcoming assertions promoted by management today. This is important because quality management so far has mainly drawn upon these traditional assertions. Chapter 5 argues that traditional ideas are not really adequate and restrict what can be achieved with any quality innovation. It therefore highlights weaknesses in the old ways and in this shows the value of bringing in new more relevant ones. The new assertions stress the value of a complementarist approach introduced in Chapter 2.

Chapter 6: A Creative Approach to 'Problem Solving'

Chapter 6 builds on the ground won in Chapter 5. New assertions are put in place. A new approach called Total Systems Intervention (TSI) incorporating the new assertions is reviewed in this chapter. The review prepares for Part 3, providing a framework in which a theory of TQM can be constructed. The practice of TQM follows this.

Part 3: A New Understanding of TQM

Chapter 7: A Theory of TQM: A Deeper Understanding of the Philosophy and Principles

The new approach to management and organisation theory, and the management and systems sciences, argued for in Part 2, is now put to work. In Chapter 7 the new ideas are used to generate a deeper understanding of the principles of TQM worked out in Chapter 3. Reference is made through TSI to the main theories found in the management literature. Areas of strength and weakness are identified. The analysis paves the way for a theory for TQM. This theory helps to overcome the lack of rigour of quality ideas in terms of management and organisation theory identified in the Preface.

Chapter 8: A Theory of the Practice of TQM: Practising Freedom

In Chapter 7 a theory for TQM is put in place. The theory stresses the need for autonomy, responsibility and participation, and getting rid of coercive forces—in short, a need for human freedom. It would not be possible, therefore, to claim proper and valid use of TQM without evidence that the practice had in its principles an element of guarantee for human freedom. This evidence needs to be provided in a theory for the practice of TQM. Chapter 8 shows that the complementarist framework introduced in Chapters 2 and 5 caters adequately in its provision for human freedom to be practised.

Chapter 9: Practising TQM:
Employing the Methods and Techniques

In Part 1, a comprehensive introduction to TQM as it stands today is established. In Part 2 a new approach to management and organisation theory and the management and systems sciences is argued for. So far in Part 3 the new approach has been put to work, first in Chapter 7 to construct a theory of TQM otherwise missing in Section I and the literature. Then, Chapter 8 brings forward the theory alongside findings on complementarism from earlier in the book to realise a theory for the practice of TQM. It remains for the final step to be taken, to supply the reader with a guide that shows how the methods and techniques of quality management can most effectively be used in TQM, to come up with and implement change proposals. Chapter 9 takes this final step and hence overcomes the lack of direction of the management and systems sciences identified in the Preface.

Chapter 10: Review

In Chapter 10 a review of the main points of Section I of the book is given. These crucial points will be underlined and some new important additional material introduced through the case studies in Section II. The points will be sealed by experiences coming from participation in the exercises and games in Section III.

Section 2: Case Studies
Chapter 11: Introduction to Case Studies

Each case study in this section is designed to underline some crucial points made in Section I. New important additional material will also be introduced in the last two case studies. Chapter 11 provides a commentary explaining this to the reader.

Chapter 12: Implementing TQM Through TSI:
Diagnostic Biotechnology (Pte) Ltd

The aim of this case study is to provide an overview example of how the new understanding of TQM worked out in Section I can operate in practice.

Chapter 13: Cause and Error: Tarty Bakeries

The aim of this case study is to illustrate how two methods introduced in Section I can be used to identify causes of error, a central issue for TQM.

Chapter 14: Quality Management in the Service Sector:
North Yorkshire Police

The aim of this case study is twofold. The first aim is to extend the debate from Section I about quality in the service sector. The second aim is to explore the kinds of issue that surface when preparing to implement quality in the service sector.

Chapter 15: Supplier Development Strategy for Small and
Medium Sized Companies: Cosalt Holiday Homes

The aim of this case study is twofold. The first aim is to introduce new ideas on supplier development strategy, thus adding to the basic knowledge provided in this book. The second aim is to explore the kinds of issue that surface when attempting to implement a supplier development strategy in small or medium sized enterprises.

Section III: Exercises and Games

Chapter 16: Exercises and Games

Exercises and games are one way of promoting training and development. Each exercise and game in this section is designed to get the participant's hands dirty by having a go at working out ideas and employing methods themselves.

This book has been written for practitioners, for masters candidates studying in the area of management, and for people researching into quality management.

If you are a practitioner then concentrate on the methods and techniques in Chapter 9 and the case studies in Chapters 12 to 15 inclusive. These will help you to implement quality in your own organisation. Chapters 1 to 4 inclusive will help you to be and sound knowledgeable about the basics of quality management. They deal with the history and main gurus of quality management, provide a definition of TQM, and explain the international quality standard ISO 9000.

Masters candidates ideally should follow the argument of the book in the sequence Chapter 1 through to Chapter 10. This will help you to systematically develop a thorough understanding of TQM. Initially an understanding of quality management as it stands today is given. Underpinning management assertions are then challenged and replaced. These assertions are applied to construct a new understanding of TQM. The case studies in Chapters 11 to 15 inclusive provide practical insights to the main points being made. The exercises and games in Chapter 16 provide you with the opportunity to try out the new understanding of TQM in both practical and thinking modes.

Researchers will want to focus on the fundamental argument of the book. You should start by reading Chapters 5 and 6 where assertions of modern-day management are fundamentally challenged and replaced. The new assertions are then used in Chapter 7 to develop a theory for TQM that draws upon management and organisation theory, and the management and systems sciences. This theory emphasises human freedom as a prerequisite to successful implementation of TQM. Chapter 8 moves on to build a theory for the practice of TQM that emphasises human freedom. Chapter 9 converts the principles given in Chapter 8 into a method for the practice of TQM. Additional material of worth to researchers can be found in the case studies in Chapters 11 to 15 inclusive.

HOW THIS BOOK COMPARES WITH THE QUALITY LITERATURE

Quality ideas have had a significant and sometimes positive effect on management today. It is the contention of this work that much more can be achieved. Quality ideas can be more rigorously analysed and can be more powerfully brought together as one organised force in a new understanding of TQM. The issue that lies at the core of TQM's difficulties at the moment is that it lacks coherence and fundamental thinking.

TQM is a management philosophy of sorts but it has hardly been related to the different management and organisation theories that exist. Much could be learnt if we asked whether prominent quality ideas conform to or contradict established ideas in management and organisation theory. We would be able to ascertain when and why quality ideas are applicable and relevant and when and why they are not. At the moment quality thinking lacks this self-analysis.

Compounding with this is the inadequate attention that quality protagonists have paid to the management and systems sciences. These sciences deal with 'problem solving'. Quality management could benefit by consulting these sciences since its own claim is that it boosts organisations' 'problem solving' competence. Many techniques and methods for quality style 'problem solving' have been developed, but each is applied in a pragmatic way without prior reasoning about the organisational or societal 'problems' that they are best suited to. Management and systems sciences have on offer a wealth of helpful guidelines to steer the choice of technique and/or method. Quality management could usefully reflect upon these guidelines for direction.

Quality management thus lacks the rigour of established management and organisation theory and the direction of contemporary management and systems sciences. Quality management desperately needs these to help to ascertain which parts of its philosophy, which principles, and which methods and techniques are appropriate, when and why. The main thrust of this book is to build in this rigour and direction to make intervention using TQM an even more powerful and better understood approach for management today.

Quality management is a highly topical management subject. A profusion of books have hit the management shelves. Some of these are excellent in achieving what they set out to do. One sort of book is written by gurus who espouse their own brand of quality management. A second sort concentrates on and details particular aspects of quality management such as Statistical Process Control. In contrast, another sort provide a helicopter view that attempts, in piecemeal fashion, to introduce the entire literature of quality management. None of the works, however, have successfully made sense of quality management in terms of established management and organisation theory. None of the books have made sense of quality management in terms of the management and systems sciences. *Beyond TQM* is different from all other books written about quality management because it reflects upon that literature and tackles head-on the issues that arise. This book provides a systemic critique of TQM.

Furthermore, *Beyond TQM* brings together the theory and practice of TQM. No other book to my knowledge has successfully achieved this. A few have attempted to put together theory with case studies, but they have failed to use the two in a synergistic way. In this book key issues are identified through the philosophy, principles and methods; are explored in case studies and pressed home in exercises and games. This three-pronged approach spearheads the book.

Finally, *Beyond TQM* is a sister text to *Creative Problem Solving: Total Systems Intervention* (R. L. Flood and M. C. Jackson, 1991, Wiley, Chichester). It complements that book by developing its argument, and by adding more methods to the 'problem solving' armoury, in this case quality management ones.

ACKNOWLEDGEMENTS

The title of this book was given to me by Russell L. Ackoff.

David McCarthy inspired some and produced all figures and illustrations.

I am grateful to Lim Jui Kok, Managing Director of Diagnostic Biotechnology, for allowing me to report in Chapter 12 some aspects of our work within his company. Thanks are also extended to Keith Cullen and Steven Green, senior officers in the North Yorkshire Police Force, for agreeing to documentation in Chapter 14 of our work with them, and to David Devlin for his work on the project. A special thank-you to Mike Isaac, Managing Director of Cosalt Holiday Homes, for permitting me to give an account in Chapter 15 of the efforts of his company, some of which I have been involved in, and for much needed injections of enthusiasm. John Beckford from the Royal Bank of Scotland and now working with me provided insights into the banking service used in Section I. The cliff-hangers in Australia, a group of ten dedicated Australian managers, contributed to the critiques in Section I. Other people, including Victor Amos, made smaller contributions to case studies. I recognise the useful review of an anonymous adviser to John Wiley. Comments from the following readers were helpful; Russell L. Ackoff, Steven Green and David Schecter.

Mandy and Ross provide the love and friendship that makes everything possible for me, including writing this book.

Section I
PHILOSOPHY, PRINCIPLES AND METHODS

Part 1: TQM as it stands today

1
A Brief History of Quality Thinking

INTRODUCTION

Our first feel for the theme of this book is had in Chapter 1, that pieces together a brief history of quality thinking. This places the remainder of the text into an historical context. The roots of quality management are traced. Main events in the emergence of quality ideas are then identified. The Japanese phenomenon and how the West has not won and still lags behind are also covered.

REVIEW

Roots

The quality idea has been around for hundreds of years. The discerning customer in shops and market-places centuries ago applied 'quality techniques', prodding and turning fruits and vegetables testing for firmness, freshness and fitness for the purpose of consumption. If the product was not adequate the purchase would not take place. The potential customer reacted against poor quality products. Nearby in the hustle and bustle of cattle markets farmers argued and bartered over the fitness of animals for breeding, dairy farming or consumption, providing evidence for their case by inspection against criteria learned from their forefathers. Those shoppers and farmers passed on their knowledge to their children, and similarly it was passed on to their children's children. As a 5-year-old I too learned principles of *inspection and reaction* from my mother as she scrutinised clothes and footwear, fruits and vegetables in our town market. Eager market traders would get short shrift from my mum if clothes had weak stitching, zips got stuck when zipping, fruits were marked and bruised or swedes were 'woody' (swedes are a vegetable popular for eating in Europe and woody is a term that describes the texture of the old and unpalatable swede).

At about the same time that I was learning to prod and feel products and fend-off persuasive stall-holders, a genuine quality revolution was taking place in Japanese manufacturing. The skills of the likes of my mum were formalised and internalised in companies, in sophisticated and rigorous procedures. *Inspection and protection* was established as a management idea. Products were inspected and the quality image of the company protected by the removal of poor quality products before customers applied their own inspection and reaction. Inspection and protection, however, is little more than *reactive* management, reacting when poor quality has already entered the product.

Nowadays quality thinking has spread across the entire manufacturing and service process and extends to all management functions, making inspection of manufactured product on its own seem a rather primitive idea. Quality management has become *proactive*, making plans to bring about continuous quality improvement and to achieve a more desirable future. The aim is to get rid of poor quality from the product rather than get rid of poor quality product.

Quality management has progressed, establishing proactive rather than reactive management. In this book we move a further step ahead, introducing an *interactive* approach. TQM is a whole system concept recognising the need to manage sets of interacting issues; issues of a technical, cultural and/or political nature.

Let us now trace the development of quality thinking, chalking up some of the main events. There are many reviews that describe the origin and evolution of quality thinking. The following review is representative. Sources drawn upon are given in Further Reading at the end of this chapter.

Main Events

Traditionally, building quality into a product was the aim of skilled craftsmen. Tradesmen gained a reputation for quality products through skilled craftsmanship that was maintained over time by enforcing lengthy apprenticeship of newcomers to masters-of-the-trade. Pride of workmanship was vital. Tradesmen worked in small tightly knit and controlled firms. Monopolistic guilds were organised to ensure achievement of a high level of skill and quality throughout its membership and the trade.

The Industrial Revolution revolutionised the manufacturing of products. Mass production set in large factories employing armies of people gave rise to new management ways. There were workers, supervisors and foremen, and managers. Establishment of factories and this new organisational structure led to the withering of many small business trades, and the removal of apprentices and masters from core positions.

At the beginning of this century, Frederick Taylor's famous scientific management swept in a mechanistic 'efficient' operation to increase output through mass production. Taylor wanted jobs

to be broken down into parts and each part to be carried out by individual specialised workers. The craftsmen concept disappeared with Taylorism and so did quality achieved through skilled craftsmanship. Inspection thus remained the sole guarantor of quality. The rush to mass production left in its wake a stream of poorer quality products. Quality was no longer built into the product.

The effort of the First World War demanded yet more mass production. Quality became a pressing issue with forces requiring reliable products to arrive on time. Following the war effort there came recognition that quality had been central to the allies' success. This in part led to the formation of associations and institutes, and to the publication of formalised ideas. In Britain, for example, the Technical Inspection Association was formed in 1919, becoming incorporated as the Institution of Engineering Inspection in 1922.

In 1931, W. A. Shewhart of the famous AT&T Bell Laboratories, published *Economic Control of Quality of Manufactured Product*. This gave the Taylorian discipline a much sounder 'scientific' footing. It converted statistical methods into a manufacturing discipline. A precise and measurable definition of manufacturing control was worked out. Stringent techniques for monitoring and evaluating day-to-day production and improving quality were dictated. In 1932 Shewhart visited the University of London to lecture and to discuss his and others' research ideas. This visit attracted significant interest which led to the formation of the Industrial and Agricultural Section of the Royal Statistical Society and the publication by the British Standards Institute (BSI) of their first standard on quality control.

The Second World War again knocked industry off-balance. Operations research grew up in the war years, calculating better and more efficient plans for bombing raids and logistical support. Priority was given to meeting delivery dates at the expense of standards in the product. In the UK the SR17 statistical advisory unit of the Ministry of Supply was established. This unit made an important contribution to the industrial war effort, but quality was to have lean years in the UK after the war was over.

In North America the war-time effort had a more profound and longer lasting effect. Thousands of quality specialists that had been trained mostly by the War Production Board, formed the American Society for Quality Control (ASQC). ASQC expanded its membership to about 50 000 in 29 specialist divisions. However, the real success story for quality thinking ironically emerged in one of the defeated nations. The Japanese launched a new nationalistic drive for expansion, pursuing economic rather than military goals.

The Japanese faced a major challenge in overcoming a reputation of shoddy products. Japanese cars, for example, became notorious for stalling on the hills of San Francisco. A major thrust in Japanese manufacturing was to tackle these difficulties by employing and developing quality approaches. After the war many top industrialists were sacked and their successors subsequently promoted from operational areas. Foreign lecturers were invited to present their quality initiatives and to offer courses and training for Japanese managers.

One famous guru who played a major role in this process of improvement in Japan was W. Edwards Deming, but there were others from the United States such as J. M. Juran. They had the benefit of an intimate involvement in working out sound quality techniques during the war and in the post-war period. The two

The Rising Sun in San Francisco, 1950s style

mentioned had also worked in the mid-1920s in Western Electric Co., and were both influenced by Shewhart.

By the 1970s the Japanese had become 'masters' at achieving quality in their manufacturing sector. But they did not sit back on this achievement. They built on the technology transfer that had happened. Even today, as any academic in the West will know, the Japanese remain hungry for new innovative ideas sending their senior academicians to leading research groups in the West. They have not given up their quest for superior production by continuous improvement in knowledge, methods and techniques.

Ishikawa in Japan made a substantial contribution to achieving quality in production. Ishikawa's Statistical Quality Control (often referred to as SQC), is a system of production methods to produce economically quality goods or services while meeting consumers' requirements. Shingo recommends that we locate and eradicate errors in production as they occur. Taguchi developed a method to build quality into the design of production processes and machinery used. This brought quality back one step, to precede actual production.

The Japanese rapidly went beyond quality in production, recognising the importance of quality in management. They devised several strategies that formed the basis of much of today's international efforts. These are summarised below:

1 Senior managers must personally take charge of quality management implementation.
2 Personnel from all levels and functions of an organisation must undergo training in quality management.
3 Quality improvement must be continuous.
4 The workforce must participate in quality improvement.

The Japanese were prime in switching commercial interests from competition in productivity to competitiveness in quality. In winning the quality challenge, the Japanese were able to achieve a massive increase in their export levels that rocked Western economies. Many Western countries were hit by negative trade balances with Japan. The Japanese quality revolution enabled them to achieve immense economic power, dominating World trade.

Meanwhile the British approach, that not surprisingly has almost been forgotten in this chapter, was slow and backward compared to the establishment of quality as an important managerial issue in North America, and the tidal wave sweeping over Japan. Belatedly, in 1961, the National Council for Quality Reliability was set up as part of the British Productivity Council. Typically, at one time the Council became defunct when the Ministry of Technology withdrew financial support. Quality now finds its home in the British Quality Association, although this is still administered and dominated by die-hards and traditionalists. The British Government has more recently become sensitive to the quality issue in business and industry in Britain. Yet business and industry still suffer from minimal injection of money, few incentives and little genuine support so typical of South East Asian countries such as Singapore. But let us not dwell on the British, nor indeed the Europeans who must also admit a failure to institutionalise quality thinking.

The Japanese success story has, however, urged some managers in Western and other countries to wake up to the quality issue. People have recognised that Japanese success was not only due to national, cultural and social differences, but reflected strongly a new attitude and desire of Japanese management to ensure that consumers receive what is promised. By the 1980s Japan's huge success made evident the direct link between quality and viability of organisations and economies (a point picked up and expanded in Chapter 7).

The 1980s therefore became an era of competitive challenge with increasing numbers of companies adopting quality management. Many consultancy companies have latched on to quality training and intervention as main services they can offer. This adds significantly to the general awareness of quality management. The development of International Quality Assurance Management System Standards in the 1980s has also acted as a catalyst in many countries, setting-off joint management and quality thinking (see Chapter 4). The 1990s is therefore likely to see quality management become the international management philosophy and this surely will continue well into the next millennium.

To tie up this chapter, a summary of the process of evolution in quality thinking described above is presented as one historical sequence below. This process ends up with TQM, the approach that we will concentrate on in this book and develop into an interactive approach:

1 *Quality inspection:* salvaging, sorting, instigating corrective actions, identifying sources of non-conformance and dealing with them.
2 *Quality planning:* developing quality manuals, producing process performance data, undertaking self-inspection and product testing, planning for quality, use of statistics and paperwork control.
3 *Quality management:* Statistical Process Control, third party approval, system audit, advanced quality planning, use of quality costs, involvement of non-production operations.
4 *Total Quality Management:* continuous improvement, involve all operations at all levels, undertake performance measurement, focus on leadership, teamwork and employee participation and motivation, take a whole system perspective.

CONCLUSION

In Chapter 1 a selected history of quality thinking has been sketched out. In the text some people who have had a guiding hand in developing the ideas are named. In the next chapter the contribution of these and other main figure-heads will be reviewed in detail.

FURTHER READING

● Other examples of potted historical accounts of the history of quality thinking can be found in:

Besterfield, D. H. (1990) *Quality Control*, Prentice-Hall, London.
DelMar, D. and Sheldon, G. (1988) *Introduction to Quality Control*, West Publishing Company, St. Paul.

● The full reference of Shewhart's book, mentioned in this chapter, is:

Shewhart, W. A. (1931) *Economic Control of Quality of Manufactured Product*, Van Nostrand, New York.

2
Quality Gurus:
Their Philosophies, Principles
and Methods

INTRODUCTION

An historical background to quality ideas such as that given in Chapter 1 is essential reading. But most people who hold an interest in quality management have heard of some famous names, some of which crop up in Chapter 1, and wish for further insight into their works. Chapter 2 provides this insight with a closer look at the contributions of the gurus of quality management who have enjoyed widest recognition. The main ideas of Deming, Juran, Crosby, Shingo, Taguchi, Ishikawa and Feigenbaum are carefully reviewed. Their contributions are analysed through their philosophies, principles and methods. A critique of each one is offered. Their strongest ideas are organised in a simple complementarist framework that is developed further as the book unfolds.

W. EDWARDS DEMING

Philosophy, Principles and Methods

Deming started out on his quality endeavour in the 1940s. His early interests focused on statistical sampling techniques. He became very interested in the work of W. A. Shewhart. Shewhart was a statistician from the famous Bell Laboratories who had made major steps forward early on in the development of control charts. His effort is documented in *The Economic Control of Quality of Manufactured Product* published by Van Nostrand in 1931. For Deming, variability in manufacturing output was the main source for concern in the drive to achieve quality in production. If the causes of variability could be located, Deming argued, then they could be eradicated. Eradication of the causes would mean less variability and greater consistency in output. This would enhance the product's reputation.

Deming recognised 'special' and 'common' causes in variability. Special causes are assignable to individual machines or operators. Common causes are those shared by operations and are management's responsibility. In this way root causes can be identified, and action to remove variability taken by the appropriate persons. Statistical Process Control (SPC) charts were the main technique put forward by Deming to perform the separation and aid diagnosis.

SPC charts and methods interpret measures of key parameters taken at regular intervals, on-line from manufacturing processes. Interpretations seek to show variability and hence help analysts to locate sources of potential and actual errors in processes. SPC is widely used today, providing a rigorous means of monitoring conformance of product against set goals and hence providing information necessary to make adjustments to eradicate non-conforming product.

Deming progressed beyond statistical methods and survey work. He formulated a systematic approach to problem solving. The PDCA cycle as it has become known has four main components: to *plan*, to *do*, to *check* and to carry out *action*. Once these stages have been systematically completed the cycle starts again with further planning. As we shall see later, this kind of approach has become widespread in the problem-solving literature.

Whilst the statistical methods helped to show management's responsibility for quality over the 'common' causes of variability, the PDCA cycle emphasised the need for management to become actively involved in their company's quality initiatives. These efforts concentrated on the internal workings of organisations.

But Deming's ideas were not only confined to internal workings. He also developed ideas on consumer research. His main contribution was combining door-to-door surveys with sampling methods.

Much of Deming's contribution covered above was implemented in Japan. Deming is a national hero of the Japanese people. He is recognised as the prime mover in securing quality in Japanese manufacturing. All sorts of honours have been bestowed upon him including Japan's premier Imperial honour, the 'Second Order of the Sacred Treasure'. His systematic statistical-based methods were entirely applicable to the mechanistic needs of Japan's post-war economic rebirth. When Deming switched attention to North America, however, his ideas riding high in Japan were knocked down. Long established, deeply rooted North American practices were hard to kill off.

Whilst it could be argued that North America needed similar mechanistic advances in quality in manufacturing, the dominant set of issues that had to be tackled first were of a human origin. They were cultural and political in nature. Deming smacked straight into strong workforce resistance, from both the managers and the workers. He encountered major difficulties arising from poor motivation, leadership and training. Difficulties were also found in standards of practice, and too heavy a reliance on technology rather than people. These issues significantly affected the development of his ensuing ideas. Deming became more human orientated in his writings. He tried to work out most clearly what the fundamental issues were that North American industry faced in the 1980s. He came up with a core 'five deadly diseases' to be tackled.

The five diseases are:

1 A general lack of constancy and purpose.
2 Too much emphasis on short-term profit.
3 A lack of or unsuitable evaluation of performance, merit-rating, or annual review.
4 Management are too mobile.
5 Management decision-making too readily relies on quantitative data without paying due consideration to less tangible or hidden factors.

These core diseases have been added to in 'Fundamental Causes of Quality Failure', pages 285–7 of Section III in this book. Fourteen have been identified. The reader is asked to assess the deadliness of each one in the context of the organisation in which they work and the society in which they live.

Deming drew-up fourteen points which he believes are essential points of action required to tackle head-on the diseases plaguing North American industry:

1   Create constancy of purpose to improve product and service.
2   Adopt a new philosophy for the new economic age with management learning what their responsibilities are, and by assuming leadership for change.
3   Cease dependence on inspection to achieve quality by building quality into the product.
4   End awarding business on price. Award business on total cost and move toward single suppliers (supplier development discussed in Chapter 15 has worked on this idea).
5   Aim for continuous improvement of the system of production and service to improve productivity and quality, and to decrease costs.
6   Institute training on the job.
7   Institute leadership with the aim of supervising people to help them to do a better job.
8   Drive out fear so that everyone can work effectively together for the organisation.

9 Break down barriers between departments. Encourage research, design, sales and production (four main organisational functions) to work together to foresee difficulties in production and use.
10 Eliminate slogans, exhortations and numerical targets for the workforce since they are divisory, and anyway difficulties belong to the whole system.
11 Eliminate quotas or work standards, and management by objectives or numerical goals; leadership as declared in 7 above should be substituted instead.
12 Remove barriers that rob people of their right to pride in their work.
13 Institute a vigorous education and self-improvement programme.
14 Put everyone in the company to work to accomplish the transformation.

To help achieve these fourteen points of action, Deming drew up another seven points in his 'action plan.' The seven points of the action plan, like the fourteen points already dealt with, are methodological principles rather than forming a clear method. They recommend a change in attitude and company design:

1 Management must rigorously tackle the five deadly diseases, the fourteen points and any other relevant issues to agree a meaning for the organisation and a plan to direct it.
2 Management needs to take pride and to develop courage for the new direction.
3 Management must explain to people in the organisation why change is necessary.
4 Every company activity should be divided into stages. The customer(s) of each stage should be identified and will become the next stage.
5 The methods of each stage must be improved and those working in each stage should work together towards quality.
6 Everyone needs to participate as a team to improve the input and output of each stage.
7 The organisation will embark on the construction of organisation for quality.

Deming is thus advocating a systemic functional analysis of the stages of a company's activities alongside a number of people-orientated steps. For example, management must take pride, develop courage and explain to others why quality is necessary. This must lead to everyone's involvement in the stage in which they are based.

Deming's contribution is extensive. It will be valuable now to reflect back on his work, to sort out its main strengths and weaknesses.

Strengths and Weaknesses

Deming's contribution has clearly been path-finding. As with any major contribution, strengths and weaknesses can be found in the work. The purpose behind a critical analysis of this kind is not to run a piece of work down, but to learn from significant contributions, and to bring together the positive worth from this and a diverse range of other findings. This is how we can develop a strong quality discipline and improve upon the efforts made so far.

The main strengths are:

1 A systemic functional logic provides an insightful way of reasoning about organisations; e.g., identification of stages and their interrelationship, and the mutual dependence linking an organisation and its suppliers.
2 Deming makes a notable prioritisation—that management comes before technology.
3 Leadership and motivation of employees are recognised as important.
4 The work is strong on statistical and quantitative methods which are needed in some circumstances.
5 The different contexts of Japan and North America are recognised and responded to in different ways.

The main weaknesses are:

1 The action plan and methodological principles are too vague to be readily put into practice. There is no clear 'Deming method'.

2 Following 3 above, the literature dealing with motivation and leadership has not been adequately drawn upon.
3 The principles and methods have nothing to say about intervention in situations that are political and coercive, even though Deming explicitly recognises this difficult area in his philosophy.

JOSEPH M. JURAN

Philosophy, Principles and Methods

Juran is another path-finder. His early achievements in Japan have been rewarded with the same main honours that Deming received. As with Deming and the bulk of pioneering quality initiatives, Juran's early work was technical in nature. He rapidly moved on however.

Unlike Deming, Juran did not hesitate early on in his work to emphasise top and middle management's involvement in achieving quality. In fact, it is Juran's view that the vast majority of quality issues are the direct responsibility of management. On this account he differs with Crosby who, as we shall see, has founded his quality drive on the idea that things are the other way around; the main portion of quality issues occur because the workers are not adequately motivated or caring and that management's job is to correct this. Juran's main points in contrast indicate that the bulk of responsibility for success or failure in getting quality right lies with management.

Introducing quality into an organisation must start at the top. Management must get used to this idea. They can start first by taking on board the simple lesson captured in Juran's trilogy. The trilogy was derived from financial management; to undertake financial planning, financial control and financial improvement. This translates to quality planning, quality control and quality improvement.

Quality planning has the following steps:

1 Determine quality goals.
2 Develop plans to meet those goals.
3 Identify the resources to meet those goals.

4 Translate the goals into quality.
5 Summarise 1 to 4 into a quality plan.

Quality control means having a simple feedback structure:

1 Evaluate performance.
2 Compare performance with set goals.
3 Take action on the difference.

Quality improvement means:

Improve on the past by
- reducing wastage
- improving delivery
- enhancing employees' satisfaction
- becoming more profitable
- ensuring greater customer satisfaction
- etc.

For Juran, concentrating on these main management tasks must be the primary concern. He is worried that too much recent work in quality management has lost touch with the basic management needs of organisations. Quality has become too gimmicky, full of platitudes and supposed good intentions, but short on real substance for action. Many quality campaigns are nothing more than sexy slogans. Behind the dressing there is little worth looking at.

We must return to the basics. Management must be fully aware of the nature and details of the quality crisis in the 1980s and beyond. Quality planning, control and improvement are the only way out of the crisis. To help, an emphasis must be placed on training. 'Quality awareness' must be instigated as a prerequisite to changing management's behaviour. Having made inroads in management's behaviour, we can spill-down the new attitude to supporting layers of management.

Juran's philosophy and main principles are clear enough. He has also advocated methods for implementing quality. The clearest and most helpful is his 'quality-planning road map'. The road map traverses issues and has to be related to the customer and their needs. In this he demands that we escape yet one more long-standing management fallacy. Too often we assume that the customer is the consumer, the end receiver of the product or service. The customer, according to Juran, should be both internal and external; anyone who we are providing a product or service to. The road map has nine junctions:

1   Identify the customers (internal and external).
2   Determine the needs of those customers.
3   Translate those needs into our language.
4   Develop a product that can respond to those needs.
5   Optimise the product features to help meet our needs as well as the customers' needs.
6   Develop a process that is able to produce the product.
7   Optimise the process.
8   Prove that the process can produce the product under operating conditions.
9   Transfer the process to operations.

As stated, the road map leads us to understand customers and their needs. Putting this into action then sets new demands on the organisation. An organisation must be geared up to cope with the new set of customers and can only do this if it follows ten steps to quality improvement:

1   Ensure that all employees are aware of the need for quality improvement—this requires leadership.

2 Set specific goals for the continuous improvement of quality in all activities.
3 Establish an organisation to ensure goals are set and a process for achieving them established.
4 Ensure that all employees are trained to understand their role in quality improvement—this must include upper management since they are the cause of most of the quality problems.
5 Ensure that problems which prevent quality improvement from happening are eliminated by setting up problem solving project teams.
6 Ensure that quality improvement progress is monitored.
7 Ensure that outstanding contributions to quality improvement are recognised.
8 Ensure that progress and outstanding contributions are publicised.
9 Measure all processes and improvements.
10 Make sure that the continuous improvement of quality and the setting of new quality goals is incorporated into the management systems of the company. Make sure rewards are based on the results achieved.

Strengths and Weaknesses

As with Deming, Juran's huge contribution can be critically assessed in terms of its strengths and weaknesses.

The main strengths are:

1 There is a strong desire to move away from quality-hype, away from empty or non-penetrating slogans etc., to concentrate on genuine issues of management practice.
2 The work establishes a new understanding of the customer, referring to both internal and external customers.
3 Management involvement and commitment is stressed.

The main weaknesses are:

1 The emphasis on management's responsibility for quality ironically fails to get to grips with the literature on motivation and leadership.

2 The contribution that the worker can make is under-valued, rejecting in principle bottom up initiatives in the West.
3 The methods advocated in many ways are traditional and old-fashioned, getting at the basic control systems but failing actually to deal adequately with the human dimension of organisations. Cultural and political issues are not meaningfully managed.

PHILIP B. CROSBY

Philosophy, Principles and Methods

The roots of Crosby's philosophy can be found in his five absolutes of quality management:

1 Quality is defined as conformance to requirements, not as 'goodness' nor 'elegance'.
2 There is no such thing as a quality problem.
3 It is always cheaper to do it right first time.
4 The only performance measurement is the cost of quality.
5 The only performance standard is zero defects.

The main ideas that Crosby promotes are found in these five absolutes. Zero defects (often referred to as ZD) or 'do it right first time', and 'conformance to requirements' are the most commonly encountered slogans. Zero defects means that errors should not be expected or accepted as inevitable. It is a management goal encouraging prevention of errors and is not meant to suggest performance of every activity perfectly. Conformance to requirements is what Crosby means by quality. If you want quality then it must be defined in terms of requirements and measures must be taken continually to determine conformance to those requirements. Finally, it is interesting to note Crosby's more recently added absolute, stating that there is no such thing as a quality problem. What he means is that problems are created by poor management; they do not create themselves or exist as separate entities from the management process.

The management style that Crosby advocates is for managers to take a lead with the belief that workers will follow the quality example being set. In essence, management have to get things started before triggering the real efforts to get at problems which are located in workers' attitudes and activities. To help promote this process workers are consulted about tasks that they perform. Goals are set for employees to achieve, and for those who outstandingly achieved them non-financial recognition is given through award programmes.

Like other gurus, Crosby has come up with his own programme for action. His is a 14-step programme for quality improvement. The 14 steps offer a rather straightforward method:

1 Establish management commitment—they must be personally committed to participating in the programme to raise visibility and ensure everyone's co-operation is received.
2 Form a quality improvement team with representatives from each department.
3 Establish quality measures for each activity, throughout the company—there are innumerable ways to measure any procedure.
4 Evaluate the cost of quality by providing an indication of where corrective action will be profitable for a company.
5 Establish quality awareness of employees by training supervisors and communicating through booklets, films and posters.
6 Instigate corrective action by encouraging working people to identify and put right defects, or pass on defects to the next supervisory level who have authority to deal with them.
7 Establish an *ad hoc* committee for the ZD programme to investigate the ZD concept and ways to implement the programme.
8 Undertake supervisor and employee training so that all managers understand and can explain each step in the Quality Improvement Programme.
9 Hold a ZD day to establish the new attitude.
10 Employee goal setting should take place; usually on a 30-, 60-, 90-day basis.
11 Error cause removal should follow the identification of problems that prevent error-free work from being achieved.

12 Establish recognition for those who meet goals or perform outstandingly by (non-financial) award programmes.
13 Establish and hold regular meetings of Quality Councils composed of quality professionals and team chairpersons, to communicate with each other and to determine action necessary to improve the quality programme.
14 Do it all over again.

Quality Councils have just been mentioned. Quality Councils develop quality improvement plans. Councils set a mission to design the improvement process, develop guidelines, establish educational modules, measure progress and assist in implementation. They become an overall monitor and guider of the business' quality programme.

Crosby helps further. He has provided a number of tools to help operate the 14-step method. The main ones are the 'Quality Maturity Grid', the 'Make Certain Programme', 'Management Style Evaluation', and 'Quality Vaccine'.

The Quality Maturity Grid provides a way for management to measure their progress as a quality company. Its purpose is to point out what quality management can do for an organisation and can be used to help persuade budget heads to spend money now to prevent failure in the future. Long-range programmes can be deduced intellectually from the grid.

The grid is divided into five stages of maturity. Six management categories serve as measurement categories. Each of the 30 blocks arising from this leads to identification of key issues characterising a business context. The five stages are:

1 *Uncertainty*—Management are confused by and uncommitted to quality.
2 *Awakening*—Management is beginning to recognise quality management can help but is unwilling to devote time or money to make it happen.
3 *Enlightenment*—Management establishes a quality policy and admits that they cause their own problems.
4 *Wisdom*—Management have the chance to make the quality improvement stick. Cost reductions are in effect and problems that do occur are handled and disappear. But in-depth reviews must be continually conducted.

5 *Certainty*—Management know why they do not have problems with quality. Quality management is an absolutely vital part of company management.

Each stage can be assessed through six measurement categories. The categories and their extremes are:

1 Management understanding and attitude—from no comprehension, to quality being an integral part of day-to-day work.
2 Quality organisation status—where in the hierarchy the quality people reside; from non-existent to on the Board of Directors.
3 Problem handling—from fire-fighting to prevention.
4 Cost of quality as a percentage of sales—from 20% to 2.5%.
5 Quality improvement actions—from no activity to continuous activity.
6 Summation of company quality posture—from not knowing why problems occur to knowing why problems do not occur.

The Make Certain Programme instigates an on-going examination of procedures and methods by the personnel involved to help them contribute to defect prevention activities on a regular basis. It asks people in groups guided by a facilitator what their biggest problem is and points out that in most cases the problems selected are caused for them by others, not themselves. The participants are asked to work out how these can be tackled. Feedback is given. More problems are identified that now include self-created ones. Participants are encouraged to get together with their supervisors to set up a defect programme to tackle them. Make Certain is successful when this happens.

Management Style Evaluation encourages managers to evaluate themselves as either ordinary, super or spectacular for the following;

1 Listening—taking time to understand people.
2 Co-operating—being part of a team.
3 Helping—letting someone lean on you without leaning back.
4 Transmitting—in writing, prepared speaking and conversation.
5 Creating—developing original concepts or expanding on the ideas of others.

6   Implementing—figuring out how to do it, and doing it right.
7   Learning—pursuing personal development programmes.
8   Leading—stating objectives clearly, getting commitment of others to those objectives, defining methods of measurement and providing the impetus to get things done.
9   Following—achieving the intent of superior's requests.
10 Pretending—acting; a dangerous method of management.

This evaluation helps managers to evaluate what assets they have and is the basis for learning about them and subsequently exploiting them.

The Quality Vaccine uses a medical analogy, bringing forward the idea of vaccinating an organisation against non-conformance. There are antibodies that prevent hassle. Some are managerial and others are procedural common sense. Vaccine preparation should have the following ingredients:

1   Integrity—everyone is dedicated to having the customer receive what is promised.
2   Systems—main systems must be in place; e.g., financial measurement, measurement of company's services, quality education, etc.
3   Communications—continual supply of information helping to identify error, waste and missed opportunities.
4   Operations—educate suppliers, continuous examination of procedures, routine training, etc.
5   Policies—clear and unambiguous.

The vaccine is administered through:

1   Determination—action is the only way forward.
2   Education—developing a common language, understanding each other's role and acquiring a quality knowledge.
3   Implementation—guiding the flow of improvement.

Strengths and Weaknesses

Like other approaches, Crosby's can be assessed in terms of strengths and weaknesses.

The main strengths are:

1   The Crosby approach is clearer than those of Deming and Juran, and is supported by a number of tools that are easy to grasp and to make work.
2   Worker participation is recognised as having value.
3   The idea of a quality problem is rejected, removing the idea that problems exist as real tangible things to be solved.
4   Crosby is very creative in getting ideas across, using metaphors like 'vaccine' and 'maturity'.
5   Crosby as a person is a great motivator and starter for quality programmes, getting things going. Attending one of his seminars convinces most people that they must straight away launch their own quality improvement programme.

The main weaknesses are:

1   The philosophy implies that workers are 'to blame' for quality problems. This can mislead management to believe that their own efforts will be only a fraction of what they turn out to be, only needing to trigger off the drive for quality. This lack of forewarning to management can be a primary cause for failure of quality programmes.

2   The ideas are heavily marketed, promoted through slogans and too often full of platitudes, raising insufficient awareness of genuine difficulties that will be encountered when implementing quality initiatives.
3   The 14-stage method is strongly management and goal orientated. This does not harness the full potential of Crosby's philosophy, that wants to free workers from externally generated goals.
4   Zero defects is often misunderstood to mean avoidance of risk and hence may have a negative effect on creativity.
5   The philosophy assumes that people will be prepared to work in an open and conciliatory way. It would not be effective in political or coercive contexts where openness does not happen.

Deming, Juran and Crosby are the most popular and well-cited characters on the quality scene. Other names that are likely to be encountered include Shingo, Taguchi, Ishikawa and Feigenbaum. We will now take a brief look at their contributions.

SHIGEO SHINGO

Philosophy, Principles and Methods

Shingo has passed through various stages of thinking in his management career. Three can be identified that are relevant to this book. Very early on in his career he held an interest in scientific management. This was followed by an interest in, and application of, Statistical Quality Control (SQC). Shingo's contribution to quality management, however, arose from a personal realisation that statistical methods detect errors too late in the manufacturing process. What is needed is to identify errors as they happen and to correct or deal with them right away.

To this end, Shingo proposed his own version of zero defects. This method is called 'Poka-Yoke', or 'defect$=0$'. The idea, as stated, is to handle errors as they occur. Initially potential error sources in the manufacturing process are identified. Since this identification procedure is vital to the success of Poka-Yoke, it must be carried out rigorously and thoroughly. All potential points of error must be located. Then, at each point, monitoring for error is undertaken. Monitoring is mechanised because human assessment is inconsistent and prone to error. When errors are found, people are then employed to establish what caused the error and to get rid of the cause. This can mean halting the manufacturing process until the error is located and eradicated. Alternatively the error may be dealt with by making alterations to the product and/or process whilst the manufacturing process continues. Whichever, the error is prevented from becoming a defect in the final product. Over time, the process is cleaned out of all the likely recurring errors. Only exceptional cases have to be dealt with. Production therefore runs smoothly and more or less continuously.

Strengths and Weaknesses

As with all the gurus reviewed above, we will assess the strengths and weaknesses of Shingo's contribution.

The main strengths are:

1 The method provides on-line, real-time measures for immediate use. This prevents over-reaction in the processes

that ordinarily occur when information about errors is used that is out of date.

2 Poka-Yoke emphasises dealing with technological issues with a relevant technical feedback and control system. It does not rely on exhortations and slogans aiming to motivate people to zero defects, which leaves fallible human beings at the centre of the zero-defect process.

The main weaknesses are:

1 The emphasis on source inspection by non-human instruments can only effectively be employed in manufacturing. Substantial redevelopment of the ideas is required to check whether they can be adapted to the service sector.
2 Shingo's ideas have nothing to say about human beings in terms of them as social, cultural or political beings.

GENICHI TAGUCHI

Philosophy, Principles and Methods

In Chapter 1 the earliest quality method was said to be inspection and reaction by end customers to the suitability of a product. This was then brought into the factory, with quality inspectors testing the end product. Gurus that we have already discussed have in different ways brought quality control forward, earlier in the process. Some have shown a concern for the technical side of things, looking for points in the process where errors occur. Some have stressed aspects of the human dimension of managing people. Taguchi steps back one further stage on the technical side. He pulls back quality management into design, offering a prototyping method. The prototyping method can be thought of as having three stages:

1 System design.
2 Parameter design.
3 Tolerance design.

The method starts up with system design reasoning. This involves both product design and process design. The aim is to get out some first attempt figures to work from, to take forward to parameter design. Product design includes choice of materials and parts, and calculating starting figures for product levels. Process design includes choice of equipment and taking a first shot at deriving process factors levels.

Next, the method calls for parameter design. The aim is to find, from the start points already determined, an optimal mix of product parameter levels and process operating levels. Emphasis is placed on sensitivity to environmental perturbations and anything else that cannot normally be dealt with using control procedures of the organisation. Reducing sensitivity is the aim. Securing minimum sensitivity relies on the help of techniques. Taguchi's techniques include ones that are efficient in searching for the optimal, workable, survivable mix.

Tolerance design then builds in tolerance to factors that can significantly affect the variation of the product. This might mean investment of money to improve equipment and materials. Tolerance design concludes the prototyping.

Once prototyping is complete implementation is undertaken. At this stage use of SQC would be relevant. Quality in design and process control clearly follow on.

The main statistical concept Taguchi brings forward is his quadratic loss function (see Figure 2.1). First of all we take a particular quality characteristic (x) and set a target value (T). The success of meeting the target can be calculated as $(x - T)$. Because the result of not achieving T or going beyond T means a financial

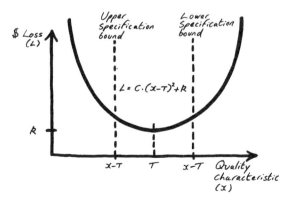

Figure 2.1 *Taguchi's quadratic loss function*

loss, the result of the calculation $(x-T)$ must always be positive. This need can be satisfied by squaring the result, i.e., $(x-T)^2$ which multiplies $(x-T)$ by $(x-T)$ thus converting all negative to positive numbers. This is then multiplied by a cost coefficient (c) that puts a price on the cost of failing to meet the target (T), i.e., $c(x-T)^2$. Finally, in accordance with Taguchi's concern about loss to society, another coefficient is set that represents the minimum loss to society (k, which is always equal to, $=$, or greater than, $>$, 0). This is added to loss associated with the target to give total loss (L) as represented by the quadratic loss function:

$$L = c(x-T)^2 + k \qquad (2.1)$$

Strengths and Weaknesses

We will now subject Taguchi's ideas to critical analysis.
    The main strengths are:

1   Taguchi's method pulls quality right back into the design stage rather than relying on adjustments to the process on-line, or inspection of final product.
2   The philosophy recognises quality as a societal issue and not just an organisational one. Quality is the minimum loss imparted by the product to society from the time the product is shipped.
3   The method is developed for practising engineers rather than theoretical statisticians.
4   The method helps a company to determine the best method of process control, reducing process costs incurring only small amounts of capital expenditure.

    The main weaknesses are:

1   The method has little relevance to processes where measurement will not produce data that can be assessed through sensitivity analysis and minimisation; i.e., it is not relevant to many important success factors in the service sector.
2   Following 3 above, there are no directives about how to manage a quality-orientated organisation, particularly the people.

Quality is placed firmly in the hands of a specialised team of expert designers and does not involve managers and workers. Taguchi's method is designed for engineers and not managers.

3 A corollary to 2 is that Taguchi has nothing to say about humans as social, cultural or political beings, and therefore makes no contribution to managing employees.

KAORU ISHIKAWA

Philosophy, Principles and Methods

Ishikawa's philosophy for organisations is Company-Wide Quality. This involves both vertical and horizontal co-operation. Vertical co-operation occurs between managers, supervisors and the workers. Horizontal co-operation means looking beyond the internal organisation, caring about end customers through customer service, and the quality that suppliers offer.

Overall, there is a functional co-operation. All functions of an organisation are brought together. This includes those, for example: responsible for strategic and corporate planning; for gathering intelligence about opportunities and constraints internally and externally; for offering control services such as personnel and training, accounting control and audit; for co-ordinating the organisation's primary activities; and for actually implementing primary activities.

All staff must be able to contribute to Company-Wide Quality. Training to achieve a high standard of knowledge about a number of key technical tools is given. Tools emphasised include: fishbone diagrams (simple cause-and-effect diagrams—see Chapter 9), control charts and graphs (see Chapter 9), histograms, scatter diagrams, and Pareto charts.

Control charts are a graphical method to help to evaluate whether a process is in a state of statistical control within predefined statistical limits. If statistical control is not maintained, the control charts have identified an area for further investigation.

Histograms are diagrams that display columns representing the frequency of various ranges of values of a quantity. They may show too high a frequency of measures outside control limits.

Scatter diagrams compare two characteristics to see if a relationship exists between them. For example, we may be able to relate temperature in a workshop to faulty product.

Pareto charts analyse procedures with the assumption that 80% of a problem is accounted for by 20% of the causes. Identifying principal causes therefore enables solutions to be implemented that will have maximum impact.

To help implement the philosophy of participation and to get the tools just mentioned to work, Ishikawa has developed Quality Control Circles (QCCs). The circles work in the following way. A small number of volunteer workers from a unit of an organisation form a group called a quality circle. The circle can be led by any person, be they supervisor or worker. The circles have regular meetings to discuss how their tasks can be done effectively and efficiently. Difficulties and issues are raised and change proposals suggested. If possible, the circles go ahead and implement their own ideas. If they cannot do so because of a lack of resources or insufficient local responsibility then management are approached. Management must be responsive, listening to and acting upon the suggestions being put forward.

Strengths and Weaknesses

There are several points that we can make on the strengths and weaknesses of Ishikawa's ideas.

The main strengths are:

1 There is a strong emphasis on the importance of people participating in the problem-solving process, and to provide them with the tools to guide their thinking and acting. This helps to improve motivation, creativity and a wider under-standing of other people's roles in the organisation.
2 A mix of statistical and human orientated techniques and methods are provided.
3 A whole system view is stressed, wanting to achieve quality thinking within the company and in all its external relations.
4 QCCs are relevant to manufacturing and service sectors.

The main weaknesses are:

1 Although fishbone diagrams are extremely helpful when organising thoughts about causes of variation of quality in production and service, relationships are represented as simple causal ones and do not show interrelationships between causes. They do not explicitly show how causes and effects can feedback on each other. They do not show the issues as a whole interactive system. The fishbone approach uses systematic but not systemic logic.
2 If management are not prepared to listen to the ideas generated by the circles, then the whole process breaks down. This is a particular difficulty in the West where the relationship between managers and workers is often conflictual and best understood as 'us and them'.
3 A corollary to 2 is that Ishikawa's ideas would struggle in a political and/or coercive environment.

ARMAND V. FEIGENBAUM

Philosophy, Principles and Methods

The thrust of Feigenbaum's contribution is a whole approach, an approach to Total Quality Control. There is a need to manage company-wide; co-ordinating and controlling all management and operational functions, bringing together social and technical aspects of the organisation. This is achieved at the same time as paying due respect to external satisfaction of consumers, as well as focusing on supplies and suppliers.

Feigenbaum's philosophy can be reduced to a rather simple four-step approach:

1 Set quality standards.
2 Appraise conformance to standards.
3 Act when standards are not met.
4 Plan to make improvements.

The four steps are, in fact, control steps. Control needs to be achieved over supplies, design, production, delivery and after-delivery service. The use of statistical methods may become a part of Feigenbaum's quality control only if they are seen to be relevant. Statistical methods are not the core ones necessary to achieve quality control for Feigenbaum.

Quality control can only be realised if the organisation has an all pervading quality consciousness. This means that adequate communication channels must be in place so that participation can be achieved. The exchange of information enables employees of an organisation to share in the company's strategy and progress.

Strengths and Weaknesses

Feigenbaum's ideas are found to have the following strengths and weaknesses.

The main strengths are:

1 A total or whole approach to quality control is advocated, kicking into touch the dangers of piecemeal quality management.
2 Feigenbaum places an emphasis on the importance of management.
3 The value of socio-technical systems thinking is taken into account.
4 Participation is promoted, harnessing everyone's contribution, leading to people having a greater sense of belonging and generating more creativity.

The main weaknesses are:

1 Although Feigenbaum's principles go beyond what we have seen so far, towards a whole systems approach, he has not worked out the relevance of different methods, be they people or technically orientated, to different kinds of quality context.
2 Although Feigenbaum has recognised the availability of different management theories, he has failed to adequately bring them together as one force for quality management.
3 Nothing is said about how to operate in a political or coercive context.

This completes the individual reviews of the most widely known quality gurus. Let us now assess their efforts as a whole.

OVERVIEW AND CRITIQUE

Each quality guru has their own knowledge base and interests. Each has worked in different situations, and several have contributed in contrasting eras. This naturally has profoundly influenced the way their ideas have developed. When contrasting their works, it is not surprising that we find a great diversity in their philosophies, principles and methods. Unfortunately this diversity has led to friction. Arguments about which one is right and which other ones are wrong have emerged. Such argumentation is not necessary. It is possible to organise the contributions according to what they are and what they are not good at doing. This process has already begun in the analyses above. Main strengths and weaknesses of each guru's contribution have been proposed. We must, however, go a step further to sort out what the gurus offer as a whole.

There are two main areas of focus; on the technical needs of quality control and on the human dimension of quality management.

Technical needs of prediction and control are catered for largely by statistical and quantitative methods. Some gurus place emphasis on inspection at the end of the process, on the process itself, or on the design stage. If we take them together we find that they cover technical needs from design right through to inspection of final product. If we have technical needs, then we can decide which approaches, if not all, are relevant to those needs.

The gurus have provided well for our technical mechanistic needs. One area they say little about in respect to technical interests, however, is organisational design. The traditional organisational hierarchical tree is implicitly assumed in most circumstances. Some gurus have made reference to the systemic nature of organisations but do not go far enough, for example, by explaining in detail how this translates to organisational design. This gap needs to be filled, a point taken up later in the book.

Management of the human dimension of organisations is not at all clearly provided for. The gurus commonly declare their interest in managing people in their philosophies, but on analysis offer few tangible principles and virtually no usable methods. QCCs, perhaps, provide the clearest exposition in the quality literature of how to encourage participation to generate motivation, autonomy and creativity through an approach that is clearly defined. As we have seen, QCCs target groups of people. Individuals have been targeted by management methods not found in the above review, like quality of working life.

Quality of working life shifts the key perspective to the individual worker as regards her or his potential and skills, and feelings about the job. It promotes meaningful recognition for workers and members as individuals. Employee suggestion programmes and a great variety of other job enrichment programmes can also be drawn in from the management literature to complement what the gurus have said.

One dimension not dealt with by the quality gurus beyond simple comment, nor indeed adequately covered in popular management theory as such, is the political and coercive character of organisational decision making; either formal or informal. Ultimately, we could ask, whose interests are being served?

Any practising manager will know that the hardest part of their job is coping with internal politics; struggling to pursue their own interests, to make an influence, to have a say, or even to survive. And the workforce may be very suspicious with quality management, wondering who ultimately will be the beneficiaries and the victims. So why is it that virtually nothing has been provided for the quality enthusiast wanting to deal with issues raised by the question, 'Whose interests are being served?'

The answer probably is that the pressure is on to please the powerful to ensure that something gets done. This is particularly the case for consultants. After all, quality gurus would look rather silly or become quite poor if they kept failing to implement their cherished ideas because they challenge the dominant wisdom of a few. This is despite the likelihood that on many occasions the dominant wisdom would not lead to the greatest benefits overall.

Since there is no magic wand, no wizardry to simply magic away the grip that the powerful have over organisations, it is not surprising to find quality protagonists joining forces with management. This may happen in the form of methods and techniques supporting the technical interest in achieving management's goals more efficiently through available technology. It may be more manipulative, however, proposing how the workforce can be influenced to work in particular ways, to effectively achieve management's goals.

Although it is easy to understand why quality protagonists have on the whole slipped into this way of thinking and acting, there is no excuse for us in this book to turn a blind eye to the political and coercive dimension of organisations. In fact, we will find later on that the logic of TQM demands dealing with even this most tricky aspect of organisational life.

Two further points are noteworthy. First, the gurus are almost exclusively concerned with commercial organisations. Second, the gurus make little mention of quality in society. Each issue is topical and should be addressed in the philosophy, principles and methods of quality management. The first point is tackled later in this book, while the second demands another complete book.

CONCLUSION

The overview and critique just completed has helped to make sense of the quality discipline as a whole as it stands today. It pulls together the contributions made by quality gurus. The simple framework, distinguishing between the different types of technical interest and their complementary relationship with types of human orientated interest, is the basis of an effective way of organising the multitude of ideas being promoted in quality management. After further preparatory material in Chapters 3 and 4, this idea will be picked up, again developed and further use made of it.

FURTHER READING

The main texts of each guru are:

Crosby, P. B. (1979) *Quality is Free*, Mentor, New York.
Crosby, P. B. (1981) *The Art of Getting Your Own Sweet Way*, McGraw-Hill, New York.

Crosby, P. B. (1984) *Quality Without Tears*, McGraw-Hill, New York.

Deming, E. W. (1966) *Some Theory of Sampling*, Wiley, New York.

Deming, E. W. (1982) *Quality, Productivity and Competitive Position*, MIT, Cambridge, Ma.

Deming, E. W. (1986) *Out of the Crisis*, MIT, Cambridge, Ma.

Feigenbaum, A. V. (1986) *Total Quality Control*, McGraw-Hill, New York.

Ishikawa, K. (1976) *Guide to Quality Control*, Asian Productivity Organisation, Tokyo.

Ishikawa, K. (1984) Quality and standardisation: Progress for economic success, *Quality Progress*, 1, pp. 16–20.

Juran, J. M. (1964) *Managerial Breakthrough*, McGraw-Hill, New York.

Juran, J. M. (1980) *Quality Planning and Analysis*, McGraw-Hill, New York.

Juran, J. M. (1982) *Upper Management and Quality*, Juran Institute, New York.

Juran, J. M. (1988) *Juran on Planning for Quality*, Free Press, New York.

Juran, J. M. (1988) *Quality Control Handbook*, McGraw-Hill, New York.

Shingo, S. (1986) *Zero Quality Control: Source Inspection and the Poka-Yoke System*, Productivity Press, Cambridge, Ma.

Taguchi, G. (1976) *Experimental Designs* (volumes 1 and 2 in Japanese), Maruzen, Tokyo.

Taguchi, G. (1982) Design and Design of Experiments, *Annual Meeting of the American Association for the Advancement of Science*, Washington DC.

Taguchi, G. (1985) *What is Total Quality Control? The Japanese Way*, Prentice-Hall, Englewood Cliffs, New Jersey.

Taguchi, G. (1986) *Introduction to Quality Engineering: Designing Quality into Products and Processes*, Kraus, New York.

● The full reference of Shewhart's book mentioned in this chapter is:

Shewhart, W. A. (1931) *Economic Control of Quality of Manufactured Product*, Van Nostrand, New York.

● A document that provides another overview of the quality gurus is:

Bendell, T. (1988) *The Quality Gurus; What Can They do for Your Company?*, Department of Trade and Industry, United Kingdom.

3
TQM: Philosophy and Principles

INTRODUCTION

Chapters 1 and 2 deal with the history and main figureheads in quality management and provide a framework through which their contributions can be understood. This information is now synthesised within a whole system, or holistic, perspective labelled TQM. Chapter 3 captures the main concepts and ideas of quality management within a definition of TQM. The definition of TQM is systematically worked out by analysing the parts; 'total', 'quality', and 'management'. This analysis uncovers further concepts and ideas to be explored. These include 'customer', '(agreed) requirements', 'first time, every time', and 'at lowest cost'.

PHILOSOPHY

Our interest in quality builds upon contemporary premises of systems thinking. Systems thinking proposes a whole or total approach to quality management. The word 'total' is very important in this expression because it states that we seek comprehensive ways of dealing with complex sets of interacting issues—involving everyone at all levels, addressing all major issues. It will not surprise the reader, therefore, to hear that the brand of quality that is of greatest interest to systems thinkers is TQM. There are several versions of TQM already available, but these tend to be ultra-pragmatic brands that suffer from a lack of fundamental thinking about the nature of businesses and organisations. Explicit use of systems thinking will help to redress this weakness.

A systemic understanding can be developed by taking the term TQM and systematically working out a definition of it. This we will achieve by defining the three component words and explaining how they should be read as a whole expression. The order of unfolding will be first to define 'quality', then to reason what is 'total quality' and complete by adding in 'management', constructing a rich understanding of TQM.

Quality has been defined in a variety of ways:

1   Quality is a predictable degree of uniformity and dependability, at low cost and suited to the market—Deming.
2   Quality is fitness for use—Juran.
3   Quality is conformance to requirements—Crosby.
4   Quality is the (minimum) loss imparted by the product to society from the time the product is shipped—Taguchi.
5   Quality is in its essence a way of managing the organisation—Feigenbaum.
6   Quality is correcting and preventing loss, not living with loss—Hoshin.
7   Quality is the totality of features and characteristics of a product, service or process, which bear on its ability to satisfy a given need; from the customer's viewpoint—British Standard Definition.

Of course, there are as many definitions of quality as there are books, authors and protagonists. Each holds a strong but limited vision of quality. What is needed is a general appreciation that reflects the wealth of ideas covered in Chapters 1 and 2. This is the immediate task.

A synthesis of ideas so far encountered is captured in the following statement about quality:

Quality means meeting customers' (agreed) requirements, formal and informal, at lowest cost, first time every time.

There are several quality ideas embedded in this statement. To find out what these are the statement can be broken down into component parts, each part with its own meaning:

1 *Customers* are all those to whom we supply products, services and information. They may be *internal* or *external* to the organisation. In other words we extend in meaning the traditional idea that customers are people external to the organisation who buy or utilise its products, services or information, to include people within an organisation to whom we supply or from whom we receive products, services and/or information. An organisation, for example, will have many departments, divisions, and jobs, some of which interact, and all of which must handle this interaction in the same spirit as if they were dealing with external customers. Dealing with customers is an interactive process.

2 *Agreed* means that there is an ideal to strive for but it needs to be agreed by all parties concerned. External customers are one party that naturally have their demands and desires. Another party is the decision maker within an organisation. They must make the final decision about what to supply and at what price, taking into consideration the external customers' needs.

Banking, for example, features two types of 'agreed' requirements. The first of these is a passive agreement in which the external customer accepts the terms and conditions regulating the particular banking products purchased. There is in this case no scope for negotiation of price or quality— the product(s) is/are the standard. This type of agreement applies principally to 'personal customers'. The range of products and the level of personal service are the features that distinguish mass-market from upper-end personal account customers (i.e., wealthy or highly paid individuals). There is, however, little scope for negotiation of this level of service or the price to be paid.

The second type of 'agreed' requirement in banking is active agreement. This most usually applies in the business banking market and is distinguished by the participation of the customer in a negotiating process that determines not only the banking products to be purchased but the price to be paid and to a great extent the level of service (i.e., service quality) to be provided.

Any company has a quality image that it needs to sustain. A quality line has to be drawn to reflect quality policy decisions made by members of the organisation. Quality is not entirely dictated by the external customer. A good example of this is Apple Computers whose 1980s business policy was to produce an exceptional product, sophisticated and versatile, at a cost mostly above that of other personal computers. The strategy assumed that businesses could not afford to be without Apple Computers. Apple computers above all others had created and would meet certain customers' needs. Judging by their 1980s success the quality decision seems to have been a winner.

The nature of the customer relationship with Apple Computers differs significantly from that in the banking sector. The purchase of a computer is essentially a single transaction (notwithstanding the need for service support) whereas a banking relationship continues over time, with daily transactions. To be successful a consistent level of service must be provided over the life of the relationship.

The comparison between banking and Apple Computers serves to show how diverse is the meaning of 'agreed'.

3 *Requirements* are measurable specifications and cover such things as durability, reliability, accuracy, speed, method of delivery and price. Measurable specifications are the basic parameters by which assessment of quality will be guided. The choice of specification is a critical one. The tendency is to go for specifications that have obvious quantitative measures like the examples given above. In manufacturing this can often be achieved, but the service sector is not so easily quantifiable. Qualitative specifications may be more appropriate in some circumstances.

The level of service provided to banking customers, to stick with this example, is often difficult to quantify. A customer will be content if they perceive that a level of service appropriate to expectations is being enjoyed. But there is no absolute determinant of quality. Bank customers often have differing expectations at different times for banking products.

The 'theory of measurement' is key knowledge here. It tells us what kind of manipulations, statistical, mathematical or others, can be made on which sorts of measures. The social empirical sciences deal with the most difficult aspects of measurement and are more prone to break the clearly defined rules of measurement. Proofs have been claimed when only spurious results were given. In quality management it is crucial that we prove as accurately as possible that we meet set requirements. The theory of measurement must be learnt and adhered to (see Further Reading).

4 *Formal and informal* makes reference to agreements made both in a formal business-like manner, and to those informally established through interaction. Informal agreements naturally develop through interaction and may be positive or negative and therefore must be assessed and managed. Informal kinds of expectation are not easily specified. These expectations are best described as an attitude. They are at least as important as formal specifications, helping to develop and maintain a quality image over time.

5 *At lowest cost* means that there is no unnecessary loss or waste in time, effort or material in the production and delivery of the product or service. The aim is for commercially orientated companies to improve viability often measured by profitability.

Non-profit making organisations aim to improve services, for example.

Unfortunately, lowest cost is a misunderstood idea. A local businessman in Hull, a Director at Hull Industry Inc., read it as, 'cut costs increase profits'. He cut and removed a tier of middle managers. For two years the size of the profit rose. He became a hero and was head-hunted. The next two years saw the company reeling. The managers of the future were gone. The business was no longer managed and lost its market position. The removed tier was not waste, it was as valuable as gold-dust. The businessman is now destroying another company.

This parallel reinforces our previously mentioned need, to maintain stable service levels over time with a continuous relationship. By removing middle managers there are no future senior managers to maintain relationships.

For banks, the need is to carefully design systems and procedures that support the delivery of service to customers. It is vital too that non-income earning areas organise themselves to provide help to income generating activities. Neither area must exist only to pursue their own objectives.

6   *First time, every time*, sets an ideal to carry through a policy of 'no licences to fail'. In other words, according to agreed requirements, a company will not accept standards in product or service that fall below those expectations.

For banking, an agreed requirement could be to deliver bank statements to customers within 48 hours of the extract date, with no more than 1% later and containing no accounting errors. There can be no licence to deliver statements within 24 hours containing errors.

These six ideas are the core ones that underpin the notion of quality proposed in this volume. But what is meant by 'total quality'?

Total quality means that everyone should be involved in quality, at all levels and across all functions, ensuring that quality is achieved according to the requirements in everything they do. 'Total' injects a systemic meaning of wholeness into quality. We argue that quality cannot be guaranteed without involving the whole organisation, across all functions and through all levels. Every job is crucial and can add to or detract from the quality endeavour.

And lastly, by integrating the term management, the value of management responsibility is projected into the meaning of quality and wholeness already established. This responsibility is everyone's as 'total' implies. Management responsibility does not necessarily refer to the company's Managers (with big M) as it does in the entire quality literature that we have reviewed. It can, and in this text does, refer to the need for everyone to be responsible for managing their own jobs, which incorporates managers with workers and anyone else associated with the organisation.

As we have seen, TQM portrays a whole systems view for quality management. TQM builds on the idea that an organisation is an interactive network of communication and control. The network shows the interaction between suppliers and consumers, with an organisation carrying out a transformation between the two with a quality purpose in mind. All organisations can be understood to operate at different hierarchical levels, each one characterised by its own attributes but vertically integrated to form a whole organisation with different properties at different levels. Quality management must ensure that horizontal integration across networks and vertical integration through hierarchies is achieved. Any total quality approach must look at an organisation as a whole in this way.

Failure to achieve either horizontal or vertical integration accordingly will limit the success of establishing a quality organisation.

PRINCIPLES

The main principles of TQM can now be drawn out from the philosophy in place:

1 There must be agreed requirements, for both internal and external customers.
2 Customers' requirements must be met first time, every time.
3 Quality improvement will reduce waste and total costs.
4 There must be a focus on the prevention of problems, rather than an acceptance to cope in a fire-fighting manner.
5 Quality improvement can only result from planned management action.
6 Every job must add value.
7 Everybody must be involved, from all levels and across all functions.
8 There must be an emphasis on measurement to help to assess and to meet requirements and objectives.
9 A culture of continuous improvement must be established (continuous includes the desirability of dramatic leaps forward as well as steady improvement).
10 An emphasis should be placed on promoting creativity.

As seen, there are ten main principles. These provide a concise understanding of TQM as it stands today. The chapter will now be concluded.

CONCLUSION

A systemic, or whole system, understanding of TQM as it stands today has been put in place. The main philosophy and principles have been documented. Each principle, however, avoids as far as possible being interpreted and understood through management and organisation theory. They remain relatively neutral. Later on in Chapter 7 the task of interpreting and putting deeper meaning into these principles with traditional and contemporary management theories will be undertaken. This will lead to a theory of TQM. There is some way to go yet before the theory can be established. Other things need to be achieved first. The next piece of preparation will be to describe and discuss the international standards on quality, which have a direct bearing for many organisations today wanting to implement TQM.

FURTHER READING

●The theory of measurement is reviewed in Chapter 3 of:

Flood, R. L. and Carson, E. R. (1993) *Dealing With Complexity: An Introduction to the Theory and Application of Systems Science* (2nd edition), Plenum, New York.

4
International Standards: Philosophy, Principles and Model

INTRODUCTION

TQM explained in Chapter 3 has emerged as the latest and most comprehensive vision of quality management. Of growing interest and importance to modern-day managers wanting to implement TQM, however, is to win accreditation, to be awarded the seal of ISO 9000 (or one of its equivalents). These standards are general models that propose a set of clauses to follow. The clauses are guidelines about what needs to be done to win accreditation. They say little about how to do it. This does not matter to us because Chapter 9 will help to achieve that. ISO 9000, then, directs attention to the main quality fault areas whilst TQM provides the techniques and methods to tackle the faults. In Chapter 4 the philosophy, principles and the model that ISO 9000 offers are analysed. A critique is provided.

BACKGROUND

The central need for reliable products in the Second World War defence procurement focused on tight specifications and consistency in product, as mentioned in Chapter 1. This was essential if the operational researchers were to see the efficiency of their models converted into military victory. The responsibility was seen quite naturally to rest with the suppliers because checks could not reasonably or effectively be carried out on the battle-ground. Not surprisingly, therefore, post-war developments saw the quality drive being governed by different industries with different systems of standards. Many of these still exist today, but in 1979 the British Standards Institute (BSI) in the United Kingdom published the first general standards (BS 5750) that applied to a broad range of businesses and organisations. Other standards were subsequently developed for the European Community (EN) and the International Organisation for Standards (ISO) whose work was completed in 1987. The ISO 9000 series was heavily based on BS 5750, but reflected international requirements and lessons learnt from eight years use of BS 5750. Now, ISO 9000, BS 5750 and EN 29000 have been harmonised and are equivalent.

THE STANDARDS

Introduction

We will now explore the philosophy, principles and model of the International Quality Assurance Management System Standards (IQAMSS—the three series listed above). Throughout the presentation reference will be made to manufacturing and service sectors (using banking to represent the service industry).

Philosophy

IQAMSS are general standards that apply to a broad range of businesses and organisations. They are not product specification standards, but management system standards. Their aim is to help organisations to achieve quality for their customers all the time. This necessarily involves all functions and departments. Documentation required for accreditation (see below) places an emphasis on organisational structure and employee participation, but the documentation itself does not dictate a management style.

The standards concentrate on those in direct contact with clients and suppliers, but does recognise the importance of the 'in between and less obvious' aspects of organisations. A BSI seminar on the IQAMSS, available on video and audio tape, argues for the following understanding. Quality affects 'people at the top', the commitment of senior people is the source from which quality can be achieved. The Chief Executive or Managing Director, or Executive group, must set quality objectives, work out how to delegate responsibility for implementation and determine how quality audits are to be carried out.

Commercial details are mainly the responsibility of the sales and marketing functions. Sales assess customers' agreed requirements, ensuring that they get what they want, how they want it, according to agreed terms and price. In the standards this is called 'contract review'.

Marketing works out other aspects of the commercial detail. They produce literature with characteristics and performance statements about the product. They develop packaging and labelling, and claims to be made through advertising and promotions. Marketing defines pricing policy and allocates production codes. They supply literature describing after-sales services.

The seminar continues, concentrating more on manufacturing, reflecting a genuine bias in the IQAMSS. Design adds the technical to the commercial details. There needs to be a clear definition of technical specifications and a recording of this. Design must build in statutory requirements and codes of practice, laying down processing, inspection and testing requirements. Purchasing must ensure that the right materials are used, communicate those needs to suppliers and make sure that they have the capability to supply. Checking procedures must be applied to ensure that there is conformance.

In manufacturing, production, processing, repair, despatch, storage, handling, installation, site contracting and servicing all have a bearing on quality. They must conform to standards, equipment must be suitable and staff adequately trained. Administration and support also play a role although this may be less obvious. For example, invoicing and credit notes must be prepared accurately.

In the service sector, let us say banking, there are similar

general needs. Banking 'products' are services as opposed to physical items. What becomes important therefore are the processes through which they are delivered. The 'product' is in effect remanufactured each time a customer requests it. Staff training is a priority—the staff member is a prime product delivery point but this must be supported by quality in the physical delivery systems, that is the 'Information Systems' (computers), 'through the wall' cash systems, Branch design, internal processes for lending and other decision making, and of course the delivery system must be initially designed to match the agreed requirements of the customer. Administration and support has a strong role in banking, internal accounting and record-keeping processes are unseen by the external customer but must be completed both accurately and on time.

Although we mentioned earlier that no management style is absolutely dictated in the documentation of the IQAMSS, many advocates of the standards do place an emphasis on authority by seniority, that is, top management control. There is a suggestion of this in the earlier comment extracted from the BSI seminar, that policy and objectives for quality management systems must come from the top. The standards' advocates are opinionated on this matter and clear evidence is found in the need to protect *senior management* from day-to-day detail. The standards look for clear evidence of delegation to management representatives, whose authority is given directly from their seniors. The role of management representatives is to co-ordinate and to analyse results, to resolve routine difficulties and to bring forward proposals for improvement for approval by senior management.

Participation, according to the standards' advocates, comes only through traditional management ideas of legitimate authority according to an organisational tree. They have ignored modern-day management literature that emphasises participation through autonomy and loading responsibility down as far as possible in an organisation. Thankfully the IQAMSS models are general enough to take on board other management styles that we can offer, such as those worked out in Chapter 8. Now we will complete the philosophy behind IQAMSS underlining the importance that they attach to documentation.

To win accreditation through third-party certification bodies, an organisation must document its quality management system. This task may lead to streamlining benefits in any case. Many organisations find that their documentation is piecemeal, with duplication and redundancy. A total systems review, which is what the standards require, will help to improve documentation and make clear how the organisation is supposed to function.

Documentation needs to be done for three levels of detail. The first level of detail is recorded in a relatively short overview, the quality assurance manual. This provides with clarity and brevity the management statement on policy and objectives. The organisational structure, a definition of responsibilities and limits of authority, and management representatives are set out. This manual defines the organisation's quality system.

The second level in more detail documents how the quality system declared in the first manual is to be implemented. Procedures are worked out that make clear who is to undertake what tasks, how the tasks inter-relate and where authority is held. Job descriptions are an excellent way of achieving this. The quality system has to undergo audit to identify weaknesses to be overcome. Documentation here must describe how audit procedures will work. Since documentation is the blueprint that explains how the organisation is to work, and as just stated this will be continually improved, it must itself be subject to change. Details of how revision to documentation will be carried out must be given. Who is to be responsible for revision and who will approve revision must be declared.

To complete the details of implementation, procedures for human resources development are needed. Staff proficiency in terms of skills and qualifications require appraisal. Accordingly training requirements will need to be determined. A training, learning and development programme has to be convincingly established.

Very detailed instructions that spell out how the quality management system will work on a day-to-day basis are documented in the third manual. A manufacturing company will want to provide details of routine procedures for the following:

1 Task instructions for activities on the factory floor and in offices.
2 Stock records and issue dockets.
3 Work and progress schedules.
4 Orders in progress.
5 Safety instructions.
6 Instructions for testing, measuring, inspecting and approving work done.
7 Records of quality control activity and any other controls that will guarantee effective organisational management.

With banking, our example from the service sector, the following would be relevant:

1 Details of clerical activities for providing customer service (the product).
2 Lending processes and record-keeping requirements.

The management of these activities will generally fulfil both service delivery functions, i.e.:

1 Lending.
2 Customer meetings and negotiations.

Routines for these will be similarly documented, detailing how the clerical workers manage through:

1 Legal compliance procedures.
2 Checking routines.

3 Trend allocation.
4 Workload monitoring systems.
5 Determination of service standards.
6 Maintenance of stock records (cash and deposits), stationery supplies, in addition to records of service quality.

The philosophy that lies behind the IQAMSS model has the following main underlying principles (the model is dealt with later).

Principles

The main principles that fall out of the above analysis of the philosophy behind IQAMSS can reasonably be listed as six. The first three are technical details of the operation of the total system, the fourth stresses human resources development, while the remaining two deal with management style and responsibility:

1 A total systems perspective is fundamental to the effective operation of a quality management system.
2 Continual quality auditing in the form of monitoring and controlling is essential.
3 The objectives and functioning of the total system—the blueprint—must be documented in three vertically integrated manuals providing an overview, details of implementation and detailed operational procedures.
4 Staff must be adequately skilled and/or hold appropriate qualifications.
5 There must be a commitment from senior personnel.
6 Traditional management ideas of legitimate authority according to an organisational hierarchical tree are emphasised.

At this point it is helpful to reiterate that the management style and ideas about responsibility are not an indetachable part of IQAMSS. We could easily implement the blueprint replacing Principle 6 with other ideas developed in the quality and management literature. For example, the value of the Viable System Model for diagnosis and redesign is shown in Chapters 7,

8 and 9. The key thing for certification is clarity and being convincing when stating how the organisation will run as a quality management system. There is plenty of scope for us to shape-up this aspect of the standards, being able to adopt different ways of implementation, each promoting different management styles. Now let us investigate the IQAMSS model in detail.

Model

The ISO 9000 series comprises 9000, 9001, 9002, 9003 and 9004. ISO 9000 is called 'Guide to Selection and Use'. It provides an introduction to the standards and guidelines for the selection and use of one particular ISO standard, or model. The standards are laid down in ISO 9001, 9002 and 9003, each targeting different types of organisation, and together spanning many businesses and companies. The title to each one indicates its use. ISO 9001 is the most comprehensive model called 'Specification for Design, Development, Production, Installation and Servicing'. The next two models are, in fact, submodels of ISO 9001. ISO 9002 is titled 'Specification for Production and Installation', omitting the design development and servicing functions. And ISO 9003 is named 'Specification for Final Inspection and Testing'. The remaining publication ISO 9004 is called 'Quality Management and Quality Systems Elements Guidelines' and outlines technical, administrative and human factors affecting the quality of products or services. We will now concentrate on the standards that are used for certification set out in 9001–9003, dealing with 9001 that details all clauses found in the other two.

The model ISO 9001 starts with three introductory clauses. The fourth group of clauses offer guidance on quality system elements, containing all the main clauses relevant for certification. We will focus on these, but will mark the ISO 9002 elements with an asterisk and ISO 9003 with a sword. Comments about the model will be made in the context of manufacturing and service sectors, continuing with the banking example for service sectors.

Clause 4.1*† covers *management responsibility*. It asks for clear statements about what the organisation is setting out to achieve, how this is to be done, by who, and what monitoring and auditing procedures will be employed for checking it.

A *quality policy* has to be documented. The policy must deal with satisfying external customers and hold a policy to enable employees to understand and implement quality plans. *Responsibility and authority* in a structured organisation is also required, to help achieve company policy. This narrows down to focus on personnel who control key functions of the declared quality system. Their jobs should be defined in terms of quality requirements. Main areas of concern are:

1   Control and maintenance of the quality system.
2   Control functions to eradicate quality deficiencies.
3   Feedback to ensure effective operation of both controls is being achieved.
4   Review of the declared quality system to ensure that it reflects policy.

Verification, resources and personnel target the delivery of product or service in accordance with quality objectives already laid down. Emphasis here is on inspection testing of products or services, checking outputs of internal services and establishing satisfaction of internal and external customers. Any such audits must be carried out by an independent third party. Management has to appoint a *management representative* to oversee the progress of the implementation of quality ideas. The management representative should have authority to oversee the whole quality effort and must not have an inherent conflict of interests. Clause 4.1 calls for *management review* in two areas:

1 Regular review of documented policies and procedures already mentioned.
2 Review of internal quality audit findings to keep the quality management system in line with declared policies and procedures.

Achieving a quality policy in the manufacturing sector is relatively straighforward, but for the service sector things are more difficult. A quality policy in banking together with the other aspects of Clause 4.1 must recognise that service, which is the bank's main product, whilst delivered locally, is often constrained by central functions. The bank's information system, for example, will be developed and controlled separately. The responsibility and authority for implementing and achieving the standards of the quality policy must therefore be properly separated between achievements that can be sought locally and those that must be obtained through central development. For example, a standard which is related to a bank's computerised information system is not controllable by the manager of a local branch.

Clause 4.2*† covers *the quality system* of the organisation and its documentation. Initially the *system organisation* is dealt with and recognised to be a part of TQM. Output from each function or part must meet agreed customers' requirements, be they internal or external. The quality system is understood to be interrelated aspects of:

1 Supplier's needs and interests.
2 Customer's needs and expectations.

Therefore a well-planned and managed quality system has to be defined and documented, which are dealt with by *quality plan* and *quality manual* sub-clauses. The quality system and plan should be documented in enough detail so that suppliers and customers can understand it and audit the quality system themselves.

This clause requires that the different parts of a manufacturing company or a bank recognise that they are both customers of and suppliers to other parts of the organisation as well as to the external customers, e.g., branch/department/division-to-branch/department/division, or branch-to-head-office, or branch/department/division-to-end-customer.

Clause 4.3* is *contract review*. Where purchases of materials and sales of equipment and services are covered by contracts, there must be clear evidence of a review of terms and conditions. Attention should be paid to the following:

1 Ensuring requirements are agreed and clearly understood by all involved parties.
2 Identification of non-conformance to agreed requirements and how they will be overcome.
3 Checking that all parties have the necessary resources, organisation and facilities.

Again in manufacturing this task is relatively clear, but requires careful thinking out for the service sector. Constraints between the bank and its suppliers will usually be explicit and conformance verifiable. Between the branches and its customers the situation varies—some contracts are negotiated and agreed, some are implicit in the customers' acceptance of the 'product' specialisation, i.e., agreements to open an account as advertised in the brochure/promotional literature. The bank must document its means of ensuring that it delivers that which is promised.

Clause 4.4 deals with *design control* and is particularly relevant where an organisation's product or service specification has a significant technical content. In manufacturing, personnel responsible for design tasks need to be identified and assigned tasks if they are appropriately qualified. Each one must be properly equipped. Communication between design personnel must be checked and any weaknesses found, such as ambiguity or conflict, must be resolved. A monitor and control function for design must be established to verify that the designs conform to the starting brief. If they do not, perhaps alterations need to be made, then changes must be verified. All statutory requirements must be met and client involvement guaranteed.

The design function in banking must cope with the total system. It is not enough to specify the type and terms of a product, the design must incorporate staff training, changes to the information systems and the means of delivery to the customer. Banking products are often designed by marketing staff without reference to technology, training or other areas which support that product.

Clause 4.5*† covers *document control*. This deals with how the documentation should be treated. All documents in manufacturing companies must be checked before issue or reissue after revision. Documents must be positioned in an organisation so that all persons concerned have easy access to them. A master record file has to be kept. People responsible for revision and issuing must be identified.

This clause demands an effective mechanism in banking for disseminating information through a distributed network of offices. Documentation can be provided in this way. Paper copies for revision and issues must be circulated throughout the network.

Clause 4.6* deals with *purchasing*. In the procurement of materials or external services, quality needs to be assessed in respect to agreed specifications. *Assessment of subcontractors* ensures that all subcontractors have the capability of supplying materials or services of the required quality. A formal assessment of capability is needed, possibly through an audit of a subcontractor's quality system or by way of other evidence. Documentary evidence on the formal assessment is required. *Purchasing data* when placing orders should amount to a formal procedure that ensures all necessary information is given to a subcontractor. Communication links are a central issue here. A record of performance is needed.

In the service sector different slants to the Clause are relevant. This clause applies in its totality to banks as purchasers of external services and supplies. It must be remembered, however, that banks also 'purchase' from customers in terms of their deposits which enable the bank to undertake its lending activities. It follows therefore that Clause 4.6 must be applied to this aspect of the organisation. With the occasional exception of very large customers (for example major companies) it is not possible to examine individual customers within the terms of this Clause. The behaviour of customers *en masse* must therefore be the items documented and audited for charging patterns.

Clause 4.7* deals with purchaser *supplies*. Here, purchaser means external customer or consumer. In manufacturing the external customer may make 'free issue', which is where they provide materials for incorporation in products it ultimately buys back. The onus is on the issuer to check quality, but this does not absolve an organisation from knowingly incorporating poor quality parts into the product or service supplied to the customer.

This clause is also relevant in the service sector. The branch of a bank, our case at hand, becomes involved in providing services from other suppliers. For example, 'key man' life insurance is tied to a lending agreement where the branch introduces a life insurance company. The branch must ensure, both in its own interests and that of the customer, that the insurance company is reputable and the product is suited to the customer's needs.

Clause 4.8*† deals with *product identification and traceability*. A manufactured product must be traced through the various stages of its production, delivery and installation if relevant. This is crucial to help identify the stage and hence the cause of any product failure. Where differing products are visually similar or identical, the products must be identified using a method of labelling or coding.

This is a difficult area where much of the product is service. It is, however, strongly relevant to internal customer claims and paper processing where at each stage of a process the output can be verified.

Clause 4.9* covers *process control*. There are many significantly different processes in both the manufacturing *and* service sector.

Accordingly only principles are set out in Clause 4.9, details having to be put in place by each organisation. The main point is that process steps need to be identified, and a plan to implement (and where relevant to deliver and install) needs to be declared and documented. The process must be carried out in a controlled way, so that plans are to hand, equipment and personnel used are adequate and that the general conditions are amenable to achieving the plans.

To ensure that a process is carried out in a controlled manner, particularly in the service sector, the process must be well documented and the staff well trained. In banking it is not possible to verify the quality of each individual transaction by a cashier for example. It is possible, however, to train staff to ask the right questions in the right manner to ensure customer satisfaction. Internal processes are subject to much simpler verification through banking procedures and batch checking of processed items.

Clause 4.10*† brings in *inspection and testing* for incoming goods, in-processing and final inspection. Inspection of incoming materials must be directed by a sampling plan. The plan details the selection of materials for testing from each received batch. Results need to be documented, describing material tested, number of rejects, reasons for rejection and corrective actions to be taken. In-process inspection similarly needs to be dealt with, tying in with Clause 4.8. Upon completion all products must undergo clearly specified final inspection. Clause 4.10 is self-evident for manufacturing companies and equally pertinent to the service sector.

The goods purchased by banks are generally items which support delivery of service rather than being incorporated in other products. These items whether computer hardware or paper supplies, must be inspected and checked for their 'suitability for use'. Records of this activity should be documented as already described.

Clause 4.11*† covers *inspection, measuring and test equipment*. It deals with the equipment used in inspection and testing, ensuring that it is suitable for its purpose. Frequency of calibration of equipment used in manufacturing should be based on stability, purpose and degree of utilisation. Records of maintenance work must be retained. Recalibration must be in line with official standards or, where this is not the case, with a clearly documented method.

For the service sector this clause must focus on the means utilised by the organisation for ensuring the quality of service, both to internal and external customers. Surveys must be substantiated with sampling used to ensure that quality of service standards are achieved and form the basis for corrective measures. There must also be inspection and testing of new products prior to their launch to customers; 'Do they match market needs?', and 'Do delivery systems support the pre-determined service standards?'

Clause 4.12*† deals with *inspection and test status*. There needs to be an indicator that states what tests a product or service has been through and whether it passed or failed.

Again two areas are mentioned here, new and established products. A new product, inspected and tested prior to customer launch is readily tracked. Established and traditional products must be reviewed fully and where necessary redesigned to ensure that current management will accept responsibility for its performance. These are equally relevant to both manufacturing and service sectors.

Clause 4.13*† stresses *control of non-conforming product*. The aim here is to ensure that non-conforming product is not used by mistake. They must be isolated and clearly marked. Each non-conforming lot must be accompanied by a report detailing the item and reasons for rejection. Defects and claims should be sent to vendors promptly.

This again is a difficult area when 'service' is the product. Only the physical aspects of banking activity; for example, statements, cheque books and plastic cards can be isolated in the suggested manner.

Clause 4.14* looks to establish *corrective action*. This basically provides for detailed and timely documentation of corrective actions taken. Time must be taken to learn from mistakes. But strictly speaking, Clause 4.14 wants avoidance of mistakes to be

achieved following analysis of quality records, service reports and customer complaints. In either case corrective action should be monitored.

Corrective action in banking must have two elements—the first is the need to redesign products/delivery systems which do not conform. This may involve addressing staff training rather than product failure. The failure identified will be an accounting error. It is vital that this is rectified immediately it is noticed with appropriate interest and service charge adjustments. This corrective action should be advanced to the customer.

Clause 4.15*† is about *handling, storage, packaging and delivery*. A policy must be set for handling, storage and packaging. Handling of products, e.g., when loading and unloading, must be done with due care for the product. Storage areas must be clean and the environment properly controlled (e.g., heat, humidity, light). Access to storage areas should be controlled. Controls should also be implemented to identify slow-moving, obsolete, deteriorated and damaged items. These points are again self-evident for manufacturing companies, but require a bit more thought for the service sector.

A bank's physical products, for example, can and should be handled in the specified manner. It is particularly important that paper which easily deteriorates is carefully dealt with. Delivery is also conducted through electronic, customer devised means

and these must be designed to give due care to the product-service, i.e., machines must be user friendly and reliable.

Clause 4.16*† covers *quality records* and is of an administrative nature. They are the routine control and reporting documents that show the progress of the quality management system. They should be kept over a reasonable length of time and stored safely. The following, extracted from above, are key records to be kept:

1 Audit of the quality system.
2 Calibration of test and measuring equipment.
3 Analyses of process control data.
4 Records of corrective actions.
5 Records of concessions.
6 Records of the product test data.

Clause 4.17* deals with another administrative matter, *internal quality audit.* Planned and documented checks on the implementation and operation of the quality management system help to confirm that it is being operated correctly and effectively. Internal quality audits must be conducted on a regular basis. Coverage, schedules and standard procedures for each audit must be predetermined. Records must be kept, such as the following:

1 Deficiencies found.
2 Corrective action required.
3 Time agreed for corrective action to be carried out.
4 Personnel responsible for corrective action.

Clause 4.18*† underlines the need for *training*. Training of personnel is concerned with the competence of personnel to do their assigned task. Where a lack of skill or qualifications is found, staff need to be sent on continued education courses and seminars. If a member of staff is new to the task then efforts must be made to train them.

Staff performance needs to be regularly appraised and recorded. Know-how is kept up to date, enabling staff to operate adequately the machinery that they are responsible for.

Clause 4.18 is a crucial one for the service sector. Staff are the key providers and producers of, for example, the bank's products—a high level of skill training coupled with detailed product knowledge is vital if a quality service is to be provided. Appraisal and development records are essential in this process.

Clause 4.19 deals with *servicing*. An 'after-sales service' in manufacturing must be offered, for example, in the following areas:

1 Instructions for use.
2 Logistical back-ups like technical advice, spares and parts availability, competent servicing.

Bank products are rarely based on one-off transactions—they are normally continuous services over time, with service of the facility being the product. The 'after-sales' service is therefore the element which is most vital.

Clause 4.20*† stresses the value of measurement using *statistical techniques*. Techniques should be used to assess, for example, the following in manufacturing when appropriate:

1 Market analysis.
2 Product design.
3 Reliability such as longevity and durability.
4 Process control/capability studies.
5 Determining quality levels and thus inspection plans.
6 Data analysis, performance assessment and defect analysis.

These aspects must in the case of banking be founded on statistical techniques for surveying customer satisfaction with the services provided. They should be used for the modification of existing services and the development of new ones. Particular aspects such as longevity and durability will be derived from the length of customer relationships rather than the apparent product—this stems from the ability to maintain a suitable level of customer service. Measurement of a less quantitative nature will also be highly relevant in banking and the service sector. For example, customer comments of all sorts are useful data-banks from which indicators can be derived.

CRITICAL ANALYSIS

IQAMSS on the face of it make sensible recommendations for any organisation. The benefits offered are common sense. Like all approaches, however, this is not the end of the story. Strengths and opportunities need to be carefully weighed up against weaknesses and threats. This critical analysis is carried out below.
  The main strengths are:

1 They offer an organised method of analysing an organisation for quality.
2 A continuous approach is recommended.
3 Consistency should be achieved.
4 Receiving the stamp of the standards may lead to a positive image, with greater credibility and acceptability.

5 In the long run it should cut overall costs.
6 Good and thorough documentation is achieved that promotes knowledge transfer and improves chances of tracing causes of error.
7 The standards promote a total systems approach.

The main weaknesses are:

1 The process of winning accreditation is very time consuming.
2 The process is resource intensive.
3 Adaptability, flexibility and responsiveness of an organisation may be reduced.
4 No methods for implementation are offered.
5 The language and concepts are geared up for the manufacturing sector, leaving much reinterpretation to be done for the service sector (currently under way).
6 Implementation may hit cultural resistance.
7 It is difficult to be sure that organisations consistently maintain their quality standards.

The main opportunities that arise are:

1 An organisation can become more competitive with respect to quality.
2 Strategic marketing opportunities arise through the prestige of an internationally recognised standard.
3 Job recruitment and satisfaction may improve with employees being proud to be members of a recognised company.

The main threats that have to be guarded against are:

1 Elaborate   documentation   encourages   undesirable bureaucracy.
2 The process of striving for accreditation can drain vital resources better deployed elsewhere.
3 The international standards are not immune to poor image. Accredited companies may not maintain standards leading to scepticism. This negates the strengths and opportunities, thus wasting resources deployed.

CONCLUSION

The model ISO 9001 has been presented. The clauses that make-up 9002 and 9003 have been marked. Comments have been given on each one in respect to manufacturing and the service sector, using banking as an example for the latter. The quality standards have been written in general terms with specific reference to manufacturing. The value to the service sector is less obvious. Where service is the product, however, the ideas need further working out. For example, it needs to be recognised that a bank's major products are not simply types of account, lending facilities, money transmission services and safe custody, but the delivery of service to a level matching customer expectations. It is that service which is the product. Procedures to enable and support service delivery can be documented, services monitored and improvements developed (turn to page 226 for more ideas about quality in the service sector). To complete this chapter a critical analysis of ISO 9000 was given, showing that despite the apparent common-sense ideas offered by the philosophy and principles, implementation of the model may encounter some severe difficulties as well as leading to benefits.

FURTHER READING

● Details of the ISO 9000 series and the video mentioned in this chapter can be obtained from the British Standards Institute at Milton Keynes, UK. Many countries have their own standards institute that will be able to provide information on the ISO 9000 series.

Section I
PHILOSOPHY, PRINCIPLES AND METHODS

Part 2: A new understanding of management today

5
Changing Assertions of Management Today

INTRODUCTION

A comprehensive introduction to TQM as it stands today has been established in Part 1. To harness the true worth of TQM, however, necessitates challenging and overcoming assertions promoted by management today. This is important because quality management so far has mainly drawn upon these traditional assertions. Chapter 5 argues that traditional ideas are not really adequate and restrict what can be achieved with a quality innovation. It therefore highlights weaknesses in the old ways and in this shows the value of bringing in new more relevant ones. The new assertions stress the value of a complementarist approach introduced in Chapter 2.

Much more is demanded of the reader to get to grips with ideas emerging from the following debates than has been expected in preceding chapters. Two incentives are on offer. First, that new ideas emerging from the discussion will help to establish a deeper understanding of the philosophy and principles of TQM. Second, the ideas suggest a powerful way of using the quality methods as a whole organised force to get at the diversity of issues faced when implementing TQM. Both incentives are rewarded in Part 3 where a theory for TQM, a theory for the practice of TQM, and practising TQM are all established.

The style of presentation shifts from straight explanation and analysis of ideas used in Part 1, to one of exploration and discussion in Part 2. The main areas of discussion in this chapter are 'the problem with problems and problem solving', 'thinking about thinking', 'systems thinking', and 'thinking about problem solving approaches'. Let us start, however, with a challenge.

THE CHALLENGE

Management today is trapped. It is trapped by its own assertions. The most common assertions are that:

1 Organisations have problems that need to be solved.
2 The correct problem solving approach is required to relieve management of all their troubles.
3 Organisations must be maintained in, or restored to, normal life.

It is the contention of this chapter that:

1 There is no such thing as a problem nor a solution.
2 There is no single problem solving approach correct for all circumstances.
3 There is no such thing as normal organisational life.

If these three counter assertions can be shown below to have value, then, for the (quality) management of tomorrow to progress, it must overcome the assertions of management today.

Achieving a change in management assertions will not be easy in any case. As the famous old Zen saying goes, and this applies to all of us, 'those who are full of their own opinions will be deaf to words of wisdom from others, asserting only their views'. Of course the wisdom of others may be rubbish, but this can only be known if we open up our minds and pay proper attention to what is being argued. This book has its own words of wisdom. Only by open and critical thinking can you determine whether or not it is rubbish. Let us explore the contentions set out in the challenge above.

THE 'PROBLEM' WITH PROBLEMS

As stated, there is a 'problem' with the idea of problems and hence problem solving. The notion of a problem always springs to my mind the idea of a 'gremlin in the works'. It is a particularly elusive one at that. A gremlin is a creature often blamed for meddling with things and causing problems, but it is never seen or found doing this. If something goes wrong, that is we encounter a problem, we tend to blame an invisible gremlin.

Solving problems is often tasked to management consultants. Management consultants come armed with all the necessary problem-solving equipment. They have a net to catch the gremlin, normally comprising a four or five stage problem-solving technique, and a desk-top gas chamber used to exterminate the gremlin following its capture in the net, hence solving the problem. This analogy is expanded in the following sketch of an imagined management consulting scenario based on the story-line that there are problems to be solved, that is, gremlins to be exterminated.

After an initial visit to and briefing by the Managing Director, a group of consultants set about locating and solving the problems of the organisation. They start off by visiting Computer Services. They can tell that the gremlin has been there because there are bugs in the software and the main computer keeps crashing. Computer Services has problems. On investigation the consultants find that the gremlin has just vanished up the air-conditioning toward the Accounting Department. The hunt begins.

On arrival in Accounting the evidence is clear enough. The gremlin has been through the books and now they will not balance. It has played tricks on the staff so that the bought ledger clerk has fallen out with the sales ledger clerk and the manager has lost control. But, as usual, the gremlin has just slipped away.

A similar story can be told for each department. The consultants find that the gremlin has been everywhere although they do not find it. And then one afternoon, possibly to save face, the consultants are seen frantically rushing along corridors net in hand dodging in and out of rooms giving rise to an air of confusion and expectancy. Suddenly there is a dash past reception and out of the door with the consultants clutching at

the net, although no one could claim to have seen the quarry. Next morning the consultants return looking cool and triumphant to report the solution to the problem, that is, how they exterminated the wretched gremlin. They recount how they did it in four or five easy steps and then leave with a cheque in hand at least the size of the story they have just strung.

The story told above is far too close to reality for comfort. Much of today's consultancy and problem solving is carried out following the three common assertions of management today. We must recognise and face up to the realities of the modern organisational world. There are no clearly definable problems. Consultants, and managers for that matter, do not solve problems. They do not return organisations to normal life. They do, however, continuously manage messes.

A mess, according to my colleague Russell Ackoff, is a set of interacting issues. A mess is characterised by compounding and related difficulties. A mess of interacting issues surely characterises the situation in the company mentioned above. Interacting issues link the software and its bugs, which affect accounting ledgers and their errors, accentuating poor relations between the two clerks and the manager, and so on. Problems are better understood as messes. Consequently, the idea of problem solving must also be abandoned.

People create messes. The only solution that gets rid of the mess is extermination of the root cause. The root causes of messes are people and their actions. So is it good-bye to the software engineer, the accounts clerks and the manager? Hardly. Management is not about exterminating people. Management is about the management of messes that arise wherever people do. Problem solving more honestly is mess management, managing sets of interacting issues.

Mess management introduces the idea of complexity, complex sets of interacting issues. Modern management has to deal with ever increasing complexity. There are many more issues to manage in today's organisations. Information in organisations today is far more voluminous and flows much more rapidly. Telephones, faxes and computers are all a part of the information age that gives rise to ever increasing complexity to be managed. This puts the spotlight on another difficulty. We human beings have a limited ability to think about the messes we create. Our minds' information processing capabilities fall far short of the demands made on it by the mass of information coming our way. Our ability to process information has not changed from hundreds of years ago when work was centred in small organisations set in local communities. Conversely the pace of change of information that has to be dealt with increases daily.

It has therefore become very difficult to co-ordinate ideas using only our mental faculties. Complexity highlights limitations in our everyday ability to understand organisations. This raises the first of two dilemmas to be tackled later in this chapter:

How can we think creatively about the messes we create?

We need to understand organisations. We also need to manage them. To this end, human ingenuity has divined many, many methods. Faced with messes, the human race has learnt to exploit its ability to conceptualise whole ideas by formulating methods that tackle the messes. People manage their working lives by systematically formalising and recording ideas in methods, some simple, others sophisticated. Each one tackles certain types of issue for which it has been developed, but none can possibly deal with all the complexity at once. In Chapter 2, for example, the overview of the contribution made by the quality gurus as a whole showed that their methods tackled either types of technical matter or human orientated ones. Unfortunately, gurus tend to claim that their approach copes adequately with most matters, in most places, most of the time. This myth naturally confuses management wanting to know which one of them is right. It leaves those willing to reason with the unenviable task of working out the strengths and weaknesses of the vast array of methods. Furthermore, there is no obvious way of knowing how to choose methods to tackle different kinds of issue in organisations. This leaves us with the second dilemma to be addressed later in this chapter:

Which models and methods are appropriate to manage which issues, when and why?

It was also stated earlier that there is no such thing as organisational normality. This follows from what has been said so far. We manage messes with a variety of models and methods, helping to move an organisation toward a more desirable future. The organisation is dynamic, that is, the issues faced are forever changing as they are managed. The only normality in this process is that it is normal for there to be no normality.

I and a colleague Michael C. Jackson have developed a creative approach to 'problem solving' called Total Systems Intervention (TSI) that overturns traditional management assertions and, we are convinced, deals with the two dilemmas noted above. The approach proposes three phases:

1 Creativity.
2 Choice.
3 Implementation.

That is, creative thinking about messes using metaphors/models of organisations, leads to informed choice about which methods can best tackle the issues surfaced during the creativity phase, which leads on to implementation of specific change proposals according to those methods. An explanation of these phases of TSI is offered in the next chapter. First it is necessary to present some thinking about thinking (i.e., how we think) that identifies the metaphors/models to be used in TSI in the creativity phase, and then some thinking about so-called problem solving approaches that provides the guidelines for our choice phase.

THINKING ABOUT THINKING

How do we think about organisations, and how can this knowledge be harnessed to help us think creatively about issues organisations face? A journey through Western occidental thought will help to answer these questions. This journey, in the form of a story, is mildly intellectual, but the terrain is not overly tough.

(The characters below could be male or female.) The journey fittingly starts in the study of a wise old manager (to be known as Wom). A bright young manager calls upon Wom seeking absolute management knowledge.

'Wom' s/he asks (to be known as Bymsak—Bright young manager(ess) seeking absolute knowledge) 'can you tell me what absolute management knowledge is?'

'I'm afraid that it will take some time and effort on your behalf', Wom said, nodding to confirm his words.

'I am not afraid to work', Bymsak enthusiastically replied. 'Just point to the beginning and I'll construct the answer.'

Wom raised one eyebrow disapprovingly, 'Take these two books as a beginning and read them. Then come back to me and tell me what the answer is that you seek.'

Bymsak returned to the office and read, meticulously keeping notes. Then, after many hours had passed, Bymsak closed the second book, having completed it, and began to summarise the findings. Accordingly, organisation and management knowledge ultimately are as follows.

Jobs are designed using scientific methods to calculate the most efficient way of doing things. The tasks of employees are broken down into parts. Observation and measurement create physical descriptions of 'the worker' and 'the job'. Therefore management is the process of planning, organising, commanding, controlling and co-ordinating the parts. This requires rational planning and efficient control of an organisation drawing upon engineering principles. The organisation is a closed system represented as a bureaucratic hierarchy.

Satisfied with this, Bymsak packed up and went home. Tonight there was no need to worry about work because all the answers had been found out and now it was simply a matter of implementing them. Tonight, Bymsak thought, I shall sit down and watch television in the comfort of my new-found knowledge. Tomorrow, s/he continued to think, I shall go to the Wom and receive much acclamation.

This particular evening's main programme was the first in a series on science. The subject was Newton's theory of the mechanical Universe. The main points were as follows. The scientific approach of observation and measurement show that the design of the Universe is based on fundamental principles and laws of physics. Laws have been formulated to calculate how objects move in a variety of circumstances. The Universe is a closed system. Newton's theory of a mechanical Universe reflects the basis of the science of mechanics. Mechanics assumes a strict hierarchy of control over and exact obedience by the parts to guarantee maximum efficiency. Mechanics draws upon and implements principles of engineering.

Bymsak, being somewhat astute, realised that Newton's theory, essential mechanics and engineering, and scientific and classical management theory (Taylor and Fayol respectively, being the authors of the two books Bymsak read) show great similarities.

'Of course, organisations are machines!' Bymsak cried aloud.

On the following day Bymsak met Wom and excitedly recounted the answer, and the confirmation that it conforms to the fundamental laws of physics, providing absolute certainty.

Wom seemed unimpressed, passed over two more books and waved his hand from his wrist indicating that Bymsak should depart and read them. Bymsak read the books and meticulously kept notes. The summary of them follows.

Organisations are complex systems made up of parts that can only be studied as a whole. Subsystems have lists of needs that must be met. Action is taken to hold the organisation in the steady-state. The organisation is open to its environment. The primary aim is to ensure survival, by transforming inputs and by adapting to changes when they occur.

Further to this we must be concerned about the nature of people at work. Individual motivation requires attention. For example, jobs can be enriched to enable people to realise higher order needs leading to greater satisfaction and productivity. The whole organisational structure should facilitate participation. Leadership should encourage democracy and autonomy being human needs orientated. There should be no bureaucratic rule.

Later, Bymsak returned home and switched the television on. Coincidentally the programme about to begin was the second in the series on science, tonight about the living world. The commentary described the organic world as follows.

Organisms are complex systems made up of parts that can only be understood as a whole. The primary aim of all organisms is to survive. They have functional parts which have needs to be satisfied. Control is held over relatively autonomous parts to achieve harmonisation and to help survival to be achieved. Organisms, for example, are open and adaptable systems that transform inputs to satisfy inner needs and have outputs.

Bymsak realised that biology and the systems and human relations theory just studied, in the two further books provided by Wom, show great similarities (authors respectively being; Parsons, Selznick, Katz and Kahn, Barnard; and Roethlisberger and Dickson, Herzberg, McGregor, Perrow). They both have an essential organic concept.

'Of course, organisations are living systems.' Bymsak confidently thought.

This wholly different organic rather than mechanistic understanding of organisations and management gave Bymsak great satisfaction. Not only was the answer to the quest now definitely spelled out, but the wrong answer that organisations were machines was also known. Knowing the wrong and the right answers provided the basis for powerful articulation of absolute knowledge in the face of peers. Feeling a sense of security with being absolutely right, the next day Bymsak visited Wom. Wom listened to the story of yesterday, the day of revelation. Unmoved, Wom passed over another two books, and then carried on working.

The books were grudgingly read by Bymsak and notes meticulously kept. A summary follows.

The essential ideas of the systems model and the human relations theory are accepted. In addition, however, an intelligence function is needed to aid learning and to enable plans for the future to be worked out. An organisation should be thought of as flows of information. The more information the greater the variety to be dealt with. Management by exception occurs only when particular management functions can no longer deal with the local variety. An organisation has an identity that can be found in all the parts.

That night, feeling a little rattled, Bymsak attempted to take his/her mind off things and watched the third in the television series on science. This time the topic was neurocybernetics, about how the human brain works. The commentary spoke of control of basic biological functions based on extensive information interchange, an intelligent mind enabling forward planning, control by exception, and overall maintenance of integrity, or identity.

Bymsak realised that the workings of the human brain and the Viable System Model show great similarities. (The two books read by Bymsak were authored by Stafford Beer, one called *Brain of the Firm*. Their content is discussed at length in Chapters 7, 8 and 9.)

'Of course, organisations are brains . . .' Bymsak mumbled uncertainly and then continued '. . . or are they like a brain in

'Of course, organisations are brains!... or are they like a brain in some ways and like a machine in other ways and an organism in yet other ways?'

some ways and like a machine in other and an organism in yet other ways?'

The following day Bymsak entered Wom's study subdued, thoughtful, and acknowledged that *there is no absolute management knowledge*. Wom nicknamed him/her Bym. Wom explained that ideas from the natural sciences had filtered into thinking about organisations and management. But that was not all. Theories developed elsewhere in the social sciences had been moved around. For example, international relations has an explanation of culture. People have beliefs, values and roles to play. They have, for example, a shared language, history, norms, dress and a common religion. There is a common sense of belonging. These are cementing characteristics of human culture. In management and organisation theory similar ideas have been used. For example, in quality management an emphasis is apparently placed on creating a corporate culture whose main identity is total quality. There is a quality language, quality norms and, with some evangelical gurus like Crosby, even a quality religion.

Furthermore, in the study of politics, much has been theorised on power relations and how coercion may come about when one party can bring greater resources to bear to serve their own interests. For example, it is often argued that managers' interests in organisations are served at the expense of the workers' interests. Political dimensions to organisation and management theory have also developed along these lines.

So, what did Bym learn on this journey? Essentially, that there are many different models, or metaphors, that have been used to provide essential and fundamental explanations of management and organisations. The five main ones that we have uncovered are; machine, organic, brain, culture and political. These form a general set, but a whole host of other related metaphors can be used, such as team, coalition and prison.

Interestingly, drawing attention to these five models/metaphors does not teach practitioners anything new. Most people use the models as metaphors on a day-to-day basis. Casual management conversation is full of metaphors. For example, when did you last hear something along the following lines?:

1 I want my department to run as efficiently as a machine.
2 The company must adapt its outlook and evolve its working practices in order to survive.
3 We must act intelligently, we must predict and prepare for the future.
4 The corporation needs a quality culture to be competitive in the 1990s.
5 A decision was made today to implement ISO 9000 following a long political fight.

The main point is, and this is an argument implicit in the Bymsak story, that Western thought has gone through a number of major shifts. Models developed in the name of science have pervaded the way managers think. So it is not surprising as noted above that managers use these different conceptions in everyday conversation. Models have been transferred from the natural and social sciences into the study of management and organisations, being employed as metaphors. Changing perceptions of organisations has also influenced strongly the development of methods used to intervene in organisations.

Each method put forward holds underlying assumptions about the nature of organisations that it has been designed to intervene in. They reflect the models of organisations already discussed. The same five metaphors can be used to illustrate this. If we think that an organisation is like a machine, as early management and organisation theory assumed, then we will try to engineer it as if we were a mechanic. If we think an organisation is like an organism or a brain then we will nurse it or operate on it when pathological conditions occur. But if it seems to lack culture then we may attempt to influence attitudes through social roles and practices. And if it is like a political system then we might explore whose motivations and self-interests are being supported. Different methods are capable of dealing with particular organisational issues because fundamentally each assumes that organisations are of a particular form or type and recommends treating them as such.

The conclusion we can reach is that each method has something to offer. They should be used in complementary fashion. We can think creatively about organisational messes by creating images of organisations with the metaphors. We can tease out important issues to be faced. Each image created by metaphors gives insights into different issues of varying importance. The participants in the analysis can then make informed judgements to identify the main organisational difficulties that currently need to be dealt with.

In day-to-day thinking we think with metaphors. Unfortunately, however, this normally occurs in a mixed, jumbled and confusing way. Metaphors are thrown around in a loose fashion and hardly clarify or crystallise main organisational issues. This can be improved on. The five main metaphors identified can be used in a mixed, organised and creative way. We need to call upon systems thinking to help out here.

SYSTEMS THINKING

Systems ideas were first popularised in the biological sciences as a response to the mechanistic vision of nature. This led systems thinking down the garden path where the belief is held that everything can be conceived of as organic. Systems thinking initially adopted the belief that all organisations are groups of interacting functional units, as the organic metaphor would suggest. Parson's systems model of organisations is a typical output of early systems thinking. But the systems idea as understood today is relevant to all the metaphors that we have discussed. Systems thinking has become much more sophisticated. To show this we need to consider the idea 'free' as far as possible from biological flavouring. We want to develop a general conception of what we mean by system. Flavourings can be introduced into the general conception later by mixing in the metaphors.

A general conception of 'a system' is a set of richly interacting elements that imports and transforms inputs and has outputs. It is distinguished from an external environment by a boundary. Communication and control are two key concepts that help to explain this. The elements communicate with each other and the environment providing the information medium in which control procedures can be brought to bear and purposeful behaviour achieved. A system therefore is a complex communication and control network.

A further two concepts help to round and fill the systems idea. They are hierarchy and emergence. Hierarchy means that each system is also a subsystem of another system and a suprasystem comprising other systems. Emergence is a concept absolutely unique to systems thinking that powerfully characterises an important phenomenon. As we pass up a hierarchy we find that each new whole is greater than the sum of its parts. There is emergence. Parts of an aeroplane do not fly on their own, but when brought together they can. Human beings are made of cells, but are not a blob of cells being able to walk and talk, love and hate, destroy and create. The whole aeroplane and the whole human being are more than the sum of their parts.

Now, what is needed is a tool for thought that can bring all the thinking about thinking together. On offer to do this is a microscope. It is a very special microscope. An ordinary traditional scientific microscope helps to see things in an ever more detailed reductionist way, showing only aggregates whose sum is equal to the sum of its parts. Our microscope is a systemic scientific microscope, capable of discriminating between richly and weakly interacting parts of networks. It displays systems as richly interactive networks and leaves out aggregates. It has numerous magnifications and so it can focus on different levels of hierarchies. Filters can be fitted, removed or replaced on to each lens. The filters that go with the microscope are the metaphors presented earlier. So the microscope helps us to see at different hierarchical levels networks flavoured by metaphors. We can see mechanistic systems, organic systems, brain systems, cultural systems and political systems. What we see simply depends on which filter we fit and which images these help to create. We can look for systems with any metaphor employed as a filter. Each metaphor will give us some insight about the main organisational issues to be dealt with. We can mix and (re)organise the metaphor analysis to create images of organisations that give us access to yet further insight.

Of course, systems are not real and do not actually exist. They are thoughts about reality raised and organised by systems metaphors. This means of raising and organising our thoughts is highly creative in what it produces. The microscope is our tool for creative thought. It helps to achieve mixed, organised and creative thinking, the goal that we set at the end of the last section. Now we need to show how this can also be employed to help to choose 'problem solving' approaches that deal with the main organisational issues in the business context that the microscope helps us to appreciate. To be able to achieve this we must learn to critically analyse and make sense of systems 'problem solving' approaches. In the context of this book we need to do some thinking about methods for implementing quality management.

THINKING ABOUT
'PROBLEM SOLVING' APPROACHES

If we are going to intervene in social contexts like businesses, firms, non-profit making organisations, or society, then we need to establish an understanding of what goes on in them. 'What do we do and why do we do what we do?' These questions are fundamental to any form of 'problem solving'. This deep thinking may seem unnecessary to people who manage, but it isn't. After all, how can a manager(ess) manage without knowing something about the people who are being managed? So, 'What do we know?'

It has been argued that there are two fundamental things we do that underpin our social and cultural way of living. These are undertaking work and getting involved in social interaction.

Work helps us to achieve goals and bring about material well-being. We make, create and do things, and we earn money or resources as remuneration for our time and skills. With money or equivalent resources we can buy or exchange things and make our lives more comfortable. The success of work depends on developing a technical mastery over the natural and social worlds. There are many cases of control over the natural world. Electricity is generated from dams. Resources are extracted from under the ground and manufactured into finished products. People also live ordered lives according to rules and practices of organisations and societies. Accounting and even quality procedures are examples of social control. Work, then, reflects what we can call a technical interest in prediction and control over natural and social processes.

Work cannot happen without social interaction. We do not work in a vacuum. We are only able to work by communicating and interacting with others. Interaction helps us to understand what is going on and to be able to operate our technical systems in co-operation with others. Developing understanding is clearly important in the workplace; without it disagreement can easily occur. Disagreement can be as much a threat to achieving goals and material well-being as failing to achieve technical mastery. The main concern is not always how sophisticated or efficient the accounting or quality system, computer technology, or machinery is. Poor relations between working people can ensure that in operation such technical systems achieve only a fraction of potential efficiency and effectiveness. Disagreement through misunderstanding, among other things, affects the 'efficiency' and 'effectiveness' of technical mastery. We must therefore have a practical interest in securing mutual understanding and learning about each other's roles and needs to enable us to employ our technical tools.

Any manager will know, however, that people at work have hidden agendas and do not always want others to understand them. It does not pay to give away what motivates one if, being politically motivated, one schemes to bring resources to bear, to control, to achieve what one wants. The prevailing group in any political struggle will be the one who has access to the most power. Of course, exercise of power can prevent the free discussions necessary to achieve learning and mutual understanding through interaction, that would help to secure technical mastery. We therefore have an emancipatory interest in achieving freedom from constraints imposed by power relations.

There is a logical interdependency between technical, practical and emancipatory interests. There is also a logical inter-dependency between the methods that support the different interests. This dependency more than anything else shows the need for complementarism. Complementarism as previously stated means that there are many different approaches to 'problem solving', but each has its strengths and weaknesses. Some are excellent at cybernetic prediction and control, in achieving technical mastery, but fail to deal with issues of humans as social and political beings. Examples are SPC and the Taguchi method. Other methods have been developed focusing on the practical interest to generate learning and understanding, but do not want to work out cybernetic blueprints for or diagnosis of organisations, and do not have the means of penetrating whose interests are being served. An example here is QCCs. Approaches with an emancipatory interest can be developed to help to overcome coercive forces, although no examples exist in the quality literature.

The idea that there are three human interests therefore offers a first way of sorting out what the methods are good at doing. It builds on the simpler version of this framework sketched out at the end of the review on the contributions of the quality gurus in Chapter 2. We will develop this framework further in Chapter 8, before putting forward a comprehensive approach to implementing TQM.

CONCLUSION

This chapter started by putting up a challenge against key assertions of management today. Evidence was given that pointed to the need to overturn the assertions. Overturning them meant that a new conception of management today had to be established.

A new conception was established. A mixed, organised and creative way of thinking about organisations and the main issues that they face was developed. This was achieved by introducing five systems metaphors offering a means to create images of organisations. The tool that employs the systems metaphors is the microscope constructed earlier. The systems metaphors can be employed through the microscope to help appreciate the main issues that an organisation faces. Accordingly, the metaphors can be used to indicate which 'problem solving' method(s) is/are most appropriate at dealing with organisational issues that they have surfaced. Each method assumes one of these metaphors as its model of organisations and hence will be more relevant to the issues surfaced by that metaphor.

A link between three human interests and the methods that logically support them was also made. This was achieved through the foundations of a complementarist framework. This critically assesses what each method is best at doing in terms of serving one of the three human interests.

A link between issues to be tackled and methods to tackle them through the metaphors and the complementarist framework was thus established. Following on, Chapter 6 provides an overview of TSI that brings together everything discussed in Chapter 5.

FURTHER READING

●The following books were mentioned in this chapter:

Beer, S. (1981) *Brain of the Firm*, Wiley, Chichester.
Flood, R. L. and Jackson, M. C. (1991) *Creative Problem Solving: Total Systems Intervention*, Wiley, Chichester.

●A comprehensive introduction to systems thinking can be found in:

Flood, R. L. and Carson, E. R. (1993) *Dealing With Complexity: An Introduction to the Theory and Application of Systems Science* (2nd edition), Plenum, New York.

●The idea of three human interests came from:

Habermas, J. (1971) *Knowledge and Human Interests*, Beacon Press, Boston.

●The history of the development of complementarism in the management and systems sciences is documented in:

Flood, R. L. and Jackson, M. C. (1991) *Critical Systems Thinking: Directed Readings*, Wiley, Chichester.

6

A Creative Approach
to 'Problem Solving'

INTRODUCTION

Chapter 6 builds on the ground won in Chapter 5. New assertions
are put in place. A new approach called Total Systems
Intervention (TSI) incorporating the new assertions is reviewed.
The review prepares for Part 3, providing a framework over
which a theory of TQM can be constructed. The practice of TQM
follows this.

TOTAL SYSTEMS INTERVENTION (TSI)

Introduction

TSI has been developed over the last five or more years. The
approach has been used, developed and refined in a wide range
of consultancies at both competitive consultancy rates in
commercial and governmental bodies and without fees in
charities, etc.

It is the argument of TSI that the search for some super-method
that can address the world's diverse mess of interacting issues
is mistaken and will fail. This is particularly pertinent for quality
management that is dominated by its gurus, each with their own
super-ideas. It would be equally wrong, however, to revert to

a heuristic, trial-and-error approach and to tackle the mess in that way. We need to retain rigorous and formalised thinking, while admitting the need for a range of 'problem solving' methods, including quality ones, and accepting the challenge which that brings. The future prospects of management science as such and quality management in particular will be much enhanced if (i) the diversity of messes confronting managers is accepted, (ii) work on developing a rich variety of methods is undertaken, and (iii) the following question is continually asked: 'What kind of mess can be managed with which sort of method?' TSI is an approach that accepts the triple challenge just detailed, so let us move on to consider its logic and process.

The Logic and Process of TSI

The logic and process of TSI can be explained as comprising three interactive phases. These initially have to be explained in sequence. The three phases of TSI are labelled Creativity, Choice, and Implementation. They require maximum participation of involved and affected people as, for example, quality management demands. We shall consider each phase in turn, looking at the task to be accomplished during that phase, the tools provided by TSI to realise that task, and the outcome or results expected from the phase.

Creativity Phase

The *task* during the creativity phase is to use systems metaphors as organising structures to help managers think creatively about their enterprises. The metaphors drawn upon by TSI are those identified in Chapter 5. The sort of questions asked are: 'Which metaphors reflect current thinking about organisational strategies, structures, and control and information systems (including past, present and future concerns)?', 'Which alternative metaphors might capture better what more desirably could be achieved with this organisation?', 'Which metaphors make sense of this organisation's difficulties and concerns?'. Essentially we are drawing up an appreciation of an organisation's main issues to be managed as illuminated by models derived from management and organisation theory. It might be the case that quality issues are highlighted. Of course, metaphors may be mixed, for example, giving rise to coerced-machines or brain-cultures.

The *tools* provided by TSI to assist this process evidently are systems metaphors. Different metaphors focus on different aspects of an organisation's functioning. Some concentrate on organisational structure, others highlight human and political aspects of an organisation. The main aspects of organisation highlighted, and those aspects neglected, by each metaphor will be disclosed in order to enhance discussion and debate.

The *outcome* (what is expected to emerge) from the creativity phase is a dominant metaphor which highlights the main interests and concerns and can become the basis for choice of an appropriate method. There may be other metaphors which it is also sensible to pursue into the next phase. The relative position of dominant and these dependent metaphors may indeed be altered by later work. If all the metaphors reveal serious issues then the organisation is obviously in a crisis state.

Choice Phase

The *task* during the choice phase is to choose an appropriate systems-based intervention method (or set of methods) to suit particular characteristics of the organisation's situation as revealed by the examination conducted in the creativity phase. Let us not forget that we consider TQM methods to be systems based, and hence a part of the TSI armoury.

The *tools* provided by TSI to help with this stage is the critical analysis of the complementarist framework introduced in Chapter 5, and set out in detail in Chapter 9. Complementarism is the idea that there is utility in all well-thought-out approaches, it is simply a matter of working out the strengths and weaknesses of each. The complementarist framework helps to get inside methods and to assess the fundamental assumptions that they hold about the nature of organisational and social reality. Knowledge of the underlying metaphors employed by systems methods is used by it. Systems and quality methods may be linked directly to systems metaphors through the complementarist framework.

The most probable *outcome* of the choice phase is selection of a dominant method, to be tempered in use by the imperatives highlighted by dependent methods.

Implementation Phase

The *task* during the implementation phase is to employ a method(s) to translate the dominant vision of the organisation, its structure, and the general orientation adopted to concerns and issues, into specific proposals for change. Examples of implementation of quality ideas are given in Section II.

The tools provided by TSI are the methods used according to the logic of TSI. These include methods designed to achieve quality that will be chosen when issues concerning inadequate quality emerge. The dominant method operationalises the vision of the organisation contained in the dominant metaphor. The logic of TSI demands, however, that consideration continues to be given to the imperatives of other methods. For example, the key difficulties in an organisation suffering from structural collapse may be best highlighted using the metaphors of organism and brain but the culture metaphor might also appear illuminating, if in a subordinate way given the immediate crisis. In these circumstances a cybernetic method would be chosen to guide the intervention, but perhaps tempered by some ideas from a human orientated method.

The outcome of the implementation stage is co-ordinated change made in those aspects of the organisation currently most vital for its effective and efficient functioning.

TSI is an iterative meta-method. It asks, during each phase, that continual reference be made, back and forth, to the likely conclusions of other phases. This idea is captured in the interactive representation shown in Figure 6.1.

REMARKS ABOUT TSI

A concluding metaphor says a lot about the nature and use of TSI. There is a famous old Zen saying that says we should not

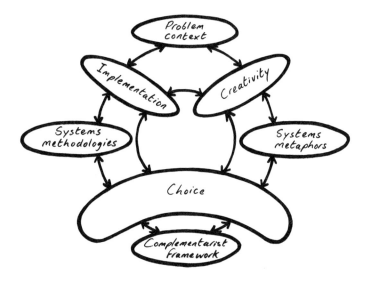

Figure 6.1   *The process of TSI*

be full of our own assertions. Zen suggests 'emptying our teacup' before greeting new guests, which means emptying our minds to make open spaces for new ideas. What I want to do with the space in your mind that you may allow me to influence is to develop an environment for thought. The idea is to wallpaper your inner skull and influence what goes on inside it. The metaphor follows.

One week an irritation starts niggling you and your partner. It is the front-room wallpaper. For six years now it has set the environment to the room and all that goes on in it, but the novelty

and usefulness of this has worn off. It is out of date and dreary in the context of new innovative ideas. A decision is made to change it. The weekend comes and the pair of you go downtown. A number of shops are visited. In each of the first six shops disappointment is felt. Hard-sell shopkeepers each having their own special style of wallpaper for sale swear to heaven and hell that theirs is the best, some genuinely believing it and sounding convincing. Each style is so unique that it is too specialised to provide an environment for all the things and activities that you want for the front-room. In terms of quality thinking, none is fit for the purpose we have set. A suitable style is found after a frustrating search. It is located in a place out of town that people always talk of but nobody seems to go to. The search involved shaking-off the most persistent and irritating shopkeepers who claim that if only you imagined hard enough you would find the generality sought. Imagination was not enough.

The chosen wallpaper has the logic and process of TSI as its motif. In this you see the microscope and the metaphors (from

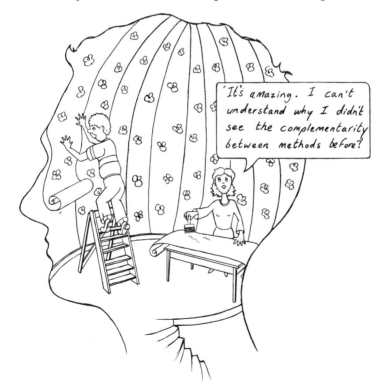

Chapter 5), the framework for choice of method (from Chapters 2 and 5, developed in Chapters 8 and 9), and a host of specialised methods. Each of the special styles offered on other wallpapers is captured in the ambience the motif offers but none loses its uniqueness. On Sunday the wallpaper is pasted-up.

Monday night you return eagerly from work to view and experience the wallpaper. A coffee is hastily made and taken into the front-room. Instead of watching the television or reading the paper, you admire the wallpaper. Your partner returns home and together you sit and enjoy the new and exciting motif. The second and third night you do the same, but on the fourth night you have a bit of a headache and there is a programme on television about cooking that is of particular interest so you watch it and pay little attention to the wallpaper. The following Saturday is your turn to have friends around and on Sunday several business colleagues visit. Most like the wallpaper, except one work colleague who chose a specialised wallpaper last month and stubbornly refuses to acknowledge the value of this new motif.

Life then returns to normal, or does it? The environment set by the new wallpaper provides a medium in which day-to-day activities are carried out in a new and rewarding way. Not everything feels perfect, but things are noticeably improved. What is not noticed is that a prime reason for this is the wallpaper. The joy of this wallpaper is its blending rather than dominating contribution.

The situation continues for several months. The in-laws then visit. They rave over the new wallpaper before greetings are exchanged. This reminds you about the wallpaper, about its motifs and contribution that it makes to the activities of the room. After the visit awareness of the wallpaper goes but the value of the ambience that it creates remains as powerful as ever.

By now my intended meaning for this metaphor should be clear. TSI is the new and exciting 'motif' that initially is prevalent in our thoughts and actions. It surrounds our thoughts as wallpaper on our inner skull. As we learn about TSI, it faces us starkly as the new motif on the wallpaper. After time and use, the motif fades from our everyday thoughts but it 'invisibly' drives our actions. We are reminded of it on special occasions. For me those special occasions are when I present the ideas in workshops, training courses and seminars. Then I think, 'yes, I rather like this wallpaper'. In years to come we may discover more satisfying motifs and changes will have to be made. This is a lesson of critical thinking that underpins our entire effort. But for now the version of TSI in this book is the best that we have got. Since we have to manage and do things now we might as well use it. Let us tie up with some concluding remarks.

CONCLUSION

Current management assertions mostly lead to the management nostrum, 'the quick fix'. The main assertions of TSI are that management needs to face up to the complexity that it should deal with and to develop formal and adequately sophisticated approaches, and to learn to use them well. To achieve this, a wholly new conception of management has to be developed. The new view abandons the notion of problems and problem solving, replacing them with a continuous approach to creative mess management.

For those that complain that TSI is too sophisticated, please remember not to blame the messenger for the bad news. The sophistication of TSI only reflects the complexity facing modern-day manager(esse)s. But TSI is more than a messenger, it also has an armoury to help to deal with the bad news. As stated earlier, however, we cannot dispose of people who are responsible for creating the bad news and causing managerial headaches. So think of TSI as an aspirin, or a paracetamol, a

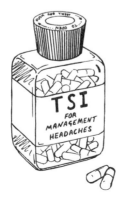

treatment that helps to ease some of the worst management headaches.

At the outset of this book, in the Preface, two main weaknesses in quality management were identified. These are, a lack of rigour in relation to management and organisation theory and the management and systems sciences. With the ideas presented in Part 2 we are now in a position to overcome these weaknesses. TSI will now be employed, first in Chapter 7 to explain TQM as a management and organisation theory, second in Chapter 8 to develop a theory for the practice of TQM, and then in Chapter 9 to suggest how to practise TQM.

FURTHER READING

●This chapter is an adaptation of Chapter 3 in:

Flood, R. L. and Jackson, M. C. (1991) *Creative Problem Solving: Total Systems Intervention*, Wiley, Chichester.

Section I
PHILOSOPHY, PRINCIPLES AND METHODS

Part 3: A new understanding of TQM

7
A Theory of TQM: A Deeper Understanding of the Philosophy and Principles

INTRODUCTION

The new approach to management and organisation theory, and the management and systems sciences, argued for in Part 2, is now put to work. In Chapter 7 the new ideas are used to generate a deeper understanding of the principles of TQM worked out in Chapter 3. Reference is made through TSI to the main theories found in the management literature. Areas of strength and weakness are identified. The analysis paves the way for a theory for TQM. This theory helps to overcome the lack of rigour of quality ideas in terms of management and organisation theory identified in the Preface.

The argument of this chapter is that quality, viability (from the brain metaphor) and culture imply each other. Unfortunately this is hardly recognised in the literature. The main quality protagonists still rely to a large extent on traditional scientific management and bureaucracy theory. And management today practise this theory. The contemporary management literature has shown that the traditional approaches to management assume mechanistic and coercive characteristics to organisations. The basis of the theory and practice of quality is therefore mechanical and coercive. In many contexts these limited conceptions contradict and neutralise much of the value that quality ideas offer to modern organisations. The aim of this chapter is to explain and to illustrate how viability and culture can step in when traditional ideas fail, to revitalise quality in management.

The plan to realise the stated argument and intention will now be revealed. In Chapter 3 we worked out a general appreciation of the quality philosophy and then extracted some main principles. These principles will now be interpreted using the traditional ideas of management and organisation theory that capture the thinking of quality protagonists. The interpretation will show that traditional mechanistic theory contradicts some main principles of quality, which threatens to dampen enthusiasm for the quality idea. This should not be the case. Up until now quality ideas have lacked two important ingredients, viability and culture. These can easily be introduced. They will be introduced, first by interpreting the quality principles with a viable and then with a socio-cultural system perspective. This will show that quality, viability and culture imply each other. The chapter will then be concluded.

QUALITY PRINCIPLES INTERPRETED THROUGH TRADITIONAL MANAGEMENT AND ORGANISATION THEORY

First, the reader will be given a quick reminder of the main premises behind traditional management and organisation theories. The theories referred to are scientific management (Frederick Taylor) and bureaucracy theory (Max Weber). These early theories are used as 'extremes' of thought that will help us to show one angle on quality principles. Of course, as we have seen in Chapter 5, more modern management theories have added a humanistic element. Management practice, however, has moved much more slowly in this direction. For ease of analysis, let us reiterate once again the main ideas of traditional management theory.

Scientific methods are used to design jobs and to calculate the most efficient way of doing things. The tasks of employees are broken down into parts. Observation and measurement create physical descriptions of 'the worker' and 'the job'. Therefore management is the process of planning, organising, commanding, controlling and co-ordinating the parts. This requires rational planning and efficient control of an organisation drawing upon engineering principles. The organisation is a closed system. A bureaucratic hierarchy defines lines of legitimate authority and power.

Embedded in this sketch are two fundamental visions of the nature of organisations. The first is a mechanical vision; the organisation operates like a machine and engineering principles are used to manage it. The second is a political vision, the organisation operates under a strict hierarchy of authority and control, the hierarchical tree showing nothing more than a power structure.

The quality principles of TQM derived in Chapter 3 can be interpreted according to this traditional model. The machine vision will be employed first and then the political one, but please remember that the political vision holds the mechanical one in the background. They lead to the following interpretations:

1 There must be agreed requirements, for both internal and external customers.
   Machine—external requirements are not seen to be relevant in the view of management.
   Political—the requirements are set internally at the top and imposed on lower levels; the mechanical setting of requirements may not take into account capability or potentiality, what could be achieved within or by removing constraints respectively.
2 Customer requirements must be met first time, every time.
   Machine—a rigid notion of objective goals to achieve in a strict internal order.
   Political—there are punishments rather than rewards; the requirements must be met otherwise demotion or dismissal may result.
3 Quality improvement will reduce waste and total costs.
   Machine—cost reduction must be pursued as a goal, which means that people must work together as cogs much more

efficiently; people must shake off what makes them unreliable (i.e., being human), there must be machine efficiency.

Political—there is a possible advantage of getting right to it, with less deliberation and thus lower costs, but higher costs could be incurred to police and supervise to achieve imposed rules. In terms of costs, there will be beneficiaries and victims. The victims often will be the employees who come under increasing pressure to achieve quality targets. A good example came to light in 1991. The Chairman of a telecom company had his salary related to profit and quality. The company have been implementing TQM for a number of years. Employees were asked to co-operate at this difficult cost cutting time. Nineteen thousand jobs were lost during the year with 10 000 more to come. Quality 'improved' and profits increased to a record £3 billion. This is not surprising since the company holds a virtual monopoly over telecommunications. The benefit to the Chairman was a 43% salary increase, up to £536 K (a substantial amount went to charity following a public outcry). The workers were the victims with 29 000 jobs taken out. During the time I consulted with the telecom company's training group I witnessed a lack of morale and fear about whose job would be next to go. The workers were an instrument by which quality and profit were improved. The viability of the company must remain in question.

4 There must be a focus on the prevention of problems, rather than an acceptance to cope in fire-fighting manner.

Machine—problems are essentially deviations from set points, and mechanisms must be installed that prevent the deviation from happening or correct it if it does happen.

Political—in authoritarian regimes, quality by inspection misses the value of quality by prevention; there will be a tendency to scapegoat and workers become good at problem avoidance and fire-fighting; more problems will occur.

5 Quality improvement can only result from planned management action.

Machine—the goals, or requirements to be met, are externalised from all but the chief governors and are implemented by leadership from the top.

Political—action is compliance to the plan, planned manipulation or coercion.

6 Every job must add value.
Machine—the mechanisms must operate systematically to increase quality at every stage.
Political—a quota or higher performance expectation.

7 Everybody must be involved from all levels and across all functions.
Machine—everyone is a cog in the machine and must work in unison strictly according to laws that must be obeyed, not necessarily because of the explicit will of some person/people, but because an organisation as a whole has a machine purpose that must be achieved; cogs (i.e., people) have no purpose.
Political—forced participation; work in unison because of the explicit will of some person/people.

8 There must be an emphasis on measurement to help to assess and to meet improvements in processes.
Machine—quantitative methods using statistics or mathematics establish how well laws are being met, how well the human cogs in the machine are performing according to machine efficiency criteria.
Political—rigid policing.

9 A culture of continuous improvement must be established.
Machine—one law that drives the machine explicitly states that the product or service must become more and more efficiently produced, but this takes no account of confounding external influences.

Political—the culture is a kind of slavery, driving not striving with little improvement likely to follow; recall the old saying—you can lead a horse to water but you cannot make it drink.

10   An emphasis should be placed on promoting creativity.
Machine—this principle is marginalised by machine thinking and is difficult to give meaning to in a mechanical context; creativity is divergent while mechanical goal-seeking is convergent.
Political—it is unlikely that people will be creative when they are merely instruments serving other people's interests.

With the machine analysis we see that the external customer has gone, continuous improvement involving external affairs has gone, and creativity has gone. This leaves a residual. This residual has a very restricted relevance. An example where it would be relevant is the nuclear industry (ignoring entirely the ethical debate that surrounds nuclear issues). Operating a nuclear industry demands adherence to strict quality standards. Laws need to be defined and documented in rule books. People's practices and the laws that govern them must be continuously refined (internal). A comprehensive measuring system needs to be installed to provide the information necessary to achieve strict control. Creativity needs to be wiped out to ensure the control of operations in a standard, predictable calculated way every time. The goals to be achieved are set-points that must not be deviated from. I suggest that you read 'Quality Management in the National Nuclear Corporation' by Churchill (listed under Further Reading) if you need convincing of this.

From the political analysis we see neutralisation or a reversal of advantages offered by quality principles. In fact, attempting to implement quality through coercive means will lead to suspicion of manipulation, demoralisation, a lack of creativity and will most likely increase costs and ultimately decrease customer satisfaction.

As already stated, traditional management and organisation theory holds both mechanical and political visions of organisations. Their individual and joint interpretation of the principles of TQM is evidence that they offer restricted possibilities to quality enthusiasts. There are two vital preservative ingredients missing from the quality literature. Viability and culture are those ingredients.

The penultimate stage of the plan of this chapter will now be implemented. Quality is interpreted below using a viable and then a socio-cultural perspective to show that quality, viability and culture imply each other.

QUALITY PRINCIPLES INTERPRETED THROUGH VIABLE SYSTEM THINKING

Viability is established and given its clearest exposition in contemporary cybernetic thought, is consolidated in Beer's Viable System Model (VSM, or brain of the firm), and its practical worth demonstrated in a number of publications. Viability is the result of two unique ideas in management. It results from a well-crafted approach to organising five main management functions as a viable system-in-focus. It also results from the employment of recursion, a special form of hierarchy. Recursion explains that a viable system-in-focus is a systemic part of a less focused viable system and contains in itself viable systems. The framework that harnesses the worth and contribution of these two ideas is the VSM. The two features and the VSM will now be reviewed. The principles of TQM will then be interpreted through the viable system perspective. First we will begin with the five main management functions and how they are organised.

The process of management has five main functions; implementation, co-ordination, control, intelligence and policy. They are organised as shown in Figure 7.1. This figure represents the VSM already mentioned. It should be consulted during the following discussion. Each function of the VSM contributes to attaining viability and, it can be argued, viability depends on the management process being carried out employing a quality approach. In other words quality and viability are complementary concepts in management. Let us briefly consider each function and make some observations about quality in each one.

Implementation is what the system is doing. It might be manufacturing or providing a service. Quality techniques found their first home in implementation in manufacturing and production. Manufacturing, for example, requires checks on the

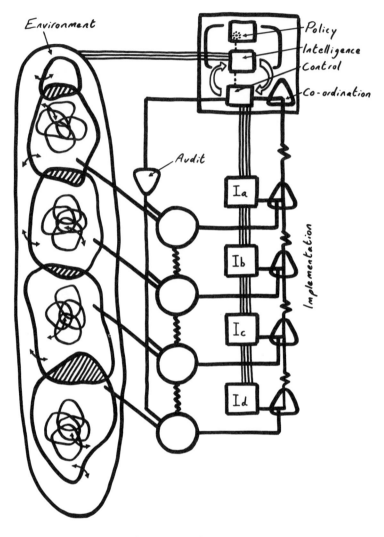

Figure 7.1   *The VSM*

quality of what is being produced, and minimising waste using statistical techniques and algorithms. Quality Assurance and SPC were initially in vogue. More recently quality ideas have spread to the other four functions that we will be dealing with below. (This progression, interestingly enough, is reflected in the evolution of quality standards such as the ISO 9000 series.)

Co-ordination manages to ensure that, in the short term, no part of the organisation is allowed to fail. It aims to overcome difficulties in implementation through co-operation between the parts for the benefit of the whole. Quality must be a characteristic of the whole. A company's quality image, that which emerges from the whole, is only as strong as its weakest part. Co-ordination in the short term can help to counter any weakness and strengthen the parts and the whole. If difficulties cannot be resolved through co-ordination and co-operation then more effective control will be required.

Control is about achieving a guarantee of internal stability. The aim is to promote the exchange of relevant information that can be used to assess how well things are going. Information is received from co-ordination when it is not able to manage, and from audit, intelligence and policy. Control has to interpret policy decisions and effect their implementation using all available information. Control allocates resources to implementation. A part of control is quality control. Audit is integral to the quality control function. The role of audit is quite general. Checks are made for all sorts of quality features of the organisation.

When difficulty in achieving control occurs and the implementation is not going according to plan, in our case for example agreed quality standards are not being met, information from *intelligence* is sought. Intelligence information details opportunities and constraints in the external environment. It represents a learning function in the organisation. If information is uncovered which is of significant long-term importance, it is sent to the corporate *policy* group along with control and co-ordination information that could not be handled locally. On the basis of this key information, internal and external opportunities are thought through and creative strategic decisions about viability and quality are made. Policy is also responsible for setting the organisation's identity. When dealing with quality, policy has to develop a quality mission in which the organisation's identity will be found.

Each of the five functions described above is precisely what it is stated to be, it is a function. *Functions* are not jobs to be filled. Each one represents the total effort of all jobs which deal with that function. Control, for example, will comprise the work activities that deal with finances, personnel, management information, quality and others. Policy will involve people from many work activities, including people with special expertise who may not reside in the organisation.

The viable system organisation allows for *participation*. Channels for resource bargaining exist between implementation and control. The means for achieving participation in quality management can be extracted directly from the quality literature. Quality Councils and QCCs are advocated by some for TQM. Other methods and techniques can be set up within the process advocated by viable system organisation. Some of these approaches can deal directly with the need to develop corporate culture (as we will see later). Importantly, they can help to overcome a main criticism levelled at the VSM, that it has little to say about how people and groups can and do work together.

A traditional approach to *measurement* to help to monitor quality standards tends to call upon short-term measures. An example is cost accounting in the form of cost and sales prices and the direction and route of cash flows. The aim is to minimise cost and to maximise profit, but ignores quality issues and long-term control instruments like latent capabilities.

An important set of measures that go with the VSM help to indicate the quality achievements of the business or organisation. The indices advocated are:

productivity = actuality/capability
latency = capability/potentiality
performance = latency × productivity

Potentiality is what could be achieved by developing resources and removing constraints. Capability is the possible achievement using existing resources within existing constraints. Actuality is the current achievement with existing resources and constraints. Two ratios can be derived from these; latency and productivity. Performance is then the product of latency and productivity. These ideas are clearly relevant to viable system thinking and address carefully the need for quality. Actual quality, capability to achieve quality within current constraints, and potential levels of quality following creative thinking about removing constraints, mark three vital things to be measured by quality management teams. In addition, the measures make it clear that quality issues do not neglect productivity, quality's forerunning management vogue.

Each function *filters variety*. It deals with most of the variety coming in but passes information on if it does not have the ability in the function to deal with issues raised. This prevents data overload occurring in any management function and allows for local autonomy. The five functions together deal comprehensively with all management information. The great variety which the organisation faces is systematically absorbed, not only by management functions as already seen, but also by recursive levels.

Recursion means that the whole can be found in the parts. That is, a whole viable system can be found in the parts of a viable system-in-focus, which is itself a part of another viable system (see Figure 7.2). This offers a novel way in which the quality mission can spill-down a business or organisation. A corporate mission is determined by policy using a participatory method that leads to the development of a corporate identity. This is the

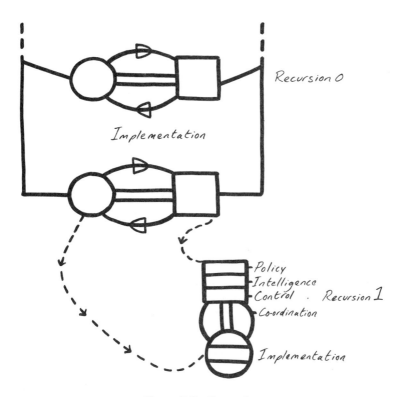

Figure 7.2 *Recursion*

quality image that we want to emerge, an aspect of identity. Sub-missions are determined locally within the identity of the whole. At higher resolution recursive levels the quality mission is interpreted and implemented. Using a recursive method helps to avoid the negative effects of coercive structures, implementing through management function, not by management authority.

Many of the key issues vital to quality management are catered for in the VSM. Recursion for example promotes *autonomy*. The parts have as much independence as is possible given the constraints that there must be when co-ordinating and controlling to maintain a whole. *Vertical loading* is encouraged. This means loading down responsibility to the 'lowest level' at which it can be managed. *Task formation* is encouraged to reverse mechanical reductionist tendencies to produce whole jobs. People then have responsibility over their work. They can determine the needs of their customers and work out for themselves how this can be best achieved. *Job grouping* is encouraged to bring together efforts that are logically related. This would bring together groups of jobs in the manufacturing process, and sales efforts, for example, by geographical location or client type.

Now let us summarise the discussion about viable system thinking and quality. The VSM shows how management functions are organised together and introduces recursion. It represents an exciting new image of organisations. The process of management in a viable system replaces systematic use of mechanical parts in organisations. Organisation through recursion replaces the traditional hierarchical tree. The VSM replaces a mechanical-coercive representation of organisations with a viable one. It brings together work activities in a logical and effective manner. This leaves the way open for participation, autonomy and responsibility to become central management concerns. Successful implementation of quality will rely on achieving these concerns in practice.

We will now use the appreciation of viability worked out above to interpret some main quality principles established in Chapter 3:

1   There must be agreed requirements, for both internal and external customers—the intelligence function helps to discover what the client requirements are and sets the agreement about

these within the quality mission; groups and individuals agree customer requirements, and by taking responsibility for their jobs are able to work out effective ways of achieving them.

2 Customer requirements must be met first time, every time—co-ordination and control at all levels aim to meet customer requirements, intelligence finds out how well the external quality goals are being met, and audit enables information about internal standards to be passed continuously to those who are responsible for controlling them (e.g., Quality Councils, groups and individuals).

3 Quality improvement will reduce waste and total costs—audit will highlight waste and total costs; real-time control helps effective decisions to be made on up-to-date information, to prevent wasteful and costly management responses to information that can often be months old.

4 There must be a focus on the prevention of problems, rather than an acceptance to cope in fire-fighting manner—the management functions get deep inside the difficulty of reactionary policies; the future is planned to enable properly co-ordinated and controlled, informed and thought-out policies to enhance efforts to achieve quality.

5 Quality improvement can only result from planned management action—management action comes from the five management functions and not from sovereign leaders according to the traditional view; strategies are conceived and implemented by those who have close involvement with them; intelligence provides information to aid the planning process; all workers must plan and manage their jobs.

6 Every job must add value—added value is achieved because customer requirements are understood; jobs and tasks are organised to be effective in achieving customer requirements.

7 Everybody must be involved from all levels and across all functions—the organisational scheme allows for involvement; goals are related to the whole and can be influenced from any management function or by any customer; quality methods like QCCs can be employed to encourage participation; supplier development is an innovative initiative in quality management that emphasises the breadth of meaning of this principle (see Chapter 15).

8 There must be an emphasis on measurement to help to assess

whether requirements and objectives are being met—a comprehensive set of performance indices that get to the heart of what is happening in an organisation are recommended and complement the five management functions.

9   A culture of continuous improvement must be established— the cybernetic principles give rise to inherent continuous change encouraging progressive quality improvement; the organisation learns through intelligence, groups and individuals learn through participation, learning provides the basis for continuous improvement.

10   An emphasis should be placed on promoting creativity— with intelligence and learning functions in place throughout the recursive organisation, and with plenty of relevant real-time information, an organisation is prepared for and can encourage creativity.

Now we have a viable system interpretation of quality principles in place. We have seen that viability and quality imply each other to a large extent. Viable system thinking *enables* an organisation to achieve customer requirements, to meet those require ments, to reduce waste, to manage issues, to plan management action, to help jobs to add value, to involve personnel at all levels across all functions, to attain meaningful measurement, and to achieve continuous improvement. Viable system thinking also *allows for* participation, autonomy, motivation, responsibility and creativity to be an integral part of organisational management. Viable system thinking will be complemented by, or even implies, the organisation being treated in these last humanistic terms. Now we will press home the positive contribution to quality management that can be achieved by effective management of an organisation assuming it is also a socio-cultural system.

QUALITY PRINCIPLES INTERPRETED THROUGH SOCIO-CULTURAL SYSTEMS THINKING

A very rich way of understanding human beings is to assume that we are interpretive beings. We are also very active, always doing things. Human beings make interpretations of things that are happening. We decide on what further actions to take based on those interpretations. We have worked out sets of action concepts to describe actions. Verbs are action concepts. Verbs are found in everyday language. They are also found in the management literature. For example, the viable system approach has five main action concepts; to implement, to co-ordinate, to control, to gather intelligence and to make policy.

Action concepts are made meaningful within the logic of a set of negotiated social rules and practices. These are not obvious, but are found to lie behind and hence explain to us what we observe being done. The rules and practices are themselves made sense of in terms of constitutive meaning. This is the fundamental assumption that underlies what is done that make meaningful why actions should be taken. It is in terms of the constitutive meaning, therefore, that we speak and act.

Let us consider a few examples of the interpretive nature of human beings. Admittedly they are extreme. In reality social rules and practices do not dictate human behaviour like the fundamental laws of physics would nature. The following examples are therefore possible cases:

1   The action 'to lay by the side of the road' would be interpreted in the UK by a set of rules that point to the practice of being hurt. Action taken would be to call for medical care. The constitutive meaning could be that UK society is caring. In another region the practice might be understood as being

drunk and perhaps no counter-action would be taken because it was perceived to be self-inflicted or each for themselves.

2   A hill tribe in Papua New Guinea greets its male visitors by feeling their genitals to determine whether they are aggressors. My acting in that way at home in the UK would probably lead to prosecution for indecent assault according to British rules and practices. The constitutive meaning that underlies this response is that physical sexual contact is only proper in private by mutual consent for sexual purposes.

3   If, as a university professor, I turned up for work groomed with spiky green hair and sporting pink pyjamas, and gave my lectures by reading poems and singing songs, then my credibility with students and colleagues would suffer. According to accepted reasoning I would be considered a 'loony'. Socio-cultural pressures prevent me from acting in that way. But leaders of other tribes elsewhere in the world dress in the way just described and pass on knowledge by chanting poems and songs.

We interpret actions of people according to a shared set of social rules and practices, and underlying constitutive meaning. These are negotiated throughout our lifetime. They constitute cultures that control people and lead overall to cohesive and orderly behaviour. Through the process of negotiation we are

'brain-washed' and 'indoctrinated' by the culture of the people who we live, work and share our lives with. 'Shared' and 'cohesive' are important concepts. We might ask, 'What kinds of action do we share that lead to cohesive behaviour?' The literatures of international relations and anthropology suggest the following:

1 Shared language (verbal and non-verbal).
2 Shared religion.
3 Shared dress.
4 Shared music.
5 A common history.
6 A common understanding.
7 A common sense of belonging.

As suggested in Chapter 5, this kind of socio-cultural reasoning has also entered management and organisation theory. People talk and write about corporate culture. Quality protagonists argue for establishment of ideal corporate cultures. Unfortunately few recognise in any depth what one is or what it entails to create one. At the moment we are mainly concerned to understand what it is. Writers in management and organisation theory cite the following important dimensions to corporate culture:

1 Company logos.
2 Company-distinct sayings.
3 Dress.
4 Stories.
5 Myths.
6 Metaphors.
7 Rites.
8 Rituals.
9 Choice of relevant issue for debate.
10 Peer-group behaviour.
11 Career patterns.
12 And many others.

Socio-cultural systems have these sorts of characteristics. They help to determine whether people interpret actions as 'correct' or 'incorrect'. They shape human behaviour. Shaping characteristics of corporate culture therefore reshapes human behaviour at work. But realising changes in the characteristics is a lengthy procedure that needs to be worked on and is too easily abused by political forces.

Treating and managing organisations as if they are cultures is a potentially powerful way of getting things done. The idea is potent. Establishing a different organisational culture means influencing people to think and act in a particular way. A quality culture requires a certain type of behaviour. For example, we treat all people that we supply information, materials or services to, as our customer, attention is focused on minimising waste, and people converse using the same quality language. Reminiscing back to my telecom consulting days, I well remember evening sessions in bars, the boozing buzzing with quality lingo such as, 'Who is the customer?', and 'What resources are being wasted?', all adapted to fit the telecommunications context.

Quality can become dominating like a religion. Corporate gods often emerge. Management representatives, advocated for example by the quality standards discussed in Chapter 4, can become quality gods. They feature on the front page of the company magazine, their picture alongside the latest details of the quality gospel, the rituals and practices. This reminds me of another consultancy experience. We discovered that the wife of a particular company's TQM management representative had registered for our 'problem solving' seminar. The effect of this on the company's training team working alongside us was profound. Every few minutes one of the team would sidle up to me, nervously saying 'Bob, did you know X's wife is on the course?' Not surprisingly this did not mean much to me, other than bringing back vague memories of a grinning portrait in a company rag. Mr X was not my corporate god. But never before and never again did the training lads act so worshipfully. Yet I was left feeling that if it had been the Finance or Sales Director's wife or husband, the whole thing would have been considered a big joke.

Successful implementation of a quality culture is never guaranteed. It has to be carefully managed. Believing that people will automatically operate a new set of social rules is optimistic. Unfortunately many attempts to implement quality have been like that. Many attempts unwittingly hope to establish a mechanical-coercive culture through a traditional management style. The most glaring evidence is use of the company's organisational hierarchical tree as the structure down which quality will spill. As we have seen, this implements quality explicitly using a formal power structure. It plays against and sees off many concepts and principles of quality management. Some of the key ones for socio-cultural systems thinking, such as participation, motivation, autonomy and others are stripped of their value or wiped out. There must be an underlying constitutive meaning that makes the rules and practices of the quality approach meaningful to employees, not just managers. Human needs must be satisfied. Everyone must have a share in the quality concept.

Perhaps now is a good time to review the discussion on socio-cultural systems thinking for quality management, using the ideas sketched out above to interpret the main quality principles set out in Chapter 3:

1 There must be agreed requirements, for both internal and external customers—all employees develop an attitude of

willingness to provide a service to all internal and external customers, and hence seek to find out what their customers' needs are; jobs are more satisfying when we deal with happy rather than irate customers. This must be part of the rules and practices.

2 Customer's requirements must be met first time, every time—all employees have a commitment to ensure that the requirements of the customers they interact with are met; this is also part of the rules and practices.

3 Quality improvement will reduce waste and total costs—those who have a commitment to quality objectives will seek out and wish to dispose of redundancy and wastage, and in this will be using their own time effectively and more meaningfully.

4 There must be a focus on the prevention of problems, rather than an acceptance to cope in a fire-fighting manner—the rules and practices of the organisation are preventative rather than reactionary.

5 Quality improvement can only result from planned management action—a management plan for action is brought into being through quality management groups and by encouraging personnel to participate in and shape the management process.

6 Every job must add value—this is another part of the rules and practices to be operated, so that all employees are working toward overall enhancement of quality in their work and personal quality of life.

7 Everybody must be involved from all levels and across all functions—the rules and practices of the quality culture pervade every corner of the organisation, which requires a cohesive underlying constitutive meaning that makes them meaningful to all employees; human needs are satisfied; everyone has a share in the quality concept.

8 A culture of continuous improvement must be established—this is another part of the rules and practices that should be normalised, relating to both work and quality of life.

9 There must be an emphasis on measurement to help to assess and to meet improvements in processes—each person when doing or redesigning their job, must achieve some kind of measure that tells them whether their quality

objectives are being met; this is another part of the rules and
practices.

10 An emphasis should be placed on creativity—all people
should participate, each understands better than most their
own job, each holds different perceptions about others' jobs,
the department or organisation as a whole; their bringing
together in participatory groups will thus release much
otherwise stifled creativity; in many ways the most valuable
resource an organisation has is its human element, not its
technology.

Socio-cultural systems thinking interprets some quality principles
as rules and practices. These need to be organised. They can be
organised using viable system thinking. Other principles are
interpreted as suggestions about how those rules and practices
can be made meaningful to employees. The importance of
achieving a shared underlying constitutive meaning is stressed.
Constitutive meaning is the unique element of socio-cultural
systems thinking that quality management must take account of.

We must allow for a humanistic element to achieve shared and
cohesive organisational culture. Viable system thinking allows
for the humanistic element. Socio-cultural systems thinking
enables it to be achieved. Viable system thinking also enables
an organisation to achieve the technical aspects of quality
management. Viable and socio-cultural system thinking
complement or indeed imply a need for each other in quality
management.

CONCLUSION

The argument of this chapter is that quality, viability and culture
in quality management imply a need for each other. TQM was
given a comprehensive exposition, being assessed by the critical
armoury offered by the creativity phase of TSI. Principles of TQM
were interpreted using the traditional mechanical-coercive vision
of organisations held in early scientific management and
bureaucracy theory. This theory dominates management
practices today. For *most* cases this interpretation was found to
contradict the main quality principles. Two vital ingredients were

missing. Viability and culture were missing. They were therefore introduced. The quality principles were reinterpreted using a viable system and a socio-cultural vision of organisations. Synergy between the two was highlighted. We saw that quality, viability and culture complement or even imply a need for each other in most circumstances. In this analytical process we injected rigour into quality ideas in terms of management and organisation theory, overcoming one of the two main weaknesses declared in the Preface. There remains the task of achieving such rigour for 'problem solving', employing management and systems sciences. To achieve this we must develop a theory for the practice of TQM that ensures human freedom is guaranteed. If nothing else, this chapter has shown that securing advantages of quality management can only happen when people have autonomy, responsibility, can participate and are not subject to coercive forces—i.e., when they are free.

FURTHER READING

●The following article was mentioned in the text:

Churchill, G. F. (1990) Quality management in the National Nuclear Corporation, in Dale, B. G. and Plunkett, J. J. (eds), *Managing Quality*, Philip Allan, Hemel Hempstead.

●Beer's trilogy on the VSM is:

Beer, S. (1979) *The Heart of the Enterprise*, Wiley, Chichester.
Beer, S. (1979) *Diagnosing the System for Organisations*, Wiley, Chichester.
Beer, S. (1981) *Brain of the Firm*, Wiley, Chichester.

●Works to consult on organisational culture include:

Allaire, J. and Firsirotu, M. E. (1984) Theories of organisational culture, *Organisation Studies*, 5, pp. 193–226.
Deal, T. E. and Kennedy, A. A. (1982) *Corporate Cultures: Rites and Rituals of Corporate Life*, Addison-Wesley, Mass.
Smicich, L. (1983) Concepts of culture and organisational analysis, *Administrative Science Quarterly*, 28, pp. 339–358.

8
A Theory for the Practice of TQM: Practising Freedom

INTRODUCTION

In Chapter 7 a theory for TQM is put in place. The theory stresses the need for autonomy, responsibility and participation, and getting rid of coercive forces—in short, a need for human freedom. It would not be possible, therefore, to claim proper and valid use of TQM without evidence that the practice had in its principles an element of guarantee for human freedom. This evidence needs to be provided in a theory for the practice of TQM. Chapter 8 shows that the complementarist framework introduced in Chapters 2 and 5 caters adequately in its provision for human freedom to be practised.

In Chapter 2 the quality gurus' contributions were found to fall into two main interest areas; a technical interest in quality control and a human interest in quality management. In Chapter 5, the human dimension split into two interests, a practical interest in learning and understanding and an emancipatory interest in overcoming coercive forces.

The technical interest in prediction and control is catered for in quality control by models that *design freedom* into organisations and society in the form of efficient cybernetic systems. The practical interest in securing through social interaction mutual understanding and learning about each other's roles and needs, to enable us to employ our technical tools, are supported by methods that have been developed that encourage growth of individual *freedom through open and meaningful debate*. The emancipatory interest in achieving freedom from constraints imposed by power relations is tackled by methods that provide an armoury to fight for individual *freedom by disemprisoning people from coercive structures*.

These three interests are logically dependent. Technical efficiency depends on understanding and learning generated through human interaction, which can only occur if coercive forces are prevented from dominating the interaction. This complementary relationship provides a systemic theory for the practice of TQM and 'problem solving' in general.

The plan for this chapter is relatively simple. We will sequentially explore methods relevant to quality management in each of the three interest areas to demonstrate how the complementarist framework caters for human freedom to be practised. The order of exploration follows the logical dependency of the interests, from designing freedom, to freedom through debate and, to complete and round off, freedom through disemprisoning.

DESIGNING FREEDOM

Although there are many methods and techniques in quality management that aim to secure efficiency in processes, there is little that parallels Beer's effort to achieve efficiency by designing in freedom. Stafford Beer has a design for freedom in his VSM. This is discussed in some detail in Chapter 7, investigating its relationship to quality management. In 1973 Beer pre-empted and smashed the arguments to be levelled by the critics of his organisational cybernetics who still fear autocratic dimensions to his work. Unfortunately Beer's 1973 masterpiece, explaining that autocracy does not have to be the case, has been left in the wilderness. Beer has made further responses but has got 'too tired' of mindless social and systems theorists to force his practical argument. But I want to bring home his unique understanding of the contribution that cybernetics can make to (quality) management and human freedom.

The message of Beer's cybernetic genius was captured for all time in the following passage from *Designing Freedom*:

> Civilisation is being dragged down by its own inefficiency. We cannot feed the starving; we cannot stop war; we are in a terrible muddle with education, transportation, the care of the sick and old; institutions are failing, and often we feel unsafe in the streets of our own cities. All this is inefficient. *Then it cannot be the case that the only way to preserve liberty is to be so damned inefficient that freedom is not even threatened.* We have to become efficient in order to solve our problems; and we have to accept the threat to freedom that this entails—and handle it. Everything that man can do contains implicit threats. This is something written in the law of requisite variety, as far as I can see. Then we have to be knowledgeable, and we have to be untrapped.

(The law of requisite variety was formulated by Ross Ashby. It states that only variety can destroy variety, i.e., the variety of a controller must be at least as large as the variety of the controlled system.)

Beer's plea is for us to understand that cybernetics will enable human activity to become more efficient, and will help to resolve many modern day problems in society. In this it will help to win freedom. He acknowledges '. . . the threat to freedom that this entails.' But the point is, why criticise and want to be rid of cybernetics, when by so doing we dispose of the design dimension to freedom? Succinctly, Beer is asking the critics of cybernetics, 'How can we be inefficient in the modern day complex world and successfully promote freedom at the same time?'

The structure of Beer's argument was engraved in 1973 in *Designing Freedom*, as the content list. It unfolds as follows. The beginning establishes 'The Real Threat To "All We Hold Most Dear"', and then reminds us of 'The Disregarded Tools Of Modern Man' (the cybernetic ones). 'A Liberty Machine In Prototype' is then proposed (machine is a misguiding metaphor—Beer uses a neurocybernetic model and this as a metaphor would be more consistent). Following on, Beer traverses science and cybernetics in 'Science In The Service Of Man' and 'The Future That Can Be Demanded Now'. The argument finishes explosively with 'The Free Man In A

Cybernetic World'. We will now review in a little more detail some of this argument.

The last 150 years, or so, has seen development from relatively simple lives in small communities with a low level of communication between them; to highly integrated national and international societies run by powerful pieces of social machinery. But the question remains, does the apparatus left over from the old civilisation, that has become established in industrial, post-industrial and information-based society, actually work in these modern times?

Old variety reducing methods involve tight structure, with organisations broken down into small chunks, all controlled from a single central source. They are governed by rules. They are rigid. As the variety that they have to handle increases, they respond by increased breaking down of the organisation into smaller and smaller chunks, with more rules to keep each chunk in place. In this machine-like cybernetic structure people become cogs operating without freedom. There is no room for freedom, not even to make local relevant decisions. Mindful people must become mindless parts. Creativity is suppressed by restricting commands and extrinsic control, originating or operating from the outside. This type of pyramidal shape can only work if, as a manager(ess) rises up the pyramid, their heads and brains get bigger to cope with escalating amounts of variety. As this does not happen literally, senior people remain out of touch with events on the ground, and their decisions become increasingly bizarre. People, already acting a cog-like role, have to turn, not only against their individuality, but now against their rationality. They become exponentially less free. Further, organisations of this sort are static and thus non-adaptive, moving only toward catastrophe, and in this sense too they threaten freedom of people belonging to them because they are not viable.

The old apparatus is catastrophic for human beings today. They are destroying the institutions that enshrine everything that we hold most dear to us. They threaten the family based on love and mutual support, the cohesion of neighbourhoods, the community, churches, businesses and growth of prosperity; all exemplified and protected by the state and international communities. They need to survive, adapt and change. What actually happens is that they clam-up and rigidify. They need to know the nature of *dynamic surviving systems*. They need to know about the *science of effective organisation*. Organisations fail because they disobey the laws of effective organisation, or variety attenuation, which in general their administrators know nothing about. The loss of freedom is a consequence of a loss of control over variety attenuation.

Only variety can reduce variety. Various components of an organisation, according to Beer's organisational cybernetics, should cope with variety relevant to them. There are five main management functions set out in recursive form to do this as seen in Chapter 7.

Now think of a human being in a viable system organisation. To have a viable organisation does mean that people receive instructions to do things, because they cannot know and understand everything that is going on everywhere else. People have to lose some potential freedom so that the whole organisation can be viable, can achieve quality and can be run efficiently. This is where freedom becomes subordinated to efficiency. The alternative that we are left with is anarchy.

We must choose between organisation or anarchy. Beer argues that if we wish to achieve freedom, then no choice exists. Although anarchy is the fight in principle for total individual freedom, in modern-day affairs it turns out to be self-defeating. Anarchy leads to disorder, chaos, catastrophe, mass inefficiency and a huge loss of freedom. In terms of Maslow's hierarchy of

needs we would crash down, ending up fighting for survival rather than, for example, enjoying self-actualisation. For each level on Maslow's hierarchy that we drop, we lose freedom. Organisation is needed, not anarchy.

A science of effective organisation is essential. This does not, Beer says, bring with it mind-blowing techniques that are already beyond most people's understanding. It is not a 'big brother' that will alienate us further from monstrous electronic machinery that governs and rules our lives.

We depend today on electronic machinery. Computers and telecommunications are vital in any organisation to help to absorb variety. Such equipment is misunderstood to be monstrous only because they contribute to the wrong side of the variety equation. If they do, they become variety amplifiers rather than absorbers, creating more variety to be managed. Such machinery can bring with it new demands that were unforeseen and hence cause rather than absorb variety. Only when electronic machines contribute to the wrong side of the variety equation are they monstrous.

With Beer we have a model of any viable system. In order to maintain viability and quality the total system must have a central regulatory model. The model ought to be created by democratic consultation but cannot dodge the truth that it will constrain variety in the parts. Some freedom has to be given up. Recursion dictates that the precise form of variety attenuation is a matter for local decision makers. We have a say in what we are prepared to give up. In short, people only need to give up as much freedom as is necessary to maintain viability of the whole. The whole returns a greater amount of freedom to people because of its efficiency, cohesion and guarantee of continuity—in short, I mean viability.

LINK 1

Beer's main contribution has been to explain how to design freedom. He is aware that other issues exist. Beer expressed a concern for a continuous process of liberating our minds from the programmes implanted in them. He makes reference to Vickers' *Freedom in a Rocking Boat*, where a mind-trap is described as '. . . only a trap for creatures which cannot solve the problems that it sets'. In this, Beer sets us up nicely for the next section. As we shall see, he links designing freedom to freedom through debate.

FREEDOM THROUGH DEBATE

Vickers' book mentioned above has stamped on its front cover, 'If we can decide upon our priorities we can use our new machines rather than be used by them.' Vickers might as well have said 'any technical system' in place of 'machines'. Beer and Vickers then make a good pair. Beer wants to design technical systems, whilst Vickers wants to work out priorities for them.

Priorities, of course, are not worked out in isolation with single minds processing away. Far from it. Priorities are established through communication. The necessary interaction ideally comes in the form of dialogue and debate, Vickers suggests.

Debate can lead to a wholly different kind of freedom, a freedom of the mind. This involves making escapes from trap-like preconceptions. Vickers' lobster-pot metaphor is a brilliant way of illustrating mind freedom. He pictures mind-traps as if they were man-traps working like lobster-pots, and says in his book *Freedom in a Rocking Boat,*

> Man-traps are dangerous only in relation to the limitations on what men can see and value and do. The nature of the trap is a function of the nature of the trapped. To describe either is to imply the other.
>
> I start with the trap, because it is more consciously familiar. We the trapped tend to take our own state of mind for granted— which is partly why we are trapped. With the shape of the trap in our minds, we shall be better able to see the relevance of our limitations and to question those assumptions about ourselves which are most inept to the activity and the experience of being human now.

Vickers' mind-trap idea can be extended to illustrate three things. First, that whichever mind-trap we are in, in principle there is a means of escape assuming that there are insufficient forces wanting to concretise them. Second, that it does not matter

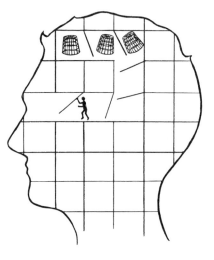

how Houdini-like we are, escaping from one mind-trap leads us straight into another. We never escape from our minds. And third, we are freer in the sense that we have a memory of all the mind-traps that once trapped us, and our means of escape from them, which have enriched our minds and our ability to make decisions with greater scope. We can pan through our history of great escapes to our advantage. We are freer. But we must never forget that we are still trapped creatures, trapped in our current thoughts. Each bit of freedom we secure, in the process described above, releases the grip of the traps, but our minds are still trapped.

The most adequate means by which we are able to work out how to escape from mind-traps, Vickers argued, is through debate. Participants may hold part of the combination for each other participant's current mind-trap. Participation in debate enables people to see more clearly the horizons of those involved. Ideally, these horizons will be brought together in one rich map that brings out new possibilities for all. This might, in practice, include working out the value of new technology, understanding friction that has evolved between finance and marketing employees, recognising that auditors are not necessarily spies, appreciating the rationale of a radical community leader, fathoming out that police officers can be genuine community officers, or learning that sending aid to undernourished people does not guarantee anything for their children's future.

In general, debate offers real possibilities for participants to learn and understand.

A great range of methods urging the use of debate have been formulated. Each one aims to release our minds from traps that otherwise restrict possibilities for innovative change proposals. QCCs make a contribution, coming directly from the quality movement. As suggested elsewhere, there are many valuable methods existing in the management and systems sciences literature that are also of value. We will now explore three of these that are relevant to quality management.

Mason and Mitroff assume, in their strategy testing approach, that mind-traps can best be escaped from by introducing adversarial debate. It is their reasoned belief that we all too easily conceive strategies whose assumptions are buried beneath our enthusiasm for them. This is as true for quality management as any other approach. It has to be recognised, they say, that if our assumptions are invalid, then the intentions we have will not be realised in action. A powerful way to get at and critique assumptions is to harness the positive gain from adversarial debate among people who subscribe to alternative strategies. After Churchman's book *The Systems Approach and its Enemies*, our best friends are our deadliest enemies.

Mason and Mitroff organise groups whose strategic positions, or perception of positions, as far as possible are homogeneous within a group and heterogeneous between the groups. Careful group formation is required. Each group declares their own strategic assumptions. Each one has to defend their assumptions against the strongest critique that other groups can put up. Where assumptions are found to be indefensible they must be changed. Where strategies fall because too many weak assumptions are found, they must be reworked or abandoned. So, throughout the whole process, participants have their most cherished plans and ideas counterposed with others. They have the roots of their preconceptions challenged. Each one has to see their own ideas in contrast with (many) others. In this process of adversarial debate there is significant learning and understanding. Each person has the chance to escape from mind-traps that they are in.

Ackoff advocates a method of Interactive Planning. In this he establishes a main principle of participation, wanting for the affected people to be involved. This is like Mason and Mitroff, except that the participatory debate is consensus seeking from the start rather than adversarial. By being involved in the planning process, which may be quality planning, members of the organisation come to understand the organisation and the role that they can play in it. They are helped to see in broader terms the main issues and possible ways forward. They learn from other people and end up appreciating things differently. In the IP methodology, Ackoff explicitly promotes challenging taken-as-given constraints, for example, working out an idealised design assuming that changes can be made to any wider 'containing system.' More than anything else, it is the process of challenging preconceptions that characterises Ackoff's interactive planning. Throughout the process mind-traps are escaped from.

Checkland and co-workers, like Ackoff, advance consensual debate. They guide participants through soft 'problem solving', a process that encourages all to contribute their own unique ideas about issues to be tackled. Many relevant ways forward are mooted and iteratively developed and debated. Participants are given every opportunity to conceptualise a given situation in challenging ways. An English pub, a favourite example, can be thought of as a social needs satisfying system, an inebriation system, an aggression making system, a profit making system, etc. Participants contribute their own ideas and are rewarded by receiving the conceptions of others. The process of debate may lead to participants changing attitudes through learning and understanding. These changes represent escapes from mind-traps.

LINK 2

We can ride with Beer and his design for freedom, but as he says, we may be ambushed if 'the threats to freedom this entails' overrun our efforts. The viable system idea designed to win freedom can easily be used to fillet freedom from an organisation.

With Vickers we may become freer people by debating, learning and understanding, for as long as no other person holds the secret combination to the traps we are in. Unfortunately, the ability to create mind-traps and to lock us in them with virtually no way of escape, may be within the power of others. Our traps may be concretised. Whatever else Ackoff, Checkland *et al.*, or Mason and Mitroff offer and do in their debates, they do not dismantle these kinds of power structure. Debate can only be effective if it is open and conciliatory. When information is purposely distorted or other political activities enter into play, the process of freedom by debate breaks down. This method of practising freedom then turns in on itself, to have the reverse effect. It either locks people inside the traps within which they already exist, or, leads them on to some other trap to the advantage of the leader (i.e., the powerful).

Designing and debating may achieve the exact opposite to the intent built into models and methods. Intentions do not guarantee a lead on to desired actions. In both instances it is possible that nothing more or less than coercion is achieved. *Designs and mind-traps can become prisons.* We therefore need another dimension to freedom, that is to disemprison.

FREEDOM BY DISEMPRISONING

When designing freedom and/or when freedom by debate fail people become emprisoned. Often this occurs because designs and debates are used to serve particular people's interests. The lack of freedom is structural and conceptual respectively. People may wittingly or unwittingly use humans as instruments for their own purposes and are able to secure this because they have sufficient 'resources' to bring to bear on and to control situations. The example provided in Chapter 3 on a telecom company may illustrate this. The imprisoned need to be released if we are to practise freedom.

There is a need to have practical ways of addressing whose interests are being served, to question this and if appropriate to change what is found. The key to opening the prison is to empower people at least with the knowledge that they are subject to the interests of others. This is not always self-evident. Such knowledge may help to break concretised conceptual traps that support coercive structures in society. A mode of critical reflection is required, to reflect upon the goals attained and means used through cybernetic models and upon the nature of consensus achieved through debating methods. Unlike designing and debating, however, disemprisoning is not flush with models or methods. Very little practical work has been done on disemprisoning.

Complicating matters further, other less well-understood coercive forces exist. Whole civilisations operate on basic premises derived from currently accepted knowledge. For example, at the moment Western civilisation is strongly influenced by traditional science, coming to the fore in society in technology and mechanistic cybernetic management practices. This dominant knowledge base is so deeply ingrained in everyday conceptual thought that convincing people their thinking and acting is shaped by some greater social consciousness is difficult indeed. But there exists a forceful argument proposed by Michel Foucault which explains that this is the case.

Much of what people think and do and the meaningfulness of it to them, rests on a set of unquestioned assumptions about the nature of and our knowledge about the world. These are invisible except to the most critically trained or minded people. They are continually reinforced by procedures established in civilisations. Institutions are central to this. Science and modern Western civilisation are our example. Schools, colleges and universities use material that rest on scientific assumptions and are prime in installing a scientific way of thought. Libraries are full of books that accept and promote the scientific way. Many books on quality management could be spotlighted as examples. Journals, magazines, television and radio are all caught up in this scheme of things. In fact, all sources of information in society are dominated by the underlying wisdom offered by science. Society also has its heroes, 'the great men of science', who we are taught to strive to emulate. Quality gurus discussed in Chapter 2, for example, are held by many to be heroes of management science. If we challenge the scientific way and the people of wisdom then micropolitical procedures switch to a more active method of operating. The challenger is subjugated. Their new ideas are prevented from being publicised. Articles are not published. Keynote talks are reserved. Ways of getting the ideas out are closed down. But if somehow the ideas break out then the dominant group have to respond. Tactics become a matter of exploitation of privileged and respected positions. The defence is simple but effective. The new ideas are 'shown' to have no sense in terms of the established rationality of science and are therefore 'shown' to be nonsense.

In terms of Vickers' mind-traps, we find a further degree of complexity to conceptual disemprisoning. As we have understood things so far, we can in principle escape from mind-traps using appropriate intervention methods. This leads us inevitably into another trap from which we may then escape. Freedom is achieved in the sense that we develop ever richer appreciations by continually escaping, although we remain trapped. But now we have to admit that this process is set only within some much larger and greater trap that captures the consciousness of civilisation. Individuals and organisations can escape from one trap into another and then another trap, but make no progress in escaping from the greater trap of their social consciousness. This trap is laid by micropolitical forces capturing the minds of whole civilisations. Our argument must then be that conceptual disemprisoning has to happen at all hierarchical levels in civilisations; from single minds, to organisational minds, to the mind of civilisations. It must tackle all types of political force, possibly including some which are not embraced by this book.

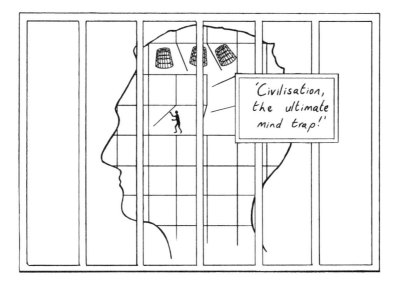

The hierarchy just mentioned has been partially tackled with a strong emancipatory theory on which is founded a set of investigative questions by Ulrich. Critical Systems Heuristics (CSH) offers a method that can be used by planners and concerned citizens alike to review the underlying value assumptions of actual and proposed designs, and to consider the consequences and side-effects for those affected by the planning. A plan to implement quality management could be interrogated by this method. CSH enables people to reveal the 'true' interests and motivations underlying proposals, assists with challenging proposals and constructing counter-proposals. It insists that no plans are rational that have not been approved by 'the affected but not involved'. It aims to disemprison people from interests and motivations of others.

The method of CSH falls into two parts. The first part helps planners to make transparent to themselves and others presuppositions that enter into social systems designs. The second part offers a practical tool which ordinary citizens can use to engage planners in rational discourse about the normative content of their plans. In the first part twelve questions are asked about the plan as it is. In the second part these questions are adapted to ask what the plan ought to be. The 'is' can be challenged by critical analysis using whichever 'oughts' that are brought forward.

The twelve questions are established around the distinction between 'involved' and 'affected' people. Those involved in the planning process are 'the client', 'the decision taker' and 'the designer'. The affected but not involved are 'the witnesses'. Questions relating to the client are about 'sources of motivation', relating to the decision taker examine 'sources of control', to the designer concern 'sources of expertise', and to the witnesses reflect on 'sources of legitimation'.

Three questions of each of the four groups just mentioned are asked, giving rise to the twelve questions altogether. The first question is about 'social roles' of the involved or affected, the second refers to the 'role specific concerns', and the third to 'key issues' surrounding the determination of boundary judgements with respect to that group.

From this procedure we establish whose interests are to be served by the goals of the organisation in plans and what conceptual assumptions are being made to support the organisation. The questions can in principle tackle coercive forces at several hierarchical levels identified earlier, but the current formation of the questions does not reach consciousness of the civilisation.

Unfortunately and as mentioned earlier, very little work has been done in this area of 'problem solving'. CSH is the only available method—but it remains on the breeding grounds and has matured very little over the last decade. For example, while the method is capable of embarrassing planners about unfair plans, it then has nothing to say about how we should proceed to bring about changes to the plans. CSH earns its place in this chapter on practising freedom by being the only genuine attempt to disemprison; rather than on the grounds that it is sophisticated and its way of use established.

Even less developed as a practical tool is the element of Liberating Systems Theory (LST) that includes the idea of freeing knowledges that are suppressed by dominant 'institutions' in society. LST attempts to get to the hierarchy at the level of the consciousness of civilisation. It shows the importance of releasing suppressed knowledge to create a greater diversity of available knowledge from which we can develop and practise systems thinking and quality management. It asks, 'How can we practise freedom adequately when so much human knowledge with all its unleashed potential is hidden?'

Much more work needs to be done on CSH and LST before we can claim to have adequate methods to disemprison. A huge effort is needed to develop these ideas for TQM. Without further substantial efforts on these two most pressing developments our hopes of practising freedom as such will remain just good ideas.

LINK 3

In Chapter 5, three human interests were explained and shown to provide a complementary theory on which we can base the practice of TQM. We can appreciate that each dimension of freedom is linked according to three human interests. We need to have efficient cybernetic designs so that society can operate effectively. The amount of efficiency realised from the cybernetic designs depends upon the following—developing learning and understanding about how to operate the designs, roles to be played by people according to the designs, how each role contributes and fits into the whole design, appreciating the benefits and meaningfulness of the whole, etc. Achieving learning and understanding requires open and free debate. On occasions when debate is subject to coercive forces a means of revealing, challenging and overcoming the forces is essential. Disemprisoning enables there to be genuine open debate for learning and understanding which leads to more meaningful work and to realisation of maximum efficiency from designs, which all adds up to maximum freedom. This is the complementarist ideal that we must strive for if we are serious about practising freedom and ultimately realising quality management consistent with the theory established in Chapter 7.

CONCLUSION

At the outset of this chapter it was stressed that proper and valid use of TQM can only be claimed if human freedom had been catered for. Three dimensions to human freedom are central to the theory of TQM established in this book. These are designing freedom, freedom through debate and freedom by disemprisoning. A logical complementary relationship between all three has been established. The relationship underlies the complementarist framework that is taken forward to Chapter 9 to promote the practice of TQM. A theory for the practice of TQM has therefore been established.

Now we are in a strong position to take forward the complementarist framework to provide the guiding force by which TQM can be practised. This is the task for the next chapter.

FURTHER READING

● Maslow's hierarchy of needs can be read up in:

Maslow, A. H. (1970) *Motivation and Personality*, 2nd edn. Harper & Row, New York.

● Russell Ackoff's work on Interactive Planning is dealt with in three main books:

Ackoff, R. L. (1974) *Redesigning the Future*. Wiley, New York.
Ackoff, R. L. (1978) *The Art of Problem Solving*. Wiley, New York.
Ackoff, R. L. (1981) *Creating the Corporate Future*. Wiley, New York.

●Details of Beer's work that explains the human freedom dimension to it are in:

Beer, S. (1973) *Designing Freedom*. Canadian Broadcasting Company, Toronto.

●Soft Systems Methodology is given a thorough exposition by:

Checkland, P. B. (1981) *Systems Thinking, Systems Practice*. Wiley, Chichester.
Checkland, P. B. and Scholes, J. (1990) *Soft Systems Methodology in Action*. Wiley, Chichester.
Wilson, B. (1983) *Systems: Concepts, Methodologies and Applications*. Wiley, Chichester.

●Ideas and methods relating to Strategic Assumption Surfacing and Testing are consolidated in:

Mason, R. O. and Mitroff, I. I. (1981) *Challenging Strategic Planning Assumptions*. Wiley, New York.

●Critical Systems Heuristics is developed and explained in:

Ulrich, W. (1983) *Critical Heuristics of Social Planning*. Haupt, Berne.

●The law of requisite variety is explained in:

Ashby, R. (1956) *An Introduction to Cybernetics*. Methuen, London.

●Michel Foucault's work can be followed through:

Foucault, M. (1965) *Madness and Civilisation*. Tavistock, London.
Foucault, M. (1974) *The Archaeology of Knowledge*. Tavistock, London.
Foucault, M. (1979) *The History of Sexuality: Volume 1: An Introduction*. Penguin, Harmondsworth.
Foucault, M. (1980) *Power/Knowledge: Selected Interviews and Other Writings 1972–1977*, C. Gordon (ed.). Harvester Press, Brighton.

●Liberating Systems Theory is argued for in:

Flood, R. L. (1990) *Liberating Systems Theory*. Plenum, New York.

●The following books were also mentioned in the text:

Churchman, C. W. (1979) *The Systems Approach and its Enemies*. Basic Books, New York.
Vickers, G. (1970) *Freedom in a Rocking Boat*. Penguin, Harmondsworth.

9
Practising TQM: Employing the Methods and Techniques

INTRODUCTION

In Part 1, a comprehensive introduction to TQM as it stands today is established. In Part 2 a new approach to management and organisation theory and the management and systems sciences was argued for. So far in Part 3 the new approach has been put to work, first in Chapter 7 to construct a theory for TQM otherwise missing in Section I and the literature. Then, Chapter 8 brings forward the theory alongside findings on complementarism from earlier in the book to realise a theory for the practice of TQM. It remains for the final step to be taken, to supply the reader with a guide that shows how the methods and techniques of quality management can most effectively be used in TQM, to come up with and implement change proposals. Chapter 9 takes this final step.

The plan for this chapter has three stages. First of all a general method to drive TQM implementation will be set out. The general method is strengthened by laying over it the TSI process to be used during TQM implementation. This enables the user to critically assess specific quality methods and techniques in terms of what contribution they will make in practice (i.e., 'Will they contribute to designing, debating or disemprisoning?'). Then some important methods and techniques already mentioned in this book will be described and assessed through the framework. The result is a comprehensive approach for TQM implementation that draws upon the management and systems sciences, and hence overcomes the lack of direction quality management was accused of in the Preface.

GENERAL METHOD TO DRIVE TQM IMPLEMENTATION

First Hints

At the outset of this presentation it is vital to note that it cannot be assumed that a quality management approach will always be the answer to an organisation's difficulties. TQM takes a particular although admittedly wide angle on customer centred issues to be managed. But, despite TQM being wide ranging and largely common sense, there is no guarantee that it will in all circumstances make the best sense. TQM *as defined in this text* must therefore only be used when TSI has led to the current conclusion that a quality approach is the most relevant way of tackling issues as they are understood at the moment.

Having stated that TQM must only be used within TSI, it is interesting to note that the approach of this chapter states clearly that the three cornerstones of TSI, Creativity, Choice and Implementation, must always be used within TQM. The plan for this chapter given in the Introduction gives that away. In effect and as shown in Figure 9.1, the focus of TSI becomes TQM for the purpose of tackling quality issues when surfaced by TSI. Figure 9.1 shows that TSI may raise quality issues to be dealt with. TSI then enters TQM. In this case the tools of the creativity phase become customer analysis guidelines and the tools of the implementation phase become quality methods and techniques. The complementarist framework is found to link customer analysis with the specific quality methods and techniques. Evidently, it would be as well to become fully versed with TSI in conjunction with this chapter. A full explication of TSI is given in the book *Creative Problem Solving* (listed in Further Readings).

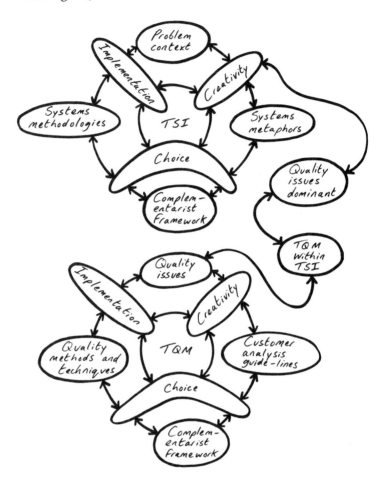

Figure 9.1   *TQM within TSI within TQM*

The General Method

(The method described below is illustrated in the case study reported in Chapter 11.) The general method that guides implementation of TQM is summarised in Figure 9.2 and detailed in the following text.

Develop an understanding of organisational design and organisational behaviour. Initially an understanding of organisational design and organisational behaviour has to be developed. This is guided by the creativity phase of TSI and will to a large extent have been

Figure 9.2 *General method for implementing TQM*

sorted out before moving on to implement TQM. For example, questions already asked will include, 'Should the organisation be designed like a VSM, an organic system or a mechanistic one; and/or managed like a cultural or a political system?' Because of the work done in Chapter 7, the implications of all these for quality management are known. The quality philosophy and principles that will guide the practice therefore will be set explicitly at this stage.

Set up a steering committee. A group of people has to be formed to steer the process of implementation according to the adopted vision of organisational design and organisational behaviour. This group is equivalent to a Quality Management Executive Council (in this case *to execute* the implementation, not necessarily to be an elite group of Executives!). The Council has to set a mission, set up the next layer(s) of Councils (deciding what depth in the organisation they must go to enable quality to penetrate the whole organisation) and design or choose educational modules (e.g., holding quality awareness courses based on this book). It will measure progress and generally assists in the implementation process. The Council assumes responsibility as the overall monitor and guider of the business's or organisation's quality programme.

Set organisational mission. The Executive Council initially sets a mission. The simple set of questions that follow can generate further and extensive debate about the organisation's mission:

1   *What do we think we do?* This normally reveals a wide range of perceptions that lead to insightful debate. In worrying circumstances it shows that participants have little conception of what they think the organisation does. In equally worrying cases conflict between participants may emerge, which feeds back into thinking about the issues to be managed, emphasising or re-emphasising the political metaphor and perhaps influencing the way the process of 'problem solving' continues. Remember, 'problem solving' is really a continuous process of surfacing and managing issues.

2   *Are we doing what we think we do?* Some honest searching here may reveal that actual activities differ from those thought to be happening.

3   *Why are we doing it?* Asking if there are good reasons for carrying out the activities currently undertaken sometimes wakes us up to the fact that we are doing things today because they have always been done, not because they need to be done.

4   *Are we doing the right thing?* Are the activities we are doing ideally what ought to be done?

5   *What else could we do?* Whether we believe that we are doing the right thing or not, it is progressive to consider what else could be done.

6   *What would be the benefit of doing something else?* Insights gained from question 5 can be tested through serious questioning about their value to the organisation.

These six questions direct attention to what it is that the participants fundamentally want to achieve. The aim is to formulate a succinct statement that captures the overall purpose and philosophy that will drive the business or organisation.

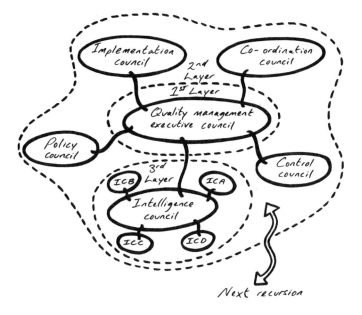

Figure 9.3 *Using the VSM to implement quality*

Set up next layer(s) of local Councils. The Executive Council ideally should represent all functions and levels since, as our whole system understanding suggests, each function will influence in some way the effectiveness of the others. The way that 'function' is thought about will depend upon the way organisational design is conceived. If the VSM is selected then representation would be sought from the functions Implementation, Co-ordination, Control, Intelligence and Policy. Deeper penetration can naturally occur, spilling down recursive levels. These then become the next layer(s) of Councils (see Figure 9.3). On the other hand, a more standard approach based upon the traditional bureaucratic model would use the organisational hierarchical tree. Functions then become subordinated to power structures and the next layer of Councils become the next most senior personnel, thus raising doubt about representation from all levels on first layer Councils.

Design or choose educational modules. The Executive Council must task itself with initial selection of educational modules through which they consider quality awareness can be best attained. They may feel the need to design special modules themselves or could approach competent independent consultants or management education bodies.

Local Councils set local missions. When the Executive Council has prepared the way for quality to be implemented the main tasks then shift to the next layer(s) of Councils. They straight away set their own local mission using the six questions listed earlier. The overall mission must be taken as given but interpreted to maintain the image or identity that must be reflected throughout the organisation. Only in this way can a coherent and cohesive quality strategy be pursued.

Undertake customer analysis. The emphasis with TQM is on the customer. A proper quality initiative will focus its thinking on customer centred issues. Requirements of the customer must be determined and agreed. Once these basic parameters have been set performance can be monitored. Performance analysis exposes weak areas where improvements must be made. Projects (a term that broadly means a way of tackling sets of quality issues) are then set up to attack weak areas and to make improvements. Customer analysis can be summarised as follows:

1 Name the customers.
2 Determine and agree customers' requirements.
3 Assess performance against the requirements.
4 Identify weak areas where improvements can be made.
5 Identify projects to make improvements.

Identifying projects to make improvements involves putting together well-thought-out and informed proposals. Guidelines to help achieve this follow:

1 The issues to be tackled by a project must be clearly identified so that all causes and symptoms are understood.
2 The ends must be clearly stated, so that a set of requirements to be met can be established and a measurable means of showing this stated. This includes setting major milestones and their expected time of completion.
3 Resource requirements must be stated.
4 Large projects should be broken down, or decomposed, into

sub-projects that are distinct but interdependent. They must be measurable against the aims of the sub-project and the project overall.

5 Rigorous measurement procedures must be highlighted that allow for failure analysis, so that the degree of failure being tackled can be compared to other proposed projects and shown to be reduced during implementation.

6 Ownership of projects and sub-projects must be clearly established so that accountability for the success of the project is unambiguous.

7 The project must be compared to other projects and their relative worth assessed.

Choose projects to be implemented. Choice of project(s) to be implemented has to be made from the set identified during customer analysis. Juran reckoned that there are two types of project:

1 The vital few.
2 The useful many.

This distinction separates the vital projects from the many other useful ones that, at least in the first instance, do not offer the same potential to improve quality. The idea is to focus on exceptional projects first so that maximum improvement can be made in the short term. A project can be identified as vital according to the following criteria:

1 How it ranks in terms of failure cost.
2 Anticipated impact on customer satisfaction.
3 That it shows a logical dependency with other vital projects and could inhibit their achievement if not dealt with. This is crucial because TQM ultimately is tackling sets of interacting issues, therefore all projects will be mutually influential.
4 If it is considered in some other way to be of vital interest to the future realisation of the overall quality mission.

The useful many should not be forgotten because, when added together, they make for further significant contributions.

We can verify the relevance of a project deemed to be of the useful many by asking the following questions:

1   Does it focus on improvement of either internal or external customer interface?
2   Does it address a significant cost of failure where measurable savings/benefits can be achieved?
3   Is it relevant in terms of achieving the local mission?
4   Does it offer the possibility of securing or consolidating on gains enjoyed when implementing the vital few projects?

Individual or joint projects ideally should be undertaken by all members of local Councils. Each member is expected to take on responsibility for a quality improvement project where practicable and desirable. Assuming responsibility in this way will help to achieve the following:

1   Demonstration of personal commitment.
2   Being seen to lead by example by those who will be encouraged to exercise a similar commitment.
3   Gaining an expertise in the ideas and means of implementation, of project management and quality improvement, in preparation to support other project leaders. After the initial phase implementing relatively easy projects, leaders of subsequent and more difficult ones will benefit significantly from the expertise of these experienced members of staff.

The choice of an initial individual project is a critical one. There is a great need for success in the early stages, since early failures could cause permanent damage to the business's or organisation's quality initiative. Projects are all about making a positive impact, but if one or more go wrong then they can backfire. The effects of a backfire could be disastrous. There is no point taking risks in the early stages of implementation. The following guidelines therefore need to be reflected upon when deciding which individual project to undertake:

1   Select a project that will be visible in the organisational context and will not be considered trivial.
2   Select a project that can easily be made more visible because

it has clear objectives that are measurable and hence can be shown to have been met.
3 Select a project that offers relatively easy possibilities for improvement.
4 Select a project that can be easily controlled from the individual's position.
5 Select a project where results are expected to be visible relatively quickly.
6 Select a project that can involve those who work with the project leader, so that they can be involved and brought together as a team.

Choose tools to implement projects. Whilst it may be the case that there are general activities to be done in any project, certain issues can be adequately tackled only by formal methods and techniques. At the beginning and throughout the process of project implementation, participants may need to draw upon a wide range of methods and techniques. Likely questions include, 'What project should we do and who will benefit from it?' Methods of debating and disemprisoning are helpful here. Then there will be the worry, 'How can we realise the project?' Methods of designing are clearly relevant to this question.

The complementarist framework from TSI comes into its own here, for it helps us to choose a method(s) or technique(s) relevant to the issues at hand. The main structure of the framework is built on the distinction between methods and techniques for designing, debating and disemprisoning. The three areas are then given depth by the five main metaphors, machine, organism, neurocybernetic, cultural and political (see Table 9.1). This builds into the framework the five main models of organisations and societies that have been proposed in management and organisation theory, and which are reflected in the methods of the management and systems sciences (see Chapter 5). This gives us:

1 Mechanistic, organismic and neurocybernetic designs.
2 Establishment of learning and understanding, coalitions and cultural cohesion through debating.
3 Ways of addressing political situations, appreciating whose interests are being served, whether the situation is coercive or not, and helping people to escape from traps.

Table 9.1   *Complementarist framework showing the main and related models/
metaphors linked to types of method*

	Type of method		
	Designing	Debating	Disemprisoning
Models/metaphors	Machine	Cultural	Political
	Organism	(Coalition)	(Prison)
	Neurocybernetic	(Learning and understanding system)	(Coercion) (Privileged interests)

For each of the three areas with its related metaphor(s)/model(s) we can extract principles for intervention. The principles fall into three types:

1 *Common principles*. Principles common to one of the three areas, designing, debating or disemprisoning.
2 *Distinguishing principles*. Principles common to several methods or techniques in one area that distinguish sub-types of method or technique.
3 *Unique principles*. Principles unique to one method or technique in one area.

Another version of the complementarist framework can be drawn up that sets out the main principles in the form just described. This highlights in what problem contexts these principles are relevant (see Table 9.2). This table has been kept relatively simple for illustrative purposes only, but can be expanded by experienced quality practitioners.

Use of the complementarist framework to aid the process of choosing a relevant method(s) or technique(s) is quite straightforward. Table 9.1 is most useful when using TSI. Table 9.2 has been constructed to help in the process of TQM, our immediate concern. Sticking with Table 9.2 then, we first need to determine two key things:

1 Whether we need to know
   ● *How* should we do it?
   ● *What* should we do?
   ● *Who* will benefit if we do this?

Table 9.2 Complementarist framework showing principles of methods relevant to quality management and their relevance to problem content

	Type of method		
	Designing	Debating	Disemprisoning
Problem context	There is a consensus view among participants about what should be done	Different conceptions and opinions exist about what should be done (non-coercive)	Agreement about what should be done cannot be reached and one party, wittingly or unwittingly, brings its resources or skills to bear to get its own way
Method answers the question	How should we do it?	What should we do?	Who will benefit if we do this?
Common principles	Communication Control Efficiency Effectiveness Efficacy Emphasis on location and elimination of cause of error	Participation Learning Understanding	Identifying whose interests are served Linking organisational power structures to biases in society (e.g., sex, race, class) Identifying how biases are mobilised in the organisation Identifying experts and their position in the power structure
Distinguishing principles	Emphasis on design control Emphasis on process control Environmental analysis Structure is prime Organisation is prime Emergence Hierarchy	Diversifying Attenuating Consensual debate Adversarial debate Group formation crucial	Identifying sources of motivation Identifying sources of control Identifying sources of expertise Identifying sources of legitimation
Unique principles	Recursion Variety filtering		

2   Whether there is
  - A consensus view among participants about what should be done.
  - Difference in perceptions and opinions about what should be done, debated in a non-coercive environment.
  - Disagreement where one party brings its resources to bear to get their own way.

Clearly, we would only be able to work out 'how to do it' if there is a consensus view among participants about 'what should be done'. Equally, we would only be concerned about what we should do if different perceptions and opinions are unresolved but can be resolved in debate without the introduction of force. If coercive forces do exist and are exerted then of prime interest would be the question asking 'Who will benefit?'.

The feel for the type of method(s) or technique(s) relevant to tackle the quality issues set for the project can be further confirmed. Confirmation can be made by checking the issues to be tackled against the common principles listed in Table 9.2 under the type of method we are considering using. For example, if it turns out that differences of opinion abound and we feel that the most relevant question to ask is, 'What should we do?', then debating methods become the obvious choice. The common principles state that participation in debate will lead to learning and understanding. Learning and understanding in non-coercive contexts substantially increase chances that agreement can be reached on what should be done.

We can then search through distinguishing and unique principles to guide us closer to the method or technique that would be most relevant. Following the example above, there may be a swing toward adversarial debate with the firm opinion that this will be most productive and will be of greatest help to establish what should be done. In this instance the complementarist framework has led us along a critically reflective route toward Strategic Assumption Surfacing and Testing (SAST). SAST would be the choice.

The complementarist framework provides the guide for choice of relevant methods or techniques during the process of implementing TQM. The following section presents the main methods and techniques mentioned in this book.

Implement educational modules and communicate details of the project. The next stage is to implement education modules and communicate details of the project to all those involved and affected. This is necessary because anything other than a trivial project will involve and affect many people. The sort of people that are assumed to be involved or affected with this style of thinking include suppliers and external customers as well as members of the organisation. A key point, actually, is to ensure that all those involved are educated so that they can be properly integrated into the project, having a clear understanding of the issues, proposed way forward and means of testing the success of the project. In some circumstances local Councils may feel the need to use or design their own specialist modules. Team members, those involved, must be capable of doing their set tasks. They must also be committed. Wide participation in setting the local mission and customer analysis will raise commitment and reduce the amount of effort needed in education and communication to build in capability.

Implement projects. Once a decision has been made about how the project is to be realised and the means of education and communication selected, project implementation switches to full steam. Actual implementation will be carried out according to the methods or techniques chosen and the project proposal itself. There are a number of other things, however, that should be taken into account. These will now be discussed.

Detailed implementation planning is vital. All those involved should be thoroughly organised, so that it is known exactly who is going to do what, when that is to be done by, and in accordance with what kinds of measurement. Resource scheduling must be calculated.

Each project must be monitored and reviewed by its relevant local Council and ultimately by the Executive Council. This puts in place a reporting system that helps:

1 To assess whether the quality initiative is realising expected benefits.
2 To assess overall success of projects.
3 To co-ordinate efforts and avoid duplication, locally and overall.

4 To promote the sharing of successes and lessons throughout.
5 To maximise benefit to the business or organisation overall.
6 To monitor overall costs and savings.
7 To agree objectives and plans for each project to be undertaken.
8 To run each project in an effective way.

Now, if the project is completely ready in terms of the factors outlined above, it can be implemented. When the project has been completed and designated benefits assessed through measurement, a report must be made to the relevant Council. A summary should be provided which contains the following information:

1 A record of the benefits achieved and the costs incurred.
2 Details of any deviations from the initial plan.
3 How the improvements that have been achieved can be consolidated and maintained.
4 Whether there are any ideas concerning wider applicability of the project.
5 How the project contributed to other related projects.
6 What lessons were learned and how these can be built upon.
7 What the key achievements were that deserve recognition.

The most relevant methods and techniques mentioned in this book are presented in the next section.

METHODS AND TECHNIQUES

Introduction

There is one common theme that links all the methods and techniques set out below. The theme is that they are relevant to the definition of quality explained in Chapter 3. Each method or technique, in some way, helps to meet agreed customers' requirements at lowest cost, first time, every time. 'In some way' means that the methods and techniques will do this broadly speaking in one of three ways; either designing, debating or disemprisoning.

A review of the contribution made by the quality gurus in Chapter 2 revealed their methods and discovered them largely to be of the designing type. The gurus have made a much smaller contribution to debating and no contribution to disemprisoning. This leaves a gap to be filled.

A search through the methods of the management and systems sciences uncovers methods relevant to quality management. These can help either to strengthen the designing armoury or to plug the gap in debating and disemprisoning (e.g., browse through the methods discussed in Chapters 7 and 8). The following methods will be drawn in from the management and systems sciences to do this job:

1 Designing
  ● Viable System Model (VSM) and its use in diagnosis.
2 Debating
  ● Strategic Assumption Surfacing and Testing (SAST)
  ● Interactive Planning (IP).
3 Disemprisoning
  ● Critical Systems Heuristics (CSH).

There are plenty of other approaches that could have been brought in. Choice of inclusion was made on the basis of their compatibility with quality thinking (all), the relative ease with which they can be explained within the frame of this book (SAST and IP; VSM following its lengthy discussion earlier), and uniqueness (CSH, the only method that contributes to disemprisoning). The reader may wish to explore other methods from the management and systems sciences after completing this book.

The methods and techniques included from the quality literature have been selected to build as much diversity as possible into the complementarist framework whilst avoiding techniques that require knowledge of sophisticated statistics and mathematics. This book has been written for managers rather than statisticians or engineers. I do believe strongly in the value of quantitative methods, but have learnt that they do not belong in a popularised book. The reader committed to developing an expertise in quality management can learn the more sophisticated quantitative techniques from other sources and immediately relate them back to the complementarist framework herein. Further Reading provides sources where the reader may start this process.

The presentation below of methods and techniques relevant to quality management follows the sequence, designing, debating and disemprisoning.

Designing

Fishbone Cause/Effect Diagrams

(Fishbone diagrams are used in the case study in Chapter 13.) The main principles of fishbone cause/effect diagrams are:

- Communication
- Control
- Efficiency
- Effectiveness
- Efficacy
- Emphasis on location and elimination of cause of error
- Hierarchy

The fishbone method is most effectively used when there is a consensus view among participants about what should be done. It helps to answer the question, 'How should we do it?'

A fishbone diagram is a hierarchical model. The main purpose of the model is to help to locate and thus facilitate elimination of cause of error. This can help within the general method for implementing TQM, pointing to areas where quality improvement projects are urgently needed.

A fishbone diagram uses the bone structure of a fish as a metaphor on which to base a model for locating cause of error. The diagram is hierarchical rather than systemic (pointed out in Chapter 2). A general version of the diagram is shown in Figure 9.4. The head of the fish is a block that is assumed to be an effect of a set of hierarchically related causes. This block is usually known as a quality characteristic. The spine of the fish provides a link to the quality characteristic on which causes can be hung. Figure 9.4 shows four categories of cause linked to the quality

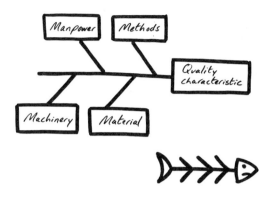

Figure 9.4 *A general version of a fishbone diagram*

characteristic via the spine. These may present a useful start to the analysis of the quality characteristic. The four are:

1 *Manpower*. People's behaviour and attitudes.
2 *Methods*. The way activities are carried out (e.g., rules, procedures, specifications, standards, etc.).
3 *Machinery*. What people work with.
4 *Material*. What people work on.

When using the fishbone diagram these general categories quickly become renamed to reflect issues of the organisation being analysed. Sub-categories are often formed that make the diagram more like a tree than fishbone.

No right and proper method exists stating how fishbone diagrams must be used. The following steps suggest one approach; identify quality characteristics, undertake initial analysis, expand analysis, discuss findings, and identify projects to be done.

Identify quality characteristics. Initially a set of errors or quality characteristics are identified for possible further analysis. They are ranked in terms of failure cost. Using the ranking and any other relevant information one or more quality characteristic(s) are chosen for cause/error analysis. This part is largely catered for within the general method for implementing TQM.

Undertake initial analysis. The four main categories are used to start up analysis. The quality characteristic is initially analysed for causes of failure in terms of manpower, methods, machinery and material. This quickly will expand.

Expand analysis. The initial analysis is expanded. New categories and sub-categories are formed. This process is like brainstorming using the fishbone diagram to structure ideas and suspicions about causes of error.

Discuss findings. Participants of the analysis must openly discuss and debate their findings, suspicions and beliefs about the cause of error and failure.

Identify projects. The result of fishbone analysis can be used in the process of selection of projects for quality improvement.

A more sophisticated approach to help with issues relating to design comes under the heading Control Charts.

Control Charts

The main principles of control charts are:
- Communication
- Control
- Efficiency
- Effectiveness
- Efficacy
- Emphasis on location and elimination of cause of error
- Emphasis on process control

Control charts are most effectively used when there is a consensus view among participants about what should be done. It helps to answer the question, 'How should we do it?'

Control charts are an essential tool of the quality manager, particularly the manager working in the manufacturing sector. The main purpose of charts is to reduce error on a real-time basis. This is achieved by calculating and plotting on graphs statistical data, and using this as a control chart to identify the occurrence and cause of error. Corrective action is taken in the presence of special causes and, more importantly, no action is taken in their absence. To understand and hence be able to use control charts, a quality manager must be conversant with some basic statistics.

Statistics is an analytical area of study that promotes understanding of numerical data. Data is collected, manipulated by techniques, is commonly presented diagrammatically or graphically and then interpreted revealing new information otherwise hidden in the data. The new information uncovered through the statistical methods of control charts brings to light where a process is centred and the degree of variation around the centre. Plotting this information enables judgements to be made about how the process is behaving. Typical errors located include:

1 *Variation around the centre is too large.* This means, for example, that there is too much defective output. In terms of our definition of TQM, agreed customers' requirements are not being met.
2 *A shift in the process occurs away from the centre to a new centre.* A shift is identified when a series of points on the control chart are consistently on one side of the centre, showing that the process is occurring around a new actual centre, away from the desired centre. This could mean, for example, that the parameters on a machine have slipped and need resetting.
3 *A trend in the process is found that is moving away from the centre.* A trend becomes apparent when a series of points on the control chart are found to consistently move away from the desired centre of the process. Faulty equipment could be the cause of this type of error

These three sorts of error can be searched for using fairly simple statistical methods. The main techniques and concepts the quality manager must understand are: the average, variation, range, standard deviation and normal distribution. Familiarity with these and how to use them in conjunction with a control chart are all that the reader needs to know within the confines of this book. This is dealt with below.

The average of a set of data is a common concept that many people use in their everyday lives. It can be written down in the form of an equation, using symbols to represent particular things that we need to know about when making the calculation. Equation (9.1) is the formal symbolic representation for calculating the average.

$$\overline{X} = \left(\sum_{i=1}^{n} X_i \right) \div n \qquad (9.1)$$

where X is the series of data, n is the number of data, ΣX signifies the series of data summed together for 1 to n, and hence the remaining division of the summed data by the number of data points produces the average figure $\overline{X}$ (pronounced 'X bar') for all the data. The average is the centre of all the data.

All processes have variation. In the previous paragraph the method for calculating averages was given. The average might be the ideal that is desired for a particular process. Very few of the data are found to be at the point of the average. They vary around the average point. There is variation. Variation of data, however, is not predictable but a range within which the variation can be allowed to occur can be set and achievement of this made predictable through control procedures. Variation can be caused by abnormal occurrences in a machine, material, people, methods, measurements or environment. If variation is found to be unacceptable (discussed below) then the cause must be traced and action taken.

The range is a straightforward measure of variation and is easy to calculate. From the series of data being analysed, the smallest number is subtracted from the largest with the result being a measure called the range. Other important and easy to understand statistics exist as measures of variation.

The standard deviation quantifies variation of a process. The standard deviation is a measure of the spread of data around the average. The closer the data lies to the average overall the smaller the standard deviation will be and vice versa. The standard deviation is calculated employing Equation (9.2).

$$s = \sqrt{\dfrac{\sum\limits_{i=1}^{n} (\overline{X} - X_i)^2}{n-1}} \qquad (9.2)$$

s is the standard deviation. Studying Equation (9.2) reveals the following. The average is calculated first of all. Then each actual data point is subtracted in turn from the average and squared (signified by the superscript 2, i.e., multiplied by itself so that the differences are all expressed as positive numbers). These

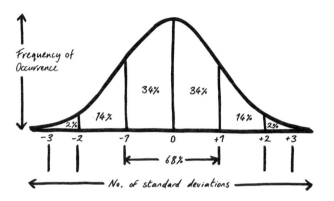

Figure 9.5 *A bell-shaped curve showing standard deviations*

calculations yield another series, the differences of the data points from the average. The resulting series is then summed to produce one overall figure. The single figure is then divided by the number of data points less one. The square root of this number is then taken—it is the measure called the standard deviation.

It is typical of measurements from manufacturing processes that when plotted on a graph, with one axis the frequency of occurrence and the other the range of measures, a bell-shaped curve is realised. The standard deviation relates to this bell-shaped curve in the following way (see Figure 9.5). Of all the data points 68% lie within one standard deviation from the average, 95% within two standard deviations and 99.7% within three standard deviations. Therefore 99.7% of the measurements taken from a manufacturing process will fall within a distribution that is plus or minus three standard deviations from the average. If the acceptable range for a manufacturing process is less than three standard deviations then it is said to be well centred and will probably meet specified requirements. If it is not, and requirements are not being met, then action has to be taken to bring the process back within acceptable variation.

Necessary statistical concepts and techniques that support control chart methods have now been put in place. We can confidently move on to look at control charts as such. A control chart is a statistical tool that provides information about a process based on measurements taken from that process. A general method for constructing a control chart follows.

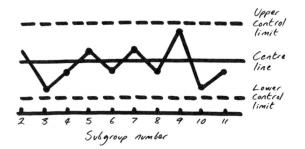

Figure 9.6 *A general representation of a control chart*

Initially, data samples from the manufacturing process called subgroups are taken at regular intervals. For example, a data series may be taken every half-hour, every hour, once per shift or once per batch—the choice of interval will depend upon the manufacturing context (production rate and process stability). A statistical measure is then derived for each subgroup from the data. The measure chosen will be in accordance with the type of control chart to be used (discussed below). This is then plotted graphically on the vertical axis of the control chart. The horizontal axis is used to represent the subgroups as they occurred over time. The control chart is therefore a series of statistical measures for a number of subgroups (say 20 to 25) which shows a measure of the behaviour of the process over time according to the chosen statistic. A centre line and upper and lower control limits can be set (see Figure 9.6). As long as the plotted points remain within the control limits (reflecting agreed requirements) that process is under control. If one or more points fall outside the limits then the process has gone out of control and remedial action has to be taken.

There are several types of control chart available to the quality manager. Selection of a chart to use depends on the type of data measurements made. Broadly speaking there are two types of data:

1   Variable data are measurements of physical parts (e.g., length, width, diameter, weight, volume, strength, etc.). $\bar{X}$ and R, that is average and range, charts are used with variable data and are described below.
2   Attribute data are measurements collected by counting defects

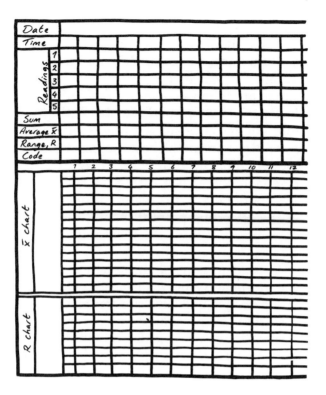

Figure 9.7 X̄ *and* R *chart*

(i.e., a unit that does not conform to requirements) and defectives (i.e., a unit that has a part that does not conform to requirements such as invoice errors, delivery errors or rejects). Attribute data are plotted on *p*, *np*, *c* or *u* charts. The more commonly used *p* and *c* charts are reviewed below (see Further Reading for *np* and *u* charts).

X̄ *and* R *charts*, as suggested by the name, are two charts combined on a single form allowing combined analysis (see Figure 9.7). Process averages X̄ and ranges R are calculated from subgroups. The usual size of a subgroup is in the region of five. The size chosen for each subgroup at the beginning must remain the same throughout the control chart exercise.

The average of each subgroup is plotted on the X̄ chart. The range of the subgroup is then plotted on the R chart. After a suitable period of, say, 20 subgroups, the average of the averages can be calculated. This is denoted $\bar{\bar{X}}$, or X double bar. This is the centre line that should be drawn across the $\bar{X}$ chart. Similarly the average of the ranges is calculated and drawn across the R chart and labelled R bar, or $\bar{R}$.

Control limits are then calculated, drawing upon the idea of standard deviation. This part of the analysis is beyond the scope of the current volume. Consult Further Reading at the end of this chapter for directions to the best sources. Control limits help to determine whether the charts are in control. Each point is assessed to see whether it lies within the control limits. If it is the process is continued. If it is not then corrective action must be taken, as the offending point turns up, to achieve real-time control. Other interpretations are then made and action taken when necessary.

A *p chart* is used to control the fraction defective (*p*) of a process. The decimal value *p* is easily calculated, dividing the number of defective units in a subgroup by the total number of units inspected. Sequential *p* values are plotted on the *p* graph. A centre line can be calculated in the usual manner and then plotted. Control limits are then calculated and plotted (see Further Reading). Each point is assessed to see whether it lies within the control limits. If it is the process is continued. If it is not then corrective action must be taken straight away. Other interpretation is then made and action taken if necessary.

A *c chart* is used to control the number of defects (*c*) in a process. It is brought into play when a large number of attributes are inspected and the total number of defects potentially are large. Subgroups of size about five are taken and kept constant in size. Note, their size may be less than the number of defects since there may be more than one defect per unit.

The number of defects for each subgroup are then plotted on the *c* chart. The centre line, *c*, is calculated by dividing the total number of defects by the total number of subgroups. Control limits are then calculated and plotted on the *c* chart (again, follow this up from Further Reading). Each point is assessed to see whether it lies within the control limits. If it is the process is continued. If it is not then corrective action must be taken. As with other charts, interpretation is then made and action taken if necessary.

Taguchi Method

The main principles of the Taguchi method are:

- Communication
- Control
- Efficiency
- Effectiveness
- Efficacy
- Emphasis on location and elimination of cause of error
- Emphasis on design control
- Emphasis on environmental analysis

The Taguchi method is most effectively used when there is a consensus view among participants about what should be done. It helps to answer the question, 'How should we do it?'

The Taguchi philosophy, principles and method were described in Chapter 2 on quality gurus. The method will be repeated in a little more detail below. Details of the statistical and mathematical techniques used by Taguchi are not dealt with in this book for managers. The method has three phases; system design, parameter design and tolerance design.

System design. The aim of system design is to apply scientific and engineering principles to develop a functional design. System design has two distinct components; product design and process design. Product design involves choice of materials and parts. Process design involves choice of equipment. Both involve calculating start design parameters; for product levels in product design and process factors levels in process design.

Parameter design. The aim of parameter design is to conduct an investigation to identify settings that minimise or reduce the performance variations in the product or process. Optimal design parameter setting demands that a distinction is made between the parameters themselves and sources of noise. Noise occurs from internal and/or external sources. Examples of internal sources include all deviations found in actual characteristics away from specified nominal settings. External sources of noise include human variability, supplier unreliability, temperature, humidity, vibration, dust and dirt.

For optimal parameter design a specific criterion for optimisation has to be selected. This usually takes the form of expected monetary loss. With Taguchi, quality is the (minimum) total loss imparted to society from the time the product is shipped. This is the expected loss experienced by an average user of the product during its lifetime due to performance variation of the product or process, including warranty and field service. Other losses may occur before shipping that must be taken into account when deriving optimal parameter settings. These include in-plant inspection, scrap and rework costs.

Experiments, the prime application for practitioners, are carried out to help the process of parameter design. Some experiments are physical, but where this cannot be achieved computer simulation will help. Experimentation helps to identify parameters that can reduce performance variation by testing their effect on noise levels. Sensitivity to environmental perturbations not normally dealt with by internal control procedures is tested. Sensitivity is reduced using techniques such as orthogonal arrays. The parameters are accordingly set. (See Further Reading for a suggested text on the Taguchi method.)

Tolerance design. The aim of tolerance design is to minimise the sum of product manufacturing and lifetime costs. The method builds in tolerance to factors that can significantly affect the variation of the product.

Taguchi's method focuses on design in machinery. The VSM, dealt with below, switches the focus to organisational design.

The Viable System Model (VSM).

The main principles of the VSM and viable system diagnosis are:

- Communication
- Control
- Efficiency
- Effectiveness
- Efficacy
- Emphasis on location and elimination of cause of error
- Organisation is prime
- Recursion
- Variety filtering

The VSM is most effectively used when there is a consensus view among participants about what should be done. It helps to answer the question, 'How should we do it?'

The VSM and recursion can be used either to design an organisation from scratch, or to test its design by viable system diagnosis and then redesign if necessary. The focus below is on diagnosis and redesign. There are two stages to viable system diagnosis, system identification and system diagnosis. Knowledge of the VSM is assumed (see Chapters 7 and 8 if uncertain).

System identification. Initially the quality ideals to be pursued are identified. The ideals are set by the Executive Council. Taking these ideals as given, a viable system for achieving them has to be determined. A VSM is drawn up to represent the quality system in terms of Implementation, Co-ordination, Control, Intelligence and Policy.

System diagnosis. Diagnosis is more complex. Diagnosis involves asking a series of questions. The questions search for cause of error.

They guide the analyst around the organisation helping to locate poor communication and control particularly as it relates to internal and external customers. Findings can be used to formulate ideas for projects among other things. Questions would include the following.

Study the Implementation of the system-in-focus (the system-in-focus means the recursion level where diagnosis is focused at the moment):

1 For each part of Implementation detail the customers, operations and localised management.
2 Study what constraints are imposed on each part of Implementation by higher management.
3 Ask how accountability is exercised for each part in terms of quality.
4 Draw up a quality model (e.g. Quality Councils) that complements the VSM diagram.

Study the Co-ordination of the system-in-focus:

1 List possible sources of oscillation or poor customer service

between the various parts of Implementation and their customers and identify the elements of the system that have a harmonising effect.
2 Ask how the image and quality of Co-ordination is perceived in the organisation.

Study the Control of the system-in-focus:

1 List the Control components of the system-in-focus.
2 Ask how Control controls quality.
3 Ask how resource bargaining with the parts of Implementation is carried out.
4 Determine who is responsible for the quality of the parts of Implementation.
5 Clarify what audit enquiries into the quality of Implementation, Control conducts.
6 Understand the relationship between Control and the Implementation elements and find out how much freedom Implementation elements possess (vital concerning issues of creativity).

Study the Intelligence of the system-in-focus:

1 List all the Intelligence activities of the system-in-focus.
2 Ask how far ahead these activities consider.
3 Question whether these activities guarantee quality into the future.
4 Determine if Intelligence is monitoring what is happening to the external customers and assessing quality opportunities with them.
5 Assess in what ways, if any, Intelligence is open to novelty (a vital consideration for continuous improvement etc.).
6 Find out whether Intelligence provides a quality centre operation, bringing together external and internal quality and providing an 'environment for quality'.
7 Question if Intelligence has facilities for alerting policy to urgent quality development.

Study the Policy of the system-in-focus:

1 Ask who participates in Policy and how it acts.

2 Assess whether Policy provides a suitable quality mission for the system-in-focus.
3 Ask how the quality ethos set by Policy affects the perception of Intelligence.
4 Determine how the ethos set by Policy affects how control and Intelligence operate together.
5 Investigate whether Policy shares a quality identity with Implementation or claims to be something different.

Debating

Quality Control Circles (QCCs)

The main principles of QCCs are:

- Participation
- Learning
- Understanding
- Diversifying
- Consensual debate
- Group formation crucial

QCCs are most effectively used when different conceptions and opinions exist about what should be done (non-coercive). It helps to answer the question, 'What should we do?'

QCCs were initially discussed in Chapter 2 because they are the idea of Ishikawa, one of the quality gurus. QCCs offer a blend of participative management and classical problem solving techniques, the latter relevant to designing rather than debating. They encompass many ideas and methods covered in this book. QCCs clearly complement the project based general method for implementing TQM. For example, the ideas could be used as a method to operate Quality Councils.

A circle is a small group of members of the organisation who operate in the same work area. This helps to create an identity for the circle. The members are volunteers who agree to meet regularly, on company time. They aim to identify quality issues, to determine possible ways forward and to implement change proposals. The groups may draw upon the technical expertise of specialists when necessary. The kinds of method and concept used in QCCs are mentioned below.

Brainstorming is commonly used. The aim is to generate many ideas and suggestions that are useful for 'problem solving' and 'problem identification'. During the process there is no room for criticism. Judgements and evaluation follow brainstorming sessions. To generate as many ideas as possible the facilitator needs to encourage everyone to contribute, perhaps by taking turns. So-called 'piggy backing' of ideas on ideas is encouraged.

Fishbone diagrams and data gathering techniques are taught and used. Pareto analysis is drawn upon. Remember, this is where 80% of quality failure cost is presumed to be held in 20% of quality issues identified. Methods to identify the vital few are taught so that the relative magnitude, say of defects, can be assessed to allow projects to be located which promise to yield the greatest benefits.

Presentation techniques are learnt to promote clear and concise communication. Group leadership and motivation are also taught, to enhance the effectiveness of group meetings. Members are educated in the use of control charts. Any other method or technique deemed to be important for the circle can become a part of their training and subsequently their quality management armoury.

The general method for QCCs is initially to brainstorm and then to identify issues and projects to work on. Following this the circle gathers data and determines causes of error. It then draws up conclusions and acts on them.

Before employing the idea of QCCs, however, some careful consideration must be undertaken. An evaluation of the readiness of the organisation for QCCs is important. Possible causes of failure need to be identified. The following questions can be asked:

1 Will management listen to the QCCs?
2 Is there too much conflict in the organisation for open participatory groups to work effectively?
3 Are there enough resources available (people, time, money)?
4 Are the staff up to it?

Strategic Assumption Surfacing and Testing (SAST).

The main principles of SAST are:

- Participation
- Learning
- Understanding
- Attenuating
- Adversarial debate
- Group formation crucial

SAST is most effectively used when different conceptions and opinions exist about what should be done (non-coercive). It helps to answer the question, 'What should we do?'

SAST has been designed to test competing strategies. It has an important role to play in TQM. For example, SAST helps progress when there are two or three competing ideas for projects to tackle a set of quality issues, but progress in synthesis or choice of project comes to a full stop. In this case advocates of each project are formed into groups and asked to defend their ideas against the strongest attack that their competitors can wage, and vice versa. The attacks guided by SAST focus on the assumptions being made about the correctness and value of the project. Differences, strengths and weaknesses are highlighted (learning and understanding). The ground is thus prepared for moving toward synthesis and/or choice of project. In this way SAST is attenuating.

SAST is normally regarded as having four main stages; group formation, assumption surfacing, adversarial debate and synthesis. Each is considered in turn.

Group Formation. The aim of this stage is to structure groups so that productive operation of the three remaining stages is facilitated. As many individuals as possible who have a bearing on the choice of project should be brought together. These individuals then form groups on the basis of one or more of the following criteria:

1 Advocates of particular projects.
2 Vested interest.
3 Managers from different functional areas.
4 Managers from different organisational levels.

Groups must be formed that share as much commonality as

possible within them, and have as much difference as possible between them. This enhances the chances of productive debate.

Assumption Surfacing. Each group should initially ensure that they have a common understanding of their preferred project. Assumption surfacing then helps each group to uncover and analyse the key assumptions on which its preferred project rests. Three techniques assist this process.

The first, *customer analysis*, asks each group to identify the key individuals, parties or groups on which the success or failure of their preferred project would depend were it adopted. These are the people who have a 'stake' in the project. The process can be helped by asking the following questions that have clear focus on the customer in quality management:

1 Who is affected by the project?
2 Who has an interest in it?
3 Who can affect its adoption, execution or implementation?
4 Who cares about it.

A set of relevant customers is thus drawn up.

The second technique is *assumption specification*. For the customers identified, each group then lists what assumptions it is making about each of them in believing that the preferred project will succeed. Each group should list all the assumptions derived from asking this question of all customers. These are the assumptions upon which the value and success of the group's preferred project depends.

The third technique is *assumption rating*. This involves each group in ranking each of the assumptions it is making with respect to two criteria. For each of the listed assumptions each group asks of itself the following:

1 How important is this assumption in terms of its influence on the success or failure of the project?
2 How certain are we that the assumption is justified?

The results are recorded on a chart (see Figure 9.8). The group would initially be concerned with assumptions that are important because they are significant for the success of the project. Those

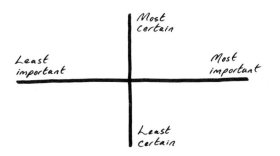

Figure 9.8 *Assumption rating chart*

that are both important and uncertain draw particular attention because they highlight weaknesses in the project.

Adversarial debate. The groups are brought together. Each one explains clearly their preferred project and their results from assumption surfacing. This is done in turn. Only points of clarification are allowed at this stage.

Adversarial debate between the groups then begins. One group defends their project whilst the other(s) look for weaknesses. The roles are then reversed. The debate may be guided by asking the following questions:

1 How are the assumptions of the groups different?
2 Which customers feature most strongly in giving rise to the significant assumptions made by each group?
3 Are similar assumptions rated differently by the groups?
4 What assumptions of the other group(s) does each group find most troubling?

The outcome might be one of the following:

1 New assumptions have to be posted on the chart.
2 Assumptions have to be moved from one quadrant to another.

Synthesis. The ideal aim of the synthesis stage is to achieve a compromise on assumptions from which a new project can be derived. In some cases synthesis may not occur but choice of project is achieved. A list of agreed assumptions can be drawn up. If the list is sufficiently long then an implied project can be worked out. This new project should hopefully bridge the gap between the old ones and go beyond them as well. The assumptions on which it is based can equally usefully be tested during implementation. If no choice or synthesis can be achieved, points of disagreement are noted and the question of what research might be done to resolve those differences is discussed.

Interactive Planning (IP).

The main principles of IP are:

- Participation
- Learning
- Understanding
- Diversifying
- Consensual debate.

IP is most effectively used when different conceptions and opinions exist about what should be done (non-coercive). It helps to answer the question, 'What should we do?'

The special feature of IP is that it challenges the future that the organisation is currently in. It leads participants to consider ideal futures that in principle the organisation could move toward. In this it is diversifying. For TQM it offers the same kind of possibilities. It can help in mission setting, leading the participants to be creative and diversify their thinking about what is possible (learning and understanding). A full-blown IP also tackles things like means planning, resource planning, and implementation and control. If carefully translated to focus on customers and projects for improvement, it could in principle support the general method for implementing TQM described earlier.

IP has five phases; formulating the mess, ends planning, means planning, resource planning, and design of implementation and control.

Formulating the mess. Initially, issues, prospects, threats and opportunities facing the Council's area of influence are highlighted. A recommended way of doing this is to work out the future they are currently in. This is a projection of the future that they would be faced with if it did nothing about things.

Customer analysis as described in the general method for implementing TQM establishes the current situation. Subsequently obstruction analysis sets out any obstacles in the way of improving quality. Then *preparation of reference projections* leads to prediction of future performance if no changes are made and trends elsewhere in the organisation continue. This analysis provides a reference scenario for the Council.

Ends planning. Ends planning concerns specifying the ends to be pursued in terms of ideals, objectives and goals. The process begins with 'ideal design'. An idealised design is a design which the participants would implement if they were free to do so. An idealised design is prepared by going through three steps; selecting a mission, specifying desired properties of the design, and designing the project.

Mission setting is already covered in the general method for implementing TQM. *Specifying desired properties of the design* amounts to a list of desired properties participants agree should be introduced by any project. *Designing the system* means setting out how all the specified properties can be obtained.

This analysis should be passed through twice. The first pass should assume no change in the 'wider system'. The second pass should assume there are no constraints (except that the ideas must not be science fiction and must be operationally viable). If the differences are great then the Executive Council must be consulted to negotiate for changes to be made so that greater scope for improvement is secured.

Means planning. Means planning looks to close the gap between the future without change and the future idealised design. Projects must be set up to close this gap where possible. Creativity is needed to discover ways of achieving the idealised future generated by the participants of the Council.

Resource planning. Four types of resource should be taken into account:

1 Inputs—materials, supplies, energy and services.
2 Facilities and equipment—capital investments.

3   Personnel.
4   Money.

For each type of resource, questions have to be asked in relation to the chosen means. For example, it must be determined how much of each resource is required, when it will be required, and how it can be obtained if it is not already held.

Design of Implementation and Control. The final phase of IP concerns itself with seeing that all the decisions made hitherto are carried out. 'Who is to do what, when and how?', is decided. Implementation is achieved and continually monitored to ensure that plans are being realised and that desired results of projects are being achieved. The outcome is fed back into the quality implementation process so that learning is possible and improvements can be devised.

Disemprisoning

Critical Systems Heuristics (CSH).

The main principles of CSH are:

- Identifying sources of motivation
- Identifying sources of control
- Identifying sources of expertise
- Identifying sources of legitimation.

CSH is most effectively used when agreement about what should be done cannot be reached and one party brings its resources to bear to get its own way. CSH helps to answer the question, 'Who will benefit if we do this?'

CSH aims to reveal whole system judgements, or presuppositions, entering into social systems designs. It is therefore highly relevant to quality management. Although quality management spreads its concern over efficient and effective designs and the management of them, it does tend to focus its attention on the technical aspects of design. It rarely, if at all, questions the political dimension. What CSH attempts to do is to explore the political dimension of the design to reveal its rationality and whose interests are being served by it. CSH also explores what other designs and rationalities ought to be adopted. This is where it answers the question, 'Who will benefit if we do this?'

The method of CSH amounts to a checklist of twelve questions. The questions penetrate the assumptions that lie behind what is inside the system design in question and what belongs to its environment. This analysis identifies the boundary judgements, i.e., the system's rationality. The assumptions in effect are tested to see whose interests are being served by the bounded rationality. These can then be challenged by other rationalities with their assumptions that people feel ought to exist inside the design. What *is* being proposed can then be compared to these new proposals of what *ought* to be the design, each one serving interests of different groups of people. CSH is therefore capable of providing insights, whether the dominant party is wittingly or unwittingly exerting its strength. Ultimately, those who would have to live with the consequences of system designs have a chance to validate its consequences on their lives.

Four groups are chosen for questioning:

1 The clients.
2 The decision takers.
3 The designers.
4 Those who are affected but not involved—the witnesses.

Questions relating to each of these seek out:

1 Sources of motivation (the client).
2 Sources of control (the decision taker).
3 Sources of expertise (the designer).
4 Sources of legitimation (the witnesses).

Three questions are asked of each getting at:

1 Social roles.
2 Role-specific concerns.
3 Key issues surrounding the determination of boundary judgements with respect to that group.

Table 9.3   *The twelve boundary questions from CSH in the 'is' mode*

(1) Who *is* the actual *client* of S's design, i.e., who belongs to the group of those whose purposes (interests and values) are served, in distinction to those who do not benefit but may have to bear the costs or other disadvantages?

(2) What is the actual *purpose* of S's design, as being measured not in terms of declared intentions of the involved but in terms of the actual consequences?

(3) What, judged by the design's consequences, is its built in *measure of success*?

(4) Who is actually the *decision taker*, i.e. who can actually change the measure of success?

(5) What *conditions* of successful planning and implementation of S are really controlled by the decision taker?

(6) What conditions are *not* controlled by the decision taker, i.e. what represents '*environment*' to him?

(7) Who is actually involved as planner?

(8) Who is involved as '*expert*', of what kind is his expertise, what role does he actually play?

(9) Where do the involved see the *guarantee* that their planning will be successful? (For example the theoretical competence of experts? In consensus among experts? In the validity of empirical data? In the relevance of mathematical models or computer simulations? In political support on the part of interest-groups? In the experience and intuition of the involved?, etc.) Can these assumed guarantors secure the design's success, or are they false guarantors?

(10) Who among the involved *witnesses* represents the concerns of the affected? Who is or may be affected without being involved?

(11) Are the affected given an opportunity to *emancipate* themselves from the experts and to take their fate into their own hands, or do the experts determine what is right for them, what quality of life means to them, etc? That is to say, are the affected used merely as means for the purposes of others, or are they also treated as 'ends in themselves', as belonging to the client?

(12) What *world view* is actually underlying the design of S? Is it the world view of (some of) the involved or of (some of) the affected?

The twelve questions in the 'is' and 'ought' mode that arise are given respectively in Tables 9.3 and 9.4. The findings can be recorded in a format such as that given in Table 9.5. Here 'is' and 'ought' answers are tabulated for each question and critical observations are then recorded. Table 9.5 is an example that shows this for social roles and clients.

It should be noted, however, that despite the unique contribution CSH makes in providing insights into whose interests are being served, it then has nothing to say about what to do with this knowledge. This is not an inherent fault of the method as such. Simply, very little work has been done on

Table 9.4 *The twelve boundary questions in the 'ought' mode*

---

(1) Who ought to be the *client* (beneficiary) of the system S to be designed or improved?

(2) What ought to be the *purpose* of S, i.e. what goal states ought S be able to achieve so as to serve the client?

(3) What ought to be S's *measure of success* (or improvement)?

(4) Who ought to be the *decision taker*, i.e. have the power to change S's measure of improvement?

(5) What *components* (resources and constraints) of S ought to be controlled by the decision taker?

(6) What resources and conditions ought to be part of S's *environment*, i.e. not be controlled by S's decision taker?

(7) Who ought to be involved as *designer* of S?

(8) What kind of *expertise* ought to flow into the design of S, i.e. who ought to be considered an expert and what should be his role?

(9) Who ought to be the *guarantor* of S, i.e. where ought the designer seek the guarantee that his design will be implemented and will prove successful, judged by S's measure of success (or improvement)?

(10) Who ought to belong to the *witnesses* representing the concerns of the citizens that will or might be affected by the design of S? That is to say, who among the affected ought to get involved?

(11) To what degree and in what way ought the affected be given the chance of *emancipation* from the premises and promises of the involved?

(12) Upon what *world views* of either the involved or the affected ought S's design be based?

---

methods for disemprisoning. More work will have to be done in due course. The theory for the practice of TQM given in Chapter 8 stresses this need.

Perhaps first steps toward employing the findings would be to bring them to the attention of the Council set up. Domination by political issues could be highlighted. Suggestions and arguments for change if deemed necessary can be made on the grounds that the quality initiative is therefore being diminished along the lines of the argument given in Chapter 7. The quality principles are being rendered ineffective. The potential benefits to the whole are being lost.

There are other bridges to cross with CSH that pose significant challenges. The challenges are:

1 The approach is relatively new and has hardly been used in practice and therefore has not matured.

2 The main source dealing with CSH is a highly theoretical and lengthy volume that requires a concerted effort to translate into a practically useful form.

Table 9.5   *A CSH recording table*

	Social roles	Role-specific concerns	Key problems
Client	'is'		
	'ought'		
	critique 'is' against 'ought'		
Decision taker			
Designer			
Witnesses			

3   The approach is asking us to challenge power structures, an alien notion for the highly conservative world of management today.

That said, the inclusion of CSH in this book is crucial because it is the only management and systems science orientated approach that represents disemprisoning. Disemprisoning holds equal status in our theory for the practice of TQM alongside designing and debating.

CONCLUSION

A general method for the implementation of TQM in any organisation has been described in this chapter. A number of valuable and relevant methods and techniques to help this process along have also been described. The general method, and specific methods and techniques for implementing TQM reflect the theory for the practice of TQM given in the previous chapter.

Part 3 of this section of the book set out to establish a new understanding of TQM. This has been achieved by developing the traditional appreciation of TQM reviewed in Part 1 with a new understanding of management today argued for in Part 2 to work out a new understanding of TQM in Part 3. A theory for TQM, a theory for the practice of TQM and practising TQM have systematically been dealt with. Section I will now be concluded.

FURTHER READING

●The methods from the management and systems sciences introduced in this chapter are extensively covered under Further Reading at the end of Chapter 8. A book that introduces them all and provides case studies of each one in action is:

Flood, R. L. and Jackson, M. C. (1991) *Creative Problem Solving: Total Systems Intervention*, Wiley, Chichester.

●The methods from the quality management literature can be explored in the following books:

Besterfield, D. H. (1990) *Quality Control*, Prentice-Hall, Englewood Cliffs, New Jersey.
DelMar, D. and Sheldon, G. (1988) *Introduction to Quality Control*, West Publishing Company, St. Paul.
Evans, J. R. and Lindsay, W. M. (1989) *The Management and Control of Quality*, West Publishing Company, St. Paul.

Feigenbaum, A. V. (1983) *Total Quality Control*, McGraw-Hill, New York.

Hradesky, J. L. (1988) *Productivity and Quality Improvement*, McGraw-Hill, New York.

Shuster, H. D. (1990) *Teaming for Quality Improvement*, Prentice-Hall, Englewood Cliffs, New Jersey.

●The reader could also consult the following texts:

Montgomery, D. C. (1990) *Introduction to Statistical Quality Control*, Wiley, Chichester.

Oakland, J. S. (1989) *Total Quality Management*, Nichols Publishing Company, New York.

Ross, P. J. (1988) *Taguchi Techniques for Quality Engineering*, McGraw-Hill, New York.

10
Review

INTRODUCTION

Section I of this book has three parts. The first part established TQM as it stands today, the second proposed a new understanding of management today whilst the third used this to rework the ideas from Part 1 moulding a new understanding of TQM. The summary of Section I from the Preface is now repeated as a recap of our progress so far.

SECTION I: PHILOSOPHY, PRINCIPLES AND METHODS

There are three parts to Section I. Part 1 puts in place an understanding of quality management as it stands today. Part 2 argues that if we are to harness the true worth of quality management, we need to make fundamental changes to modern day management assertions that underpin most of the ideas presented in Part 1. A new set of assertions are put forward. The third part of Section I applies the new assertions to construct a theory for TQM. This theory is then employed to prepare a theory for the practice of TQM. Building on this, a general method for the practice of TQM is described.

PART 1: TQM As it Stands Today

Chapter 1:   A Brief History of Quality Thinking

Our first feel for the theme of this book is had in Chapter 1, that pieces together a brief history of quality thinking. This places the remainder of the text into an historical context. The roots of quality management are traced. Main events in the emergence of quality ideas are then identified. The Japanese phenomenon and how the West has not won and still lags behind are also covered.

Chapter 2: Quality Gurus: Their Philosophies, Principles and Methods

An historical background to quality ideas such as that given in Chapter 1 is essential reading. But most people who hold an interest in quality management have heard of many famous names, some of which crop up in Chapter 1, and wish for further insight into their works. Chapter 2 provides this insight with a closer look at the contributions of the gurus of quality management who have enjoyed widest recognition. The main ideas of Deming, Juran, Crosby, Shingo, Taguchi, Ishikawa and Feigenbaum are carefully reviewed. Their contributions are analysed, studying their philosophy, principles and methods. A critique of each one is offered. Their strongest ideas are organised in a simple complementarist framework at the end of the chapter that is developed further as the book unfolds.

Chapter 3: TQM: Philosophy and Principles

Chapters 1 and 2 deal with the history and main figureheads of quality management and provide a framework through which their contributions can be understood. This information is synthesised within a whole system, or holistic, perspective labelled TQM. Chapter 3 captures the main concepts and ideas of quality management within a definition of TQM. The definition of TQM is systematically worked out by analysing its parts; 'total', 'quality', and 'management'. This analysis uncovers further concepts to be explored. These include 'customer', '(agreed) requirements', 'first time, every time', and 'at lowest cost'.

*Chapter 4: International Standards: Philosophy,
Principles and Model*

TQM as explained in Chapter 3 has emerged as the latest and most comprehensive vision of quality management. Of growing interest and importance to modern day managers wanting to implement TQM, however, is to win accreditation, to be awarded the seal of the international standard ISO 9000 (or one of its equivalents). These standards are general models that propose a set of clauses to follow. The clauses are guidelines pointing out what needs to be done to win accreditation. They say little about how to do it. ISO 9000, then, directs attention to the main quality fault areas whilst TQM provides the techniques and methods to tackle the faults. In Chapter 4 the philosophy, principles and the model that ISO 9000 offers are analysed. A critique is provided.

PART 2: A New Understanding of Management Today

Chapter 5: Changing Assertions of Management Today

A comprehensive introduction to TQM as it stands today is established in Part 1. To harness the true worth of TQM, however, necessitates challenging and overcoming assertions promoted by management today. This is important because quality management so far has mainly drawn upon these traditional assertions. Chapter 5 argues that traditional ideas are not really adequate and restrict what can be achieved with any quality innovation. It therefore highlights weaknesses in the old ways and in this shows the value of bringing in new more relevant ones. The new assertions stress the value of a complementarist approach introduced in Chapter 2.

Chapter 6: A Creative Approach to 'Problem Solving'

Chapter 6 builds on the ground won in Chapter 5. New assertions are put in place. A new approach called Total Systems Intervention (TSI) incorporating the new assertions is reviewed in this chapter. The review prepares for Part 3, providing a framework in which a theory of TQM can be constructed. The practice of TQM follows this.

PART 3: A New Understanding of TQM

Chapter 7: A Theory of TQM: A Deeper Understanding of the Philosophy and Principles

The new approach to management and organisation theory, and the management and systems sciences, argued for in Part 2, is now put to work. In Chapter 7 the new ideas are used to generate a deeper understanding of the principles of TQM worked out in Chapter 3. Reference is made through TSI to the main theories found in the management literature. Areas of strength and weakness are identified. The analysis paves the way for a theory for TQM. This theory helps to overcome the lack of rigour of quality ideas in terms of management and organisation theory identified in the Preface.

Chapter 8: A Theory for the Practice of TQM: Practising Freedom

In Chapter 7 a theory for TQM is put in place. The theory stresses the need for autonomy, responsibility and participation, and getting rid of coercive forces—in short, a need for human freedom. It would not be possible, therefore, to claim proper and valid use of TQM without evidence that the practice had in its principles an element of guarantee for human freedom. This evidence needs to be provided in a theory for the practice of TQM. Chapter 8 shows that the complementarist framework introduced in Chapters 2 and 5 caters adequately in its provision for human freedom to be practised.

Chapter 9: Practising TQM: Employing the Methods and Techniques

In Part 1, a comprehensive introduction to TQM as it stands today is established. In Part 2 a new approach to management and organisation theory and the management and systems sciences is argued for. So far in Part 3 the new approach has been put to work, first in Chapter 7 to construct a theory for TQM otherwise missing in Section I and the literature. Then, Chapter 8 brings forward the theory alongside findings on complementarism from earlier in the book to realise a theory for the practice of TQM. It remains for the final step to be taken, to supply the reader with a guide that shows how the methods and techniques of quality management can most effectively be used in TQM, to come up with and implement change proposals. Chapter 9 takes this final step and hence overcomes the lack of direction of the management and systems sciences identified in the Preface.

Chapter 10: Review

In Chapter 10, Section I of the book is reviewed. The crucial points made in Section I are underlined, and some new important additional material introduced through the case studies in Section II. These will be sealed by the exercises and games in Section III.

Section II
CASE STUDIES

11
Introduction to Case Studies

A new approach to TQM was established in Section I. This approach is better equipped than traditional approaches to TQM to guide implementation of quality thinking in organisations because it has taken the following into account:

1 The strengths and weaknesses of the philosophy, principles and methods of approaches currently in use.
2 Contributions available from management and organisation theory.
3 Contributions available from the management and systems sciences.

Now, in Section II, the emphasis will be shifted to consider in some detail the practice of TQM argued for in the previous section.

Section II presents four case studies. Each case study underlines a different set of lessons learnt in Section I. In addition, the third and fourth case studies introduce important new material vital to the reader. The third case study in Chapter 14 provides a detailed discussion about quality in the service sector. The fourth case study in Chapter 15 defines supplier development strategies. This material had no obvious place to go in Section I. It does, however, fit comfortably at the beginning of the respective case studies.

Each case study in the following four chapters roughly adopts the following structure: background information; explanation of ideas, concepts and methods (in the last two cases); employment of ideas, concepts and methods; and an analysis of the successes and failures of the implementation.

The first case study in Chapter 12 follows on from Chapter 9 where a general method for implementing TQM was given. One use of the general method to implement TQM in a company in Singapore dealing with diagnostic biotechnology (and named after this) is reported. Diagnostic Biotechnology's background is explored and the main issues that it faces are surfaced. Reasons for choosing TQM are given. The first stages of implementation are described. This includes setting up an Executive Committee and determining its mission, setting up the first layer of Quality Councils and setting their missions, and identifying projects for each Council. The case study concludes with a brief discussion of the successes and failures of the project.

Chapter 13 focuses on identifying cause of error using the fishbone technique and VSD. The study and intervention were carried out in Tarty Bakeries in North America. The main area of concern was the room where pre-baked cakes are decorated. A background to the situation is given. Fishbone analysis and then VSD are used to investigate the main difficulties and issues to be managed, with an emphasis on locating causes of error. Recommendations made are summarised. Successes and failures are discussed.

The next two case studies contain the new information already mentioned. Chapter 14 starts off with a thorough review of quality in the service sector and describes how North Yorkshire Police in the UK have set about implementing quality management in police services. A literature review is recorded uncovering a wide debate about quality in the service sector. The review then converges on quality for policing services. The views of officers about quality in their jobs gathered during lengthy fieldwork are summarised. The first stages of implementation of TQM in North Yorkshire Police are recounted and include; the national discussion about quality management for policing services, setting up a working party in North Yorkshire Police, determining strategies and missions, choosing an organisational structure for implementation (dealing with geographical rather than functional needs), and developments from there. In this case the organisation was under direct guidance from the Home

Office of the Government, which adds an interesting new dimension to the implementation of TQM.

The remaining case study in Chapter 15 moves on to explore supplier development strategies for small and medium-sized enterprises. A review of the literature in this area is given. Cosalt Holiday Homes in the UK, where a supplier development strategy is being developed and implemented, is introduced. Cosalt has been implementing a range of quality approaches over several years. A method for supplier development is given. Employment of the method in Cosalt is described. Successes and failures are reflected upon.

Together, these four case studies illustrate a wide range of efforts to achieve quality management in contrasting organisations under widely varying circumstances. None of the cases record neatly finished interventions—they are realistic and anyhow implementation of quality is an on-going process. (Please note that the name and location of Tarty Bakeries has had to be altered to maintain confidentiality.)

12
Implementing TQM Through TSI: Diagnostic Biotechnology (Pte) Ltd

INTRODUCTION

In this chapter a case study is presented that illustrates how to use the general method designed to implement TQM, through TSI, introduced in Chapter 9. Only the main features of the method are dealt with. A practical example of its use is documented. First of all the company Diagnostic Biotechnology is introduced. This is followed by a run through of the employment of the general method in Diagnostic Biotechnology. The case study is concluded with a summary of the most significant achievements and failures of the quality intervention.

BACKGROUND INFORMATION

After an introduction to TSI the Managing Director of Diagnostic Biotechnology (Pte) Ltd (DB) in Singapore, Mr Lim Jiu Kok, invited me in May 1990 to consult in his company and to apply our creative problem solving approach. As the company's name suggests, its business is diagnostics using biotechnology. In June 1990 at a further meeting in Taiwan we agreed that I should spend two days in Singapore in September that year. I was to meet people from all functions of DB and to grasp a broad understanding of the main issues that they face. The second stage of involvement would be a two-day seminar in November 1990 in the company to explore with the staff organisational difficulties and possible ways forward using systems ideas. A third phase was also discussed, possibly to be an analysis of large projects undertaken by the company, to assess their effectiveness and efficiency.

As is always the case in consulting and as we shall find out below, things do not go exactly according to plan. What was to happen, however, was exciting enough and well worth while recounting. But we need to know more about DB before the story can be told.

INTRODUCING DIAGNOSTIC BIOTECHNOLOGY (PTE) LTD

Diagnostic Biotechnology (Pte) Ltd (DB) was founded in 1984 on Sing$6M venture capital. In 1991 it had about Sing$20M authorised capital. Investors in the company include local and foreign venture capitalists. Biotech Research Laboratories Inc, (BRL), in Maryland, USA, holds the majority of the foreign equity. DB has a technology transfer agreement for a period of seven years with BRL, which manufactures diagnostics, monoclonal antibodies and other research products for the biotechnology industry. Under this agreement, DB receives technologies in immunology and immunochemistry; cell culture; hybridomamonoclonal antibody production; and recombinant DNA-genetic engineering techniques. DB also has a contract with BRL to produce products for them subject to USA Governmental approval.

DB researches into and produces diagnostic kits and offers laboratory services using the latest biotechnology.

Biotechnology is any technique that uses living organisms, or parts of organisms, to make or modify products, to improve plants or animals, or to develop micro-organisms for specific uses. Biological systems and organisms are applied to technical and industrial processes. Pharmaceuticals, speciality chemicals, foods, agriculture, and commodity chemicals, are dealt with.

Current product lines in DB are the ELISA-HTLV II assay kit and the Western Blot-HTLV III assay kit for detection of antibodies against AIDS. The first kit is used for screening, while the latter is used for conducting confirmatory tests. Other products being introduced are HTLVI assay kits, Western Blot-HTLVI assay kits and a range of Hepatitis B and EBV diagnostics. For the longer term, DB plans to move into recombinant DNA technology, adding fusion and enzyme-engineering techniques to its existing tissue culture and monoclonal antibody technologies, for production of diagnostic kits.

Let us now turn our attention to the quality intervention employing TQM through TSI in DB.

CONSULTING USING TQM THROUGH TSI

TSI: Task, Tool and Outcome

Let us pick up the story line again. The initial visit to the company in September 1990 went ahead and a report of the first phase discussions was presented to Mr Lim, and later to many other staff. The original idea to hold a two-day seminar to educate the staff about TSI was reworked following the September findings. A participatory workshop was set up instead. Personnel from all functions and many layers of the organisation were brought together. The task was to develop an appreciation of the main issues faced by DB. The tool was TQM employed through TSI. The expected outcome was recommendations for new ways forward for DB.

Creativity

The two-day session was extended to a three-day one to allow participants to be introduced to systems and management ideas. Forty employees attended. Most attendees were degree educated specialist natural scientists who had no experience of management concepts. The first day was a difficult one for all involved. Participation was negligible despite plenty of opportunity being given. A significant cultural difference which had not been taken into account explained the initial lack of success. As many participants privately informed me, it is humiliating for Chinese people to lose face in front of others. Since many participants had a lack of management knowledge and would be humiliated admitting this in front of their colleagues, Day 1 was doomed from the start. On the following days, however, things came alive.

On Day 2 TSI was employed in earnest. A frank and open discussion about the main issues faced by DB removed the barriers. All present had strong feelings for which issues were most relevant. In summary people felt:

1 A lack of mission
2 No sense of pride, commitment, confidence, role or identity of individuals
3 The company is young and so are many of the staff, giving rise to a lack of overall experience
4 Control, communication and organisation are weak
5 DB is a success story but 'Is it competitive?'
6 'The future seems to hit us before we have had a chance to prepare for it.'

Findings are also expressed in Figure 12.1.

Whilst this discussion was happening, attributes of the main metaphors used in TSI were 'slipped in' and debated along with the issues. There were two dominant concerns. First, that the company had undergone substantial expansion in 1989 but had not put in place proper communication, co-ordination and control procedures (there were cybernetic failings). Second, that the company was young and had yet to develop a corporate culture. The first concern was convincingly captured by ideas of viability portrayed by the brain metaphor, whilst the second fell in place with ideas of quality that resembled the culture metaphor. Political and machine metaphors were held in support. Participants also discovered that viability and quality implied each other (the observation that prompted the argument in Chapter 7!).

Choice

TQM was introduced to the participants. It was explained as a systemic approach to 'problem solving', acknowledging that it

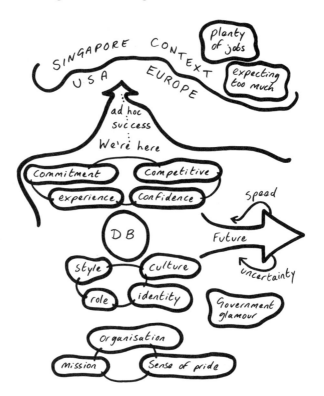

Figure 12.1   *An expression of the main issues debated by 40 participants in a workshop at Diagnostic Biotechnology (Pte) Ltd (DB)*

assumes issues stem from a lack of quality. The ideas and methods of TQM were shown to be highly relevant to DB's current difficulties. In principle TQM can tackle cybernetic and cultural difficulties. Quality was especially relevant for the task, the ideas being strongly promoted in Singapore by its Government, at that time led by Lee Kuan Yew.

There was one main worry at this stage. Traditionally quality is implemented top-down using the organisational hierarchical tree. As discussed in Chapter 7, this is hopeless because it merely implements quality according to a formal power structure and negates many of the benefits TQM has to offer. We therefore began to conceive of the organisation in different ways to develop a more useful appreciation of organisational design and organisational behaviour. Mr Lim had already been working on a highly participatory auditing and decision-making approach within DB. He had created a series of committees to act as 'think-tanks' about the organisation. Each committee was tasked to focus its attention on a particular area of the organisation. The committees were; Manpower Planning, Corporate Strategy, Customer Services, Control Systems, Research and Development, and Technical. Each member of one committee would also participate in one other committee. Thus each committee was capable of looking in a focused way at its main area of responsibility, and at the same time would understand the organisation as a whole. My own task was to ensure that Lim's innovative arrangement covered all aspects of viability and so I worked on these committees, tightening up their outlook where possible with an on-going viable system diagnosis. The arrangement of the committees is shown in Figure 12.2. This proved to be an ideal way of implementing TQM.

Implementation

TQM was implemented in the following way. First of all a company quality mission was set by all 40 participants. This took

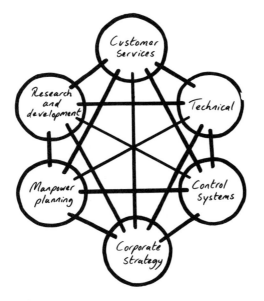

Figure 12.2. *The participatory committee structure of Diagnostic Biotechnology (Pte) Ltd used to implement the first stages of TQM*

a whole morning, but the value of the exercise was to create a company image that all participants felt they could relate to and had ownership of. Many staff commented that this was the first time that they had grasped a genuine understanding of DB as a whole. Following this, committees were reformed with specialist and non-specialist participants in each group. Committees were then asked to define their mission within the spirit of the company mission, enabling the new identity to filter throughout the company. A viable perspective was extremely useful here because it encouraged identity, through the mission, to spill down recursive levels.

The committees then identified their customers (both internal and external), customers' requirements (as far as possible at this stage), and were asked to identify weaknesses in satisfying those requirements. With this information each committee defined a number of projects which aimed to improve customer service. Some means of measuring the effectiveness of each project was requested. The concept of a vital few and useful many projects was adhered to. On completion of project definition committees were brought back together to present and share their findings. Main themes of projects were analysed and discussed. Let us now consider a few outputs from this application of the general method for implementing TQM.

The following mission for DB was agreed upon:

A quality biotechnology company excelling in manufacturing and distribution of diagnostic products across the world, striving to facilitate better health standards by continuously improving the product range through research and development.

Ideally all six committees would have been reformed, but because of shortage of people we were only able to bring together four in the short term. These were Manpower Planning, Technical, Research and Development, and Customer Services. Let us briefly look at the activities of each one.

Manpower planning set the following committee mission:

To cultivate the skills of people who provide services and products to our customers.

The customers were named internally as all DB staff; and externally as suppliers and users, distributors and agents. Weaknesses in meeting their needs were identified under two broad headings; attitudinal and technical. Attitudinal weaknesses included a lack of safety and quality consciousness, poor work intelligence and team commitment, no global outlook, closed-mindedness and limited initiative. Technical weaknesses included a poor level of technical training and required skills to do jobs properly, and a limited general knowledge of techniques and products. The main project that was identified was a massive training programme too large to document here. Performance measures were given. This project is now under way.

Technical set the following committee mission:

To enhance technical competence, co-ordination, and the implementation of all technical activities with a view to continuously improving the overall efficiency and to achieve customer satisfaction.

The customers were identified internally as Research and Development, Production, Quality Control, Technical, Administration and Finance, and Marketing; and externally as end users, distributors and dealers. Weaknesses in meeting their needs were identified. The following shortfall areas were listed: documentation on the stages of development related to the product, i.e., product specification, techniques involved, difficulties encountered, technical data and evaluation, and standard operating procedures; monitoring and reviewing the documentation and implementation process; involvement of Quality Control, Technical and Production during the final stage of research and development; introduction of process design into production; overall review of data; change when necessary; and final product evaluation. A project was set up to improve communications and establish procedures on all these technical matters. Project success was to be measured by product yield and customer feedback. This project is now under way.

Research and Development set the following committee mission:

To realise a commitment to achieve the company mission through improvement, innovation and diversification of product range by upgrading technology, forming strategic collaborations and supporting the smooth functioning of other departments.

The customers were identified internally as all DB staff and externally as end users. The need internally was to provide customers with quality and friendly service, to continuously upgrade skills and to ensure technical transfer happens; and externally, to develop quality products for accurate diagnosis and ease of use. Weaknesses in meeting their needs were identified as poor communication among colleagues, insufficient involvement of representatives from other functional areas in research and development seminars, and poor quality control in the latter phase of development of a product. The main project aimed to improve company-wide participation and communication. For example, seminars and lectures were to be arranged to update staff on the latest technological and product developments. This project is now under way.

Customer Services set the following committee mission:

To provide and improve quality services to meet customers' needs.

The customers were identified internally as all departments, the Board of Directors and shareholders; and externally as distributors, subsidiaries, end users and competitors. The main need internally was thought to be feedback; and externally, information on the company, the product range, the image, product information, response to complaints, shipping information, education about the product and technology. Weaknesses in meeting those needs were identified as poor communication and a lack of continuous updating on planning and control. A project was devised for the market information function to make the following improvements; greater teamwork and active participation, continuous review of procedures and proper documentation to help to keep abreast of market changes, and to increase emphasis on follow-up. Information was to be gathered, categorised and circulated to all departments. The main measures were formulated in terms of the amount of useful information channelled into the organisation and adaptability achieved. This project is now under way.

Achievements and Failures

In what ways did the first stages of intervention in DB tackle the main issues identified earlier? A major achievement was overcoming the lack of identity in DB by formulating a company mission. Working out of the mission not only gave direction to DB, but had the added value of sealing employee commitment through mass participation in its construction. Setting committee missions also built into individuals an identity and a way of understanding their role in the whole organisation. This did help to develop pride, as did the sense of continuous quality improvement. DB as a success story became real for all. Control, communication and organisation were being targeted by many of the defined projects and hence should improve and support preparation for the future.

The sessions were generally accepted as a breakthrough for the company by the participants, although in some ways the efforts remain bootless. For example:

1 A senior member of staff did not participate.
2 The company had to keep functioning over the duration of the workshop and so only limited contact could be made with 'shop floor' staff.
3 The amount of time available was hardly enough to 'routinise' the new attitude and quality culture with the staff.
4 The Managing Director has a powerful character and hold over the company which, despite his revolutionary management style, would probably continue to largely shape DB.

These imperfections, however, did not represent a checkmate. The following ways forward were recommended and are now under discussion:

1 To plan and design management seminars and a management resource centre in DB.
2 To help to set up the committees with carefully worked out procedures, accountability, quality aims, customer identification and requirements etc., and thus to implement quality management throughout the company.
3 To work at least initially with the Managing Director, to develop a clear understanding of how the committee structure, which promotes participation, can clearly complement the organisation of the various management functions.

Let us now conclude this chapter.

CONCLUSION

The aim of this chapter is to illustrate one use of the general method for implementing TQM through TSI described in Chapter 9. First we explored the business of Diagnostic Biotechnology (Pte) Ltd (DB). Following this, consulting in DB employing TSI through TQM was discussed. Without a doubt, this report shows only one convoluted trajectory driven by TQM (through TSI), of which there could be an infinite number. The details of the consultancy do, however, offer general lessons for consulting practice. Let us consider these.

Consultancy, or 'problem solving', is the continuous process of management of issues. Our understanding of messes is ever changing and therefore so should our management of 'it'. DB is a case at hand that shows how perceptions and needs change and how the methodologies that we choose for implementation may be appropriate in some contexts or at particular times but not others. For example, a methodology to achieve company training was slowly and effectively replaced by an intervention that employed TQM as dominant and Viable System Diagnosis in support. Now I find it hard to conceive of this relationship between the two methodologies changing in the DB consultancy. But only by continually putting into practice the logic and process of TSI will we be able to 'guarantee' that the current or some future intervention happens in a relevant and informed way.

FURTHER READING

● The source of this case study is:

Flood, R. L. (1991) Implementing Total Quality Management through Total Systems Intervention: A creative approach to problem solving in Diagnostic Biotechnology (PTE) Ltd, *Systems Practice*, 4(6), pp. 565–578.

13
Cause and Error: Tarty Bakeries

INTRODUCTION

In this chapter the theme is tracing causes of error. Two methods introduced in Chapter 9 are employed—the fishbone method and diagnosis using the Viable System Model (VSM). The aim is to illustrate the practical value of each method and to reflect upon the different and complementary contributions that they make. First of all Tarty Bakeries is introduced with particular attention being paid to recent events in the company. Our two chosen methods are then employed. The case study is concluded with a brief comparative discussion reflecting on the use of the two approaches.

BACKGROUND INFORMATION

Tarty Bakeries in the USA manufactures a variety of cakes and pastries. The processes are quite complicated. One part of cake manufacturing is hand decoration of pre-baked cakes. The project reported below was carried out in the decoration room where cake decoration is undertaken.

About six months prior to the start of the project the two production lines in today's decoration room were in their own rooms with the benefit of a full complement of managers, forewomen and charge hands. Prior to the move the individual rooms collectively were producing more than was being realised from the efforts of the new single room when the study began. This observation takes into account seasonal variations that occur, for example, at Christmas time. In the new set-up, only two managers were employed to deal with decoration (the room manager and the production manager), of which just one was directly employed in the decoration room. Staff were liable to regular changes of line to suit day-to-day production needs. The room manager and forewomen were regularly found working on the line.

The operation of the decoration room gave the appearance of being out of control. The manager and forewomen were not fully aware of the state of operations at any one time. They did not clearly understand the targets and expectations of senior management. They were confused about their roles and job scope.

The main source of information was the daily production schedule that contained only requirements by type of decoration for the day. This aided the production manager but did nothing for the other staff. No target schedule existed for each line, so the forewomen did not know what they should produce or when they should produce it. Furthermore, the forewomen had no benchmark against which they could monitor the performance of the lines. Information used was simply past experience and 'gut feeling'. The workers were never informed about how well or badly their line was doing.

When lower than desired output occurred, the standard response was to increase various throughput rates on the lines. This was successful at producing required volume. It was, however, linked to a sharp rise in the volume of rejects.

Components forewomen also had few guidelines. They were responsible for producing components for the decorated cakes such as marzipan Father Christmas figures, horseshoes and scenery. A common failure was that insufficient components were made. They were frequently used up in the middle of a cake decoration run.

Management style employed to control quality and throughput was crude. It amounted to shouting commands such as 'Watch your lines' or 'Watch your writing' or 'Watch your flowers'. The shouted orders and reprimands were completely ignored by the decorators.

A significant difficulty arose with the availability and capability of sugar-paste sheeters. Some sheeters were more reliable and faster than others. A combination of poor quality sugar-paste and poor sheeters had frequently led to significant reductions in productivity.

Machinery was not very reliable. Maintenance was not planned. Maintenance work was only carried out when machines were down. If a machine is down then decorators are not being utilised. Each lost minute leads to the loss of production of up to 10 cakes, equivalent possibly to 600 cakes per hour. To compensate for these high losses that occur decorators were employed on overtime at extra cost to the company.

Quality checks testing the appearance of cakes were conducted on a subjective basis. There was usually a difference of opinion between Quality Control and Production over the completed cakes. For example, the production manager has removed cakes that had been put on hold in the drying room, marked by stickers placed on them by the quality control team, that subsequently passed packing inspection with little difficulty. Similarly, cakes taken off the line by Quality Control Inspectors were placed back on by forewomen and passed on subsequent inspection.

Minor equipment can have a significant impact on the costs and quality of production but were largely overlooked. For example, cutters that cut basic shapes from sugar-paste had on occasions been too small, generating a need for repairs to marzipan components to make for compatibility. Another example is icing nozzles that are the key tools of cake decorators. Regular cases were noted of decorators working with damaged nozzles leading to poor quality finished product.

It was surprising to find that whilst a large number of staff wore a 'decorator's hat', a sign of being multi-skilled, many of them in fact were not multi-skilled. When production experiments were carried out, limitations in the ability of staff to fulfil the complete range of decorating functions were often encountered. Typical responses from staff were 'I only do shells' and 'I've never done writing'.

Both fishbone diagrams and the VSM are used below to surface and to analyse the errors (issues) in the decoration room. The main projects chosen to tackle the errors are sketched out. Some of the changes suggested by the VSM that were implemented are reported.

TRACKING DOWN CAUSES OF ERROR

Fishbone Diagrams

According to the method for fishbone analysis given in Chapter 9, quality characteristics should be identified first. This helps to surface errors to be dealt with. In the decoration room there was one main error troubling senior management, that productivity had fallen in recent times. Productivity therefore became the focus for initial analysis.

Initial analysis was undertaken using the four main categories; manpower, methods, machinery and materials. This was subsequently expanded. Some sub-categories were added. For example, manpower was broken down into senior managers, room manager and decorators. Machinery was broken down into main equipment and minor equipment. There were few items relating to methods and none relating to material. This is all recorded in Figure 13.1.

A glimpse at Figure 13.1 will reveal that a relatively large number of issues were linked to manpower suggesting that substantial efforts would have to be invested here. The issues linked to methods and machinery may have been fewer but did pose significant difficulties that would need to be addressed by vital projects. The three main projects identified were to change management style, to introduce a training policy, and to establish adequate organisation, procedures, communication and control. The last project was considered to be the most vital since it promised to yield the greatest benefits in the short term. Reflecting upon the complementarist framework confirms that these sorts of issue will be tackled using the VSM. Use of the VSM is discussed in the next section.

Changing management style was dealt with in two ways. First of all quality inspection as such was abandoned. Quality checks continued only as an integral part of the reorganised decorating room described later. Second, the room manager and forewomen

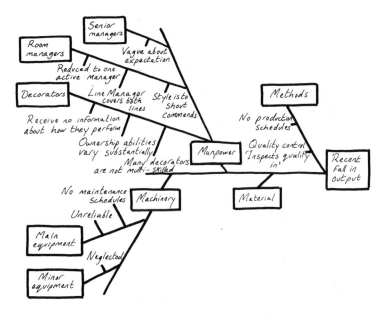

Figure 13.1   Fishbone diagram of issues faced in the decoration room of Tarty Bakeries

were requested not to shout but, after identifying errors, to approach the offender and to speak personally to them. This approach proved beneficial as indicated by reduced noise levels, improvement in the mood of the line and, as far as could be determined, reduction in numbers of rejected cakes (this was assessed under project conditions).

Training was broken down into three distinct areas of need, decorating skills, quality of work and speed of work. The room manager was tasked with locating decorators in need of training as well as finding suitable courses for them to attend. Suitable courses were found at the local college that had specialist modules in catering and related topics. The success of this project is being determined in an on-going fashion. Variables being monitored include rejection of work levels, productivity (difficult to prove that training was a key factor here), and flexibility of staff (e.g., the number of occasions when staff are unable to transfer between tasks when requested).

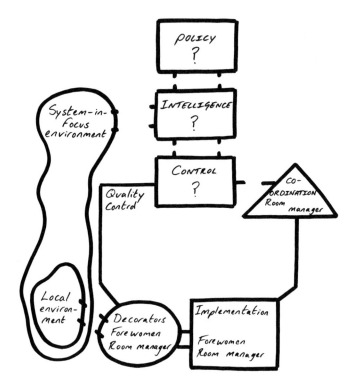

Figure 13.2   Organisation of the decoration room at Tarty Bakeries according to the VSM

VSM

The VSM was used to study the organisation of the decorating room and to propose a reorganisation that detailed new procedures, communication and control. Figure 13.2 illustrates how poorly organised the new decorating room was. When the two production lines were brought together six months previous to the study, Implementation became crushed into a single system of production and management. This was a hopeless effort to cut costs. There were no distinct jobs or roles. For example, the room manager was diverted away from the job of management by continuous crises on the production line. He persistently joined the decorators on the line to help out. Forewomen did the same. Co-ordination was done in a fire-fighting fashion. There was little management of any sort within the decorating room.

Figure 13.2 also shows that other lines of communication were broken. It was not clear who if any one was dealing with policy and intelligence. Senior management were failing to contribute here. Consequently these management functions were missing. Control amounted to nothing more than an 'external' policing exercise. Quality control performed this function, although it has to be said in an ineffective way. Furthermore, there was virtually no interaction between the decorating room and its own operational environment, let alone the wider environment of the system-in-focus. The room was operating in virtual isolation. Overall, a major change in operations had been introduced with insufficient consideration being given to procedures, communication and control and basic organisation.

System diagnosis using the VSM as set out in Chapter 9 revealed massive flaws. Some examples follow.

Studying the implementation of the system-in-focus raised questions about how accountability is exercised in terms of quality. It was discovered that accountability was not exercised. Studying the Co-ordination of the system-in-focus raised questions about how the image and quality of co-ordination is perceived in the organisation. Evidently the image was of management by command and reprimand, relying heavily on the room manager who was normally up to his neck in crisis management. Studying the control of the system-in-focus raised questions about how Control controls quality. It did this by inspection. This undesirable approach was particularly weak because people in production simply placed rejected cakes back on the line and most were subsequently passed. Studying the Intelligence of the system-in-focus led to the realisation that there were no activities of this sort undertaken. And studying the Policy of the system-in-focus raised questions about who participates in policy and how it acts. The members of Policy, at least on paper, were senior management, but their lack of guidance indicated that for all intents and purposes they were not (inter)acting with the decorating room.

A further well-planned reorganisation was essential. Figure 13.3 shows how this was done. Implementation reverted to two distinct lines each with its own line manager. The room manager took on the co-ordination function. Decorators and only decorators did the decorating. Line managers and the room manager were

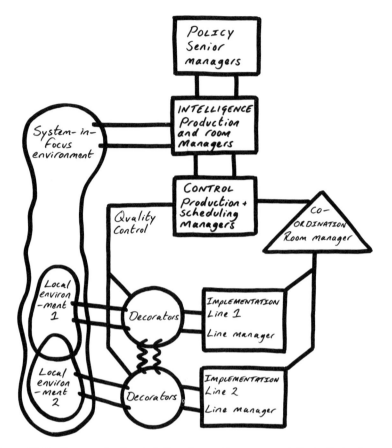

Figure 13.3 *Reorganisation of the decoration room at Tarty Bakeries, one possible VSM recommendation*

'banned' from working on the line. The control function became the responsibility of production and scheduling managers who passed on their plans to the room manager who co-ordinated the line managers to realise the targets. The room and production managers also took on responsibility for intelligence. The room manager actively sought after the best training courses available for decorators. The production manager kept in touch with the most innovative developments in manufacturing cakes and, for the decorating room, in cake decoration. The line managers kept in touch with their local operating environment.

The following principles of organisation and procedure were established:

1 Implementation:
   (a) manage the individual line from top to bottom
   (b) manage the equipment—line speeds, input rates, sheeter speed, etc.
   (c) allocate staff to particular tasks on the line
   (d) manage bottlenecks
   (e) prepare for product changes
   (f) manage line changes
   (g) manage the breaks
   (h) manage and adjust throughput to meet production targets
   (i) managers must not work on the line
2 Co-ordination:
   (a) managers must not work on the line
   (b) co-ordinate the scheduling plans
   (c) anticipate and manage cake changes
   (d) allocate decorators and other staff to lines
   (e) manage the forewomen
   (f) assist the Schedule Manager to schedule production and to set targets.
3 Control:
   (a) work out a regular maintenance schedule
   (b) schedule production in an efficient manner
   (c) carry out quality checks and feed back the results to Co-ordination and Implementation, e.g.,
      ● are forewomen or the Room Manager working on the line?
      ● provide the basis for critical analysis of production methods, staff utilisation, machine reliability and so on—one member of staff was appointed to provide information about relationships between staffing (team-work and task combination) and output and optimum manufacturing methods (through improvement trials)
      ● provide information for costing purposes
      ● help to identify critical variables thus assisting the forewomen and Room Manager (such as machine speed, belt speed, allocation of tasks, balance of jobs on the line)
      ● highlight quality issues directly with the staff involved and encourage them to take responsibility for dealing with them.

4 Intelligence:
  (a) identify weaknesses in staff ability and identify appropriate training courses for them
  (b) identify new technology and methods for cake manufacturing.
5 Policy:
  (a) choose products to be made
  (b) send clear signals to Intelligence and Control about long-term targets and expectations.

A few additional notes support the above outlined organisation and procedures.

The combination of production records and improved established practices has made it easier to develop a simple workload monitoring/productivity/costing system based on output measures of cakes per head. It has also helped in the development of a planning model to assist the production manager to more accurately forecast staff requirements and probable output against projected sales figures by cake type. More stable staffing has subsequently been achieved. Furthermore, the company has been prepared for later implementation of a Just In Time manufacturing approach.

One immediate opportunity was to undertake an overall review of the staffing levels. With better organisation spare staffing capacity was found. The extra time was split between increasing volume output and enhancing staff's skills by sending them for further training.

Quality specifications for weights and recipes of various cakes are not difficult to check. They were introduced. If difficulties occur on the line, adjustments can easily be made to rectify the situation. For example, the weight of sugar-paste can be increased/decreased to compensate for a light or heavy cake.

Quality checks on the appearance of cakes had largely been done on a subjective basis. One particular worry came to the fore and had to be hastily dealt with. The cake on the line never looked like the picture on its box. Clearly there was a high degree of variation. An agreed level of variation had not been established. The following questions became the basis of another project:

1 What is an acceptable degree of variation?
2 Who is to determine it?
3 How will it be moderated?
4 How can that subjective knowledge be passed on to other staff?

In the above listed principles of organisation and procedure it was mentioned that improvement trials were undertaken. One trial was carried out on cakes for female birthdays. This cake, along with all others, was made on a flow production basis, cakes being passed down the line for each successive item of decoration. The trial undertaken was to examine whether the cake could be made using teams. The aim was to:

1 Reduce damage caused by moving the cake on and off the line four times during decorating
2 Regulate the flow of cakes down the line
3 Increase output by reducing quality rejects.

The initial trial was conducted with teams of four. This led to difficulties since decorators were constantly changing ice bags. Staff on the line reckoned that teams of eight would be better. Their method was put on trial and proved effective with a throughput of 10 cakes per minute easily being achieved. This was increased to 12 per minute without much difficulty. Quality errors were virtually eliminated. Teaming was shown to work in this case.

The following observations can be made about the teaming trial:

1 Staff were very interested in getting involved and were keen to try out different ideas.
2 Teams were easily able to achieve self-organisation, allocating roles and duties, with minimal help from consultants and the forewomen.
3 No pressure was applied to achieve the various speed levels.
4 The suggestion for team size came from the most knowledgeable sources available, the line operators.
5 Reliance on managers was reduced freeing them to concentrate on managing rather than supervising.

6   Greater flexibility was achieved—in theory two or three cakes could be made on one line at any time.
7   Teams are self-checking for quality purposes.
8   Trainee decorators can be developed more easily.
9   Staff morale improved because they were more involved.
10   More short product runs can be accommodated.

The case study will now be concluded.

CONCLUSION

Evidently this case study focused on internal analysis of the decorating room. The fishbone method was revealed to be a systematic approach helpful in surfacing issues to be discussed. It brought these forward in the form of categories and sub-categories. The categorisation helped to break down issues to allow for detailed discussion.

A strength of the fishbone method not previously mentioned but evident in this case study, is that following detailed analysis of the issues, themes began to emerge traversing the categorisation. A reformulated understanding was realised in the three themes, management style, training needs, and organisation, procedure, communication and control. These themes provided the platform on which projects were then identified.

The VSM drew together and related the organisational issues. It showed where procedures, communication and control were lacking. The VSM was the prime source of inspiration for a rigorous reorganisation of the main activities in the decorating room. The VSM systemically penetrated difficulties in organisation, procedure, communication and control. In this way it complemented the fishbone method. The fishbone method surfaced issues and synthesised themes. The VSM generated a systemic understanding of the issues and themes.

Throughout the project continual use was made of quality ideas that have been discussed in this book. Emphasis was placed on concepts from the behavioural sciences such as autonomy and responsibility of the decorators in the redesigned room, to improve motivation and to reduce error. Critical variables were identified and worked on to improve reliability of the processes. Trial runs were also undertaken testing variations of the process seeking greater efficiency. All together the methods and concepts of quality management brought together through a TQM perspective made a significant contribution toward improving all aspects of the decorating room.

14
Quality Management in the Service Sector: North Yorkshire Police

INTRODUCTION

The aim of this chapter is to develop further the debate on quality management in the service sector already started in this book. The following summary of findings will remind the reader of the main points to pick up on.

Quality management largely developed in the manufacturing sector. The nature of the processes lent themselves to mathematical and statistical analyses. The theory and practice of quality control developed and employed quantitative methods. Transferring the concepts and methods to the service sector hit upon unforeseen difficulties. The processes were not physical nor tangible for the most part. Quality control has been replaced to some extent in the service sector by quality management, introducing some basic concepts from management and organisation theory such as participation, autonomy, motivation and leadership. This has paved the way for quality to be introduced more effectively in the service sector, although inadequate understanding of the ideas being employed has led to much controversy and debate.

The content and structure of this case study is as follows. A background to quality in the policing service in the UK is given.

A literature review of quality in the service sector and policing services is then provided. Fieldwork undertaken is summarised. Following this preparation, an account is given of the way policy on quality thinking has evolved in North Yorkshire Police (NYP). This process of policy fomulation is the main theme of the case study since it is here that the pertinent issues of general interest arise relating to quality management in the service sector. Implementation of the models and methods that emerged is still on-going and is not reported in any detail herein.

THE POLICE SERVICE AND QUALITY

Interest in quality management in the police service has external and internal origins. External pressure has come from legislative requirements. The true origin, however, is arguably the internal commitment that has grown among those in the force conscious of the potential benefits quality thinking offers to policing.

There are three key turning points that mark the origins. In 1989 the Joint Consultative Committee (comprising elements from three police staff associations) undertook a major review of issues at the heart of policing practice. The main finding was evidence of a lack of compatibility between what policemen on the street saw as their role and the service expected by the public. They were not meeting customers' expectations. At about the same time the ten-yearly British Crime Survey provided hard evidence of falling police credibility. Finally the Wolff Olins report into the Metropolitan Police identified a lack of common purpose amongst employees and significant differences in opinion about what constitutes proper police work.

Consequently great concern arose in the force. A Quality of Service Sub-committee was set up and the Association of Chief Police Officers (ACPO) launched a quality of service initiative. The fundamental aim was to conceive of adequate ways to provide a service to the community. In 1990 ACPO produced a strategic policy document with the following stated objectives:

1 To provide the police service with a corporate statement of common purpose.

2   To provide appropriate means to identify, implement and monitor the quality of service.
3   To propose further development of effective standards of service delivery by individual forces and by the service collectively.

External forces then put pressure to bear. In 1991 the Home Secretary called for changes in all organisations to ensure that service still met needs. Central Government took on a key role in the quality debate in general and within the police service in particular. The Citizen's Charter was launched. One aim was to inform the public about the standards of performance of their local police force, and to facilitate comparisons from year to year and between forces. Performance indices have been implemented to aid the complex task of auditing police forces. These have spread right across the spectrum of 'hard' traditional quantitative measures and 'soft' methods interpreting customer perception. Each approach has enjoyed only limited success.

NORTH YORKSHIRE POLICE

North Yorkshire is the largest single county policing area in England. The main industries of the area are related to tourism, pastoral and arable farming, coal mining, fishing, quarrying and confectionery.

Other major employers include local authorities, area health authorities and HM Armed Forces. There is a ratio of one officer to every 513 residents, low compared to similar forces.

Policing in the area is special. The vast majority of the area is rural which requires a particular style of policing. There are also a small number of very large and densely populated towns and cities that need a very different policing approach. Policing therefore involves balancing these two styles.

A new structure was implemented from January 1992. Seven new Divisions were created. Much greater autonomy was given to each Division. The belief was that devolving decision making to the lowest competent level would significantly aid implementation of quality on a force-wide basis. It would allow Divisional Commanders to address local issues in meeting customer requirements.

The Strategy Group of NYP in consultation with representatives of the Staff Associations discussed in full the recommendations of ACPO's policy document mentioned earlier. They accepted them as they stood. Some recommendations were implemented straight away. A force mission statement was published. The Deputy Chief Constable was designated the chief officer responsible for quality. A senior officer at Headquarters was charged with the task of researching and collating information, and producing proposals for a force policy on quality. A force strategy paper was published titled 'The Implementation of Quality in The North Yorkshire Police'.

In 1992 a Force Quality of Service Co-ordinating Group was formed. The group is chaired by the Deputy Chief Constable and included eight other police officers, seven of chief officer rank. David Devlin and I from the Centre for System Studies at the University of Hull joined this group. Diverse membership allowed for the co-ordination of many interested parties.

Later a smaller sub-committee was formed. The aim was to establish a small group that could efficiently work on the early stages of policy formulation. This group was tasked to bring forward proposals to the Co-ordination Committee. Four police officers and the Centre's representatives formed the sub-committee. Before detailing the workings of this sub-committee, let us reflect on the literature so that our efforts can be placed in the context of contemporary thought on quality in the service sector and police service.

LITERATURE REVIEW: QUALITY IN THE SERVICE SECTOR AND POLICE SERVICE

Introduction

The literature review is separated into two sections. The first section covers quality in the service sector. Findings recorded here have general relevance to the police service as well as other services such as health, education, catering and banking. The second section concentrates on quality in the police service although does offer some general lessons.

Quality in the Service Sector

There are a number of characteristics that distinguish a service as a product from a manufacturing product. Most obvious are difficulties in measurement and the greater prominence of personnel in the service environment. In short, intangibility and inseparability are characteristics of quality in the service sector.

Intangibility makes for great difficulty in describing the product to customers. It is equally difficult for them to express precisely what they desire from the product. This poses particular difficulties therefore in meeting customers' agreed requirements.

Furthermore service is not a product that can be stored. It is not possible therefore to undertake a final quality check in the same way as is possible with manufactured products. There is no equivalent to manufacturer's specifications anyhow.

Intangibility thus means that improvement in the service is difficult to measure, monitor and control. Improvements are also difficult to illustrate to customers. Quality is often judged, not on the service itself, but on the strength of tangible evidence such as appearance of personnel and premises. These are clues that consumers use to 'sense' the quality of the service.

Inseparability of the production and consumption of the service is the second characteristic of quality in the service sector. No time buffer exists in which checks can be made to assess whether the quality of service meets a required standard. Getting it right first time takes on an added importance. Customers see all mistakes. Provision of the service is the moment of truth. In addition, the instantaneous nature of the provision of service and its consumption results in an interaction between server and consumer enabling either party to influence the quality of the service.

Changes in technology and consumer awareness have had a significant impact on the service sector. Developments in Information Technology (IT) have provided the Service Manager with sophisticated tools with an increased potential for monitoring and controlling operations. There is a danger in this however. New technology can get between the consumer and provider, diminishing possibilities for 'the personal touch'. At the same time consumers are becoming better informed and more demanding.

For all these reasons mentioned above, many writers have argued that quality in the service sector demands a different approach to quality in the manufacturing sector. Priority must be given to leadership, motivation, consultation, and human resource utilisation. Well-cared-for machines are predictable, people are not. Technology, although important, plays only a supporting role to the development and management of human resources. Traditional quantitative techniques therefore play a secondary role.

The secondary role holds value and should not be neglected. For example, Federal Express employ Service Quality Indicators. This is a continuous method of checking on twelve critical failure points in their service process. The sorts of thing that are measured include lost packages and late deliveries. Failures are monitored daily and reported monthly. Each failure is weighted for their importance to the customer providing an overall indicator of customer satisfaction.

Cravens and colleagues argue that quality improvement must focus on two main factors:

1 Identifying the relevant dimensions of customer-perceived quality by interacting with them.
2 Identifying which business processes and results favourably contribute to customers' perceptions of quality.

Berry, Parasuraman and Zeithaml have devoted considerable time and effort to these issues. Their main worry is that the nature of customer expectations and how thay are formed is ambiguous. They reckoned that customer expectations and perceptions are based on five key dimensions of service:

1 Tangibles—physical facilities, equipment and appearance of personnel.
2 Reliability—an ability to perform the promised service dependably and accurately.
3 Responsiveness—willingness to help customers and to provide a prompt service.
4 Assurance—knowledge and courtesy of employees and their ability to inspire trust and confidence.
5 Empathy—caring and providing individualised attention to the customers.

These expectations are the factors against which the consumer will judge the service. All five dimensions can attract negative comments but only assurance, responsiveness and empathy are able to draw positive comments. The work has been developed by Parasuraman and co-workers and called 'Servqual', a scale for the measurement of customer perceptions within the service industries.

Meeting expectations requires consultation. The CEO of AT&T in 1988 highlighted his company's sensitivity to shifts in customer expectations. Being partners in a highly interactive relationship demands this. In this way, he says, AT&T is able to adapt quickly to meet those expectations. Others have pointed out that consultation has to be handled carefully. Consultation of clients has a secondary effect of further increasing expectations.

Rawson analysed the best of the private sector. He noted that they ask questions and listen to answers. Consultation is a good thing. Rawson recommends that consultation be a standard non-expendable part of policy and programme development.

Haywood-Farmer has proposed a conceptual model of service quality that combines three main aspects of quality with three classifications of service types. He refers to the three Ps of service quality:

1   Physical processes.
2   Procedures and facilities.
3   Professional judgement.

He relates these to a three dimensional scheme of service types that segments services according to their degree of:

1   Labour intensity.
2   Service customisation.
3   Customer contact and interaction.

This then assists decision makers when deciding on the focus for the organisation's quality efforts.

The main ideas and models proposed for quality in the service sector have now been reviewed. These hold general value for any service industry, including the police service. Many of the points were further rehearsed in the literature on policing that we looked at. They are not repeated below. Literature specifically dealing with the police service will now be reviewed.

Quality in the Police Service

The following review considers in some detail the degree to which quality management is applicable to the police service. Unique factors are highlighted. General lessons can also be found.

As already mentioned, there is a genuine awareness of the value of quality thinking within the police service. The Chairman of the Association of Chief Police Officers (ACPO) in 1991, for example, argued that consumerism, public expectation and ultimately public satisfaction are the watchwords for the 1990s. He believes firmly that quality provides a very satisfactory route toward meeting these key issue areas.

Counterparts in the USA are supportive but recognise deep inherent difficulties. The Chief of Police in Madison in 1990 espoused a positive vision of quality for the police service. He argued this despite the negative pressures that he astutely acknowledges exist in the police force such as the ever-changing world of politics colliding with the rigidity of bureaucracies. This makes quality management a difficult job indeed.

The structure and organisation of the police force poses technical as well as political difficulties (reflecting the argument in Chapter 7). Armistead stated that the organisational structure has tended to give rise to a technical core that seeks to exclude those outside the organisation. This is a troubling observation to those wanting to promote quality in the police force. It suggests a well-developed back-room operation is favoured to an open front office. This isolates the police force from the customers that a quality approach seeks to serve.

Overcoming this can be tackled in many ways. Community consultative groups are currently a statutory requirement. This allows the customer to play an active role in the formulation of policy and the management of service delivery. Consultation of this type, however, is only one side of the coin of customer expectation. It is equally important for the public to understand the limitations of the service that it can realistically expect from the police. For example, the force do have significant resource limitations. Hirst pointed out that unrealistic expectations are as damaging as unrealised ones.

Another way of counteracting inward-looking policies in NYP is to establish a permanent and generous complaints procedure allowing for interaction and feedback with the customer. Ram gave American Express and British Telecom as examples where complaints procedures provided a valuable form of feedback. Ram pointed out that currently a major reason for bad handling of complaints is a culture of defensiveness.

Added to political and technical concerns, then, are cultural ones. This was recognised by the President of the Police Superintendent's Association of England and Wales. He argued for a quality approach. He said in 1990 that quality of service needs a force committed to the concept and so must start in house. But this will take a radical change in attitudes within the organisation, particularly at the managerial level.

Not surprisingly, the intensity in enthusiasm for quality management that exists in the force has not been matched by speed in implementation. Hudson and Thompson recognise the need for a quality of service programme but admit that they are trailing behind major companies. This review points to technical, cultural and political reasons why.

Further to the technical, cultural and political difficulties commented on above, O'Connor argued that the advance of quality in the police has to date been chequered as a consequence of three more factors:

1 Professionalism—whereby police officers tend to view the public as uninformed on matters of policing the community. They are not good at second guessing the public's wants and needs.
2 Resources—there is an increasing emphasis on cost containment and resource allocation by cost centres.
3 Translation—the police are struggling to translate quality of service into policing.

Taking all these and earlier mentioned factors into account will not be an easy task. They present a supreme challenge.

For a start, tackling quality in a service organisation with a huge number of employees demands a human orientation. In a hard-hitting statement, Couper proposed changing the leadership style within the organisation from a hierarchical, paramilitary bureaucracy to a collaborative, improvement-seeking team. Equally sharp was Howard's point that policies arriving in the mail-box do not change people's behaviour and attitudes. The Audit Commission in 1990 expressed the opinion that management systems should delegate responsibility so that police staff can take decisions using individual initiative.

Whilst agreeing on the need to enlist full support, Hirst took up the issue of developing a positive sense of motivation. He asked why a hard-pressed constable should support a system that means training, more work and exposure to greater criticism. where is the *quid pro quo*? There must be a perceptible improvement in the officer's job to make it worth while. This means breaking away once and for all from promotion as the only reward system. Rewards must be linked to the quality standards of the service.

Richardson, on rewards for quality of work, noted that recruitment is bringing in an ever increasing calibre of employee. This is coupled with rising expectations in terms of career progression, training, ability to specialise and the physical working environment. Presumably, the higher calibre officers will also be able to take on more responsibility and autonomy. Not everyone agrees that this is a good idea. Some like Levitt (quoted by Armistead) still maintain that discretion is the enemy of order, standardisation and quality. Armistead counter argued that services with a high degree of uncertainty must allow for discretion by the person providing the service.

Cullen adds to individual discretion the importance of adopting a team working style. Within team working there are two factors to consider:

1 Involve people in all they can affect.
2 Inform people in all areas they cannot affect.

At the end of the day, however, there must be some evidence that efforts such as those discussed above are achieving success. Measurement causes a particular dilemma for the police service.

Traditional areas of policing, including crime investigation, traffic control, and foot patrol, have no benchmarks. There are no proven benchmarks and no commonly accepted standards of service. There is no precise definition of what should be achieved in those areas. Hirst says, a clear definition of the role of the police force is a prerequisite to negotiating and setting standards of service delivery.

New standards and subsequent measurement indices must be carefully designed. Account must be taken of the Home Secretary's point in his speech to the Police Foundation in 1991, that 75% of police time is spent on invisible matters. Attention must be paid to Warcup, who observed that too much emphasis is placed on quantity, such as crime clear-up rate, rather than quality. Statistical data has determined police policy for far too long. They do not reflect, for example, public satisfaction. As Keogh said, statistics in policing is just a numbers game and is of little or no practical value.

Indicators could be customised to reflect local circumstances and objectives. This does lead to some tensions worthy of note. Difficulties will arise if local indicators when cross correlated are not found to have some equivalent standing. The integrity and identity of the national police force is then threatened. On the other hand setting national performance indicators will lead to realisation of those indices and not necessarily satisfaction of the local customers. Armistead has developed this debate beyond the scope of this current review. The main point, however, underlines the value of a whole systems view.

Hudson and Thompson addressed this issue. They observed that police service quality is being approached from four different directions—ACPO, HM Inspector of Constabulary, the Audit Commission and by individual forces. Each is producing its own ideas and suggestions. The result as they say is rather confusing for those charged with implementing quality of service initiatives. Hudson and Thompson propose a systems approach. There must be co-ordination and consistency in the introduction of standards.

Allen, discussing a New England Police Department, found sub-optimal service delivery where sub-systems were being optimised without due regard to the total system. Systems theory would be relevant he adds because one of its precepts is that an organisation must be looked at as a whole. Allen reported that ICAP (Integrated Criminal Apprehension Programme) concentrates on the value of effective feedback and data analysis from all sub-systems in optimising the functioning of the system as a whole.

Blount has also reported that experience showed the importance of making sure that every step in the service is viewed and managed in the context of the whole. The quality of service depends on all parts of the delivery chain working in concert. Interdependencies, Blount added, must be managed and coordinated with leadership, a sense of teamwork, trust and a unified focus on satisfying customer needs.

Cravens and co-workers add one final point to our debate. They indicated that a key ingredient of successful quality improvement programmes is participative management that cuts across traditional organisational boundaries. The police force, for example, sticks closely to a departmental structure. Cross-departmental activities must be promoted.

Conclusion

The above reviews highlight a number of key points that need to be addressed in the NYP initiative. These are summarised below. The list will be of value later when reflecting upon the success of policy formulation and ideas for implementation generated by the Quality of Service Co-ordination Committee. The policy should deal with:

1 How the customers are to be consulted and their expectations incorporated in the policy.
2 How the product is to be described to the customer, explaining the constraints that have to be taken as given such as limited resources.
3 How quality is to be measured, monitored and managed, identifying
   ● hard measures,
   ● soft measures,
   ● critical failure points.
4 How the rigidity of bureaucracy, the paramilitary culture, reward by promotion, and the integration of technical and

cultural dimensions, are to be dealt with (some of these may need to be implicit rather than explicit in the policy).

5 What training and/or action should be undertaken,
   - to achieve quality awareness,
   - to improve management style including, leadership, motivation, participation, consultation, autonomy and team-work,
   - to improve individual skills including, reliability, responsiveness, courtesy, and empathy.

6 How a systems or holistic approach is being adopted.

We will now return to our involvement with NYP and the work of the Quality of Service Co-ordination Committee. Fieldwork was undertaken by David Devlin of the Centre for Systems Studies, to improve awareness in the Centre and indeed in the Committee of the current feelings about quality held by police officers and constables throughout NYP. This is reported below.

FIELDWORK

Introduction

The fieldwork consisted primarily of interviews with a carefully selected cross-section of personnel within NYP. Interviews were carried out with all ranks across all functional areas, comprised both formal and informal sessions, and employed a combination of direct question and answer techniques with relaxed and free flowing discussion methods. The main issues that emerged are summarised below.

The Main Issues

The main issues that emerged from the interviews fall into three areas that the reader will be familiar with by now—technical, cultural and political. Some issues naturally relate to two or all three of the areas. The reader will not be surprised by this either since the notion of interacting issues is fundamental to the argument of the book.

The following technical issues surfaced:

1 The NYP computer system is at the cutting edge of IT but the stored data is not being used intelligently. It does not produce frequency or trend charts for example. Its data is read literally. Some constables depend on the data and do not use their initiative.

2 Management training is inadequate. Managers need to develop improved interpersonal skills and an ability to motivate staff.

3 Management are too far removed from the practical demands of modern-day policing.

4 There are far too many external directives and audits indicating excessive amounts of external control. For example, there is little freedom for officers to manage their own budgets.

5 CID noted that inter-departmental charging put the focus on cost accounting rather than crime detection.

6 Internal communication is becoming less formal with fewer barriers, an effect of the integration of new breed officers. Some management by memo remains. Too much information, such as Force Orders, is passed on in written form.

7 Management team meetings are too infrequent.

8 Communication between shifts is inadequate.

9 Police work is reactionary with insufficient planning.

10 Greater civilianisation of roles is on the whole well received because it frees officers from administration to concentrate on policing.

11 HQ is a self-serving system. It is remote. It is a separate organisation.

12 Resources are inadequate for the set tasks.

13 Operational procedures should include (internally and externally) prompt service, fast response to incidents, fair and courteous treatment, time spent with individuals, availability, aftercare and feedback, and local familiar police presence.

14 Measures are too often quantitative and inappropriate. There is too much concern with chasing irrelevant targets. Targets must be set locally.

The main cultural issues included the following:

1 Quality can only be improved if there is a fundamental change in the culture of the force. This requires strong leadership from the front. The force culture is still grounded in bureaucratic rules.
2 Officers have learnt to be defensive since they expect criticism to be followed by discipline and punishment.
3 Sexism is still prevalent.
4 The force has lost sight of the social aspect of policing. Gone are the times when an officer was a very definite part of the social make-up of the community.
5 The calibre of officer is superior nowadays leading to a greater level of competence.

The main political issues included:

1 There is conflict between the old school trained in traditional methods, and new breed officers who are a product of a new training system which encourages individual initiative and open communication across ranks. The new breed was thought to be winning through, although is seen as cocky by the old breed.
2 Despite the more open communication already mentioned, there remains suspicion and worry about a lack of honesty. In particular, some bosses are not trusted.
3 The police image is created by the media who are more concerned about capturing the public's attention than reporting accurately. Negative accounts of police conduct and results attract attention. The local media are much fairer than the national media.
4 The police force is not good at coming forward and defending their decisions and actions through the public media.
5 NYP enjoys better than average public relations.
6 Civilian staff are downtrodden, closely controlled and frustrated. They are second-class employees.
7 Motivation is linked to promotion. Promotions mainly happen in HQ so staff aim to get into HQ to further their careers.
8 The Discipline Code is harsh.
9 The Inspectorate Department is viewed with great suspicion.

The following ideas reflected how those interviewed saw the way ahead for improved quality in the police service:

1 Enhance consultation.
2 Improve internal quality.
3 Devolve decision making.
4 Enhance interpersonal skills and quality awareness.
5 Return to community policing.
6 Co-ordinate efforts with involved and affected agencies.
7 Improve the use of civilian staff.
8 Get away from departmentalisation.
9 Set and disseminate a clear long-term strategy.
10 Identify who is responsible for quality.

Conclusion

The reasoned responses of the officers and constables in NYP show a strong consistency with the main ideas that surfaced in the literature reviews. The two sets of information combined provide an excellent backboard against which the NYP quality initiative and policy can be continuously critiqued. The policy as it is reported below is critiqued in the Conclusion using the two sets of information. The next section reports on policy formulation and some ideas for implementation.

POLICY FORMULATION

Introduction

The contribution that David Devlin and I have made through the literature reviews, fieldwork and as members of the Quality of Service Co-ordination Committee cannot be prised out of the proceedings very easily. It cannot be listed as a set of recommendations that succeeded or failed. Rather, our contribution has been the injection of knowledge and experience in an interactive process of policy formulation. Ideas presented in this book have, therefore, had an influence over policy formulation. This section concentrates on that contribution.

The Committees

The Quality of Service Co-ordination Committee met twice before sending away a sub-committee to formulate a coherent policy (four senior officers, Devlin and I were members). The committee covered much ground and debated many issues. Those two meetings established the following—a statement of purpose and terms of reference.

The Policy Sub-committee met twice. Members agreed that its primary objective was to compile a report for the Co-ordination Committee. That report has been submitted and accepted by the Co-ordination Committee. The main contents of the report were generated at a workshop run by the Centre for Systems Studies. They are described below and critiqued in the Conclusion.

The Workshop

The purpose of the workshop was to generate the essential ideas for a coherent policy for the quality initiative in NYP. Two lines of enquiry were pursued:

1 Examination of the role of the Co-ordinating Committee.
2 Employment of a general method for implementing TQM (described in Chapter 9).

Initially the findings of the literature review and the fieldwork were presented and discussed to provide a background to the proceedings.

Organisational design and behaviour were considered. The VSM was introduced and its five functions correlated to functions of NYP. This was compared and contrasted to the traditional bureaucratic structure that the officers and constables were familiar with. The model was generally well received. After some discussion it was agreed that a VSM vision of the organisation would be adopted.

The next stage of the general method is to set up a Steering Committee. Members thought that the Quality of Service Co-ordination Committee filled this role. There was agreement that this Committee would act clearly as a co-ordination group and not a control one.

Setting the organisational mission was relatively straight-forward too. The statement of purpose and terms of reference were discussed. It was suggested that an abbreviated more concise statement of purpose would be beneficial in communicating the function that the Committee aimed to fulfil throughout the organisation. The mission was agreed to be:

The co-ordination, communication, dissemination and implementation of quality thinking within North Yorkshire Police.

The formal mission statement for the Force already in existence was discussed. Members agreed that the mission statement set for the Committee was consistent with it. Discussion moved on to consider possible structures for implementing TQM in NYP bearing in mind the essential ideas of the VSM.

A sketch was drawn of the structure used within a division of the Metropolitan Force in London to improve quality through the implementation of team building. This concentrated on the development of communication and interpersonal skills as the catalysts for change. The success of this approach was compared with that of a further Metropolitan division that concentrated its efforts on technical advancement rather than interpersonal aspects of quality. It was revealed that quality had become much more a part of the fabric of the former division. In the latter case the tools for technical competence did improve efficiency in terms of meeting performance indicators but provided nothing much in meeting the community's expectations of quality. This reflected the findings of the reviews and the fieldwork.

A diagram was then drawn of the structure adopted within the urban Harrogate Division of NYP for team building (see Figure 14.1). Team composition involved Shift Inspector as team leader, shift personnel, and facilitator. The main activities of the teams were:

1 To identify the internal and external customers' requirements.
2 To disseminate feedback from management.
3 To establish and to operate performance indicators.
4 To identify and to work on specific projects.

The team structure was not specifically designed for implementation of quality but was found after discussion to be

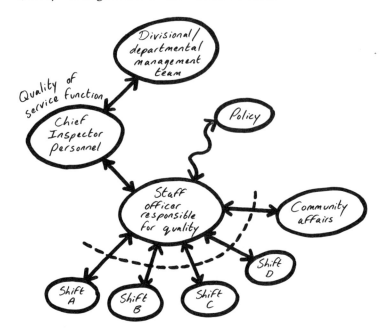

Figure 14.1 *Harrogate Division of North Yorkshire Police—team structure*

suitable as the basis for further discussion. It was tested as a general model holding an adequate blueprint for adoption in all areas of NYP.

The model for the rural division at Malton was discussed. The main driving force behind this design was the inclusion of as much consultation as possible between the operational members of staff and the community they serve. Positive aspects to the Malton model were found but it did not seem to provide a mechanism for dealing with community related quality issues. It did not allow for consideration of internal matters.

Others expressed the concern that both the last two models had bottlenecks at the 'functional inspector' point. This might impair the effectiveness of communication between the local teams and the Divisional Management Team (DMT). Representation of each team on the DMT was discussed but there was a general feeling that this was not practical because DMT comprised members on a functional basis whereas the teams were formed on a geographical or shift basis, depending on which model was being considered.

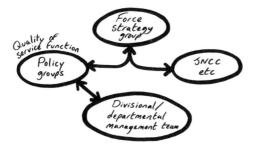

Figure 14.2 *Structure for implementing quality of service in North Yorkshire Police*

Compared with the adopted vision of the organisation design and behaviour, the models were also thought to be too hierarchical because they showed DMT at the top of a pyramid type structure. A suggestion to invert the models was warmly accepted for its symbolic value in refocusing on the importance of the customer in quality of service issues.

The Harrogate model was further developed as shown in Figure 14.2. The Force Strategy Group set strategy. The JNCC (Joint Negotiating and Consultation Committee) are responsible for negotiating and consulting with all stakeholders, involved and affected, within and outside the boundaries of the Force. Strategy formulation takes into account information received from the JNCC. Policy groups implement strategy. The groups are headed by a senior officer, with the remainder of the complement coming from departmental and divisional teams. There are six Policy Groups—CID, Operations, Personnel, Inspectorate of Development and Technology, Administration, and Community Affairs. On testing the model the sub-committee found that it could easily be customised to suit local criteria, such as geographical combination and division by function.

A potential way of operating this model using a highly simplified version of the VSM, our adopted vision for the organisation, is shown in Figure 14.3. Corporate decision making is undertaken by the Force Strategy Group with the task of creating a corporate vision and providing support. Policy and co-ordination is dealt with by the Quality of Service Co-ordination Committee, with representation from divisions, departments and the Staff Association. The main task areas are education,

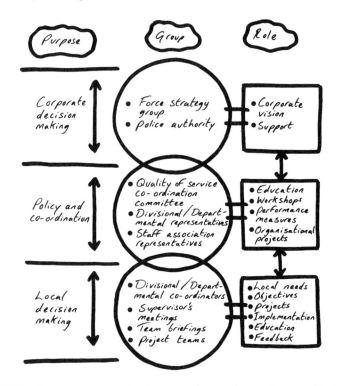

Figure 14.3 *Process to operate structure for implementing quality in North Yorkshire Police*

workshops, establishing best practice and performance measures, and co-ordinating projects. Local decision making is the responsibility of Divisional and Departmental Co-ordinators, and project teams, with contributions from supervisors' meetings and team meetings. Local decision making is responsible for meeting local needs, setting local objectives, establishing projects and implementing desired changes, providing locally relevant education, and ensuring that adequate feedback happens. The overall philosophy behind Figure 14.3 is to monitor, review and improve operations.

Discussion moved on to consider briefly some examples of quality projects suitable for implementation using the models of Figures 14.2 and 14.3. Some quality initiatives already underway were found to fit in well. This strengthened the value of the model in the view of those present. Co-ordinating the projects through the models would also strengthen them and enhance their potential for use elsewhere in the force. Lessons learnt could be disseminated quickly to a much wider audience. Some other ideas for vital projects included ideas for the development of income generation, improving techniques of generating customer feedback, establishing a marketing strategy, reviews of internal communication systems, and reviews of career systems. Discussion and debate was not extensive since project identification was carried out mainly to test the value of the models for implementation.

A report was compiled from the wealth of information generated at the workshop. The report documented much of what was discussed above. The models were put forward as a means by which quality could be implemented. The report was accepted by the Quality of Service Co-ordination Group. We will now conclude this case study by critiquing the models and other points of policy using the findings from the reviews and the field work.

Discussion

As was stated earlier, the results of the literature reviews supported by the findings uncovered by the fieldwork, provide a backboard against which the policy for implementing quality of service can be critiqued. Six points emerging from the reviews that the policy should deal with were given on pp. 233–4. We will now consider the policy in the light of these points.

The sixth point asks for an account of how a systems approach is being adopted. The pair of models shown in Figures 14.2 and 14.3 are clearly systemic. The VSM in particular helps to design in systemicity to plans, or in this case policy. The main ideas of viable system thinking are rehearsed elsewhere in this book and do not need to be reiterated here.

A benefit of having this systemic picture is that, at least in principle, all other policy matters can be taken account of. That viability and quality imply each other was argued in Chapter 7. Working through the remaining five points, then, becomes a task of checking whether they are taken into account in principle or as an explicit part of the policy. This task is undertaken below.

1 How are the customers to be consulted and their expectations incorporated in the policy? The following can be observed:
   - the JNCC is feeding opinions of all stakeholders to the Force Strategy Group;
   - the Quality of Service Co-ordination Committee represents a wide range of internal views without becoming unwieldy, and has representation from divisions/departments, the Staff Association, and externally from the Centre for Systems Studies;
   - the divisions/departments actively acting to understand local needs through the use of customer attitude surveys and improved consultative forums.

   Point 1 is therefore explicitly dealt with by the policy.

2 How is the product to be described to the customer, explaining the constraints that have to be taken as given, such as limited resources? As it stands, channels of communication are in place to achieve dissemination of information internally and externally. In practice only the internal customers are explicitly dealt with through 'official' channels, although explaining constraints and their implications to officers and constables is not well done.

3 How is quality to be measured, monitored and managed, identifying,
   - hard measures,
   - soft measures,
   - critical failure points.

   Several hard measures are already in place that can be used to provide information on quality of service. Soft measures have become the focus of attention in recent times. Performance indices are one way of providing soft measures. Some of those produced can be utilised. Critical failure points have not been seriously considered so far. At the moment the third point is not adequately built into the policy, being taken account of in principle only.

4 How are the rigidity of bureaucracy, the paramilitary culture, reward by promotion, and the integration of technical and cultural dimensions to be dealt with? A strong argument in defence of the policy catering in practice for point 4 can be made. The traditional bureaucratic structure is replaced by a viable system structure that will help to reshape the

organisation's design over time. The paramilitary culture is also replaced in this way. Figure 14.3, for example, shows that local decision making happens according to local needs. The integral nature of the models in Figures 14.2 and 14.3 highlight the integration of technical and cultural dimensions. The only question mark remaining hangs over reward by promotion. This is being addressed by the Sheery Enquiry which is expected to report in April 1993. Realistically this is unlikely to bring about change for some considerable time. Partly counteracting this negative element, however, is the likely reward officers and constables receive by way of personal satisfaction that greater autonomy and responsibility provide.

5 What training and/or action should be undertaken,
- to achieve quality awareness,
- to improve management style including, leadership, motivation, participation, consultation, autonomy and team-work,
- to improve individual skills including, reliability, responsiveness, courtesy, and empathy?

There are two complementary cuts that can be made through these needs, to provide an organisational structure that supports efforts in this direction and to actively undertake training. The organisational structure is already in place as previously made clear. Training has been attempted (not previously mentioned) but failed. The reasons given by those who attended the course all boil down to one thing, that the consultants who presented the course were patronising. The failure of such a course needs to be put down to experience, albeit bad experience, and a new programme put in place to achieve quality awareness, etc. Currently training is not sufficiently well dealt with.

In summary, in principle all findings from the literature reviews can be dealt with through the policy recently adopted by the Quality of Service Co-ordination Committee. In practice more details need to be injected in the areas of measurement and training to establish clearly how they are to be dealt with according to the policy.

CONCLUSION

The aim set at the beginning of this chapter was to develop further the debate on quality management in the service sector started earlier in this book. A project involving North Yorkshire Police was selected as a vehicle with which this aim could be achieved. In preparation, detailed discussion of quality in the service sector and police service arose from literature reviews of each. Fieldwork undertaken was summarised. Many general lessons for the service sector were recorded. Then the process of policy formulation for quality of service in North Yorkshire Police was traced, with the major points only being noted. The policy was then critiqued against the findings of the literature reviews and fieldwork. This revealed many strengths. Some weaknesses in measuring and training were found, but in principle this could be taken care of within the confines of the formulated policy.

FURTHER READING

●The following authors and articles were referred to in the text:

Allen, W. R. (1987/8) Conventional and Systems Approaches to Law Enforcement Management, *New England Journal of Business and Economics*, 14, Fall/Winter.

Armistead, C. G. (1986) Quality Assurance in the Uniform Branch of the Police Service, *International Journal of Quality and Reliability Management*, 3, pp. 8–25.

Association of Chief Police Officers (1990) *Setting Standards for Policing: Meeting Community Expectations*, ACPO Strategic Policy Document.

Berry, L. L., Zeithaml, V. A., and Parasuraman, A. (1985) Quality Counts in Services Too, *Business Horizons*, pp. 44–52, May–June.

Blount, W. F. (1988) AT&T service: Quality and Renewal, *AT&T Technology*, 3, pp. 2–7.

Couper, D. C. (1990) Police Department Learns 10 Hard Quality Lessons, *Quality Progress*, 23, pp. 37–40, October.

Cravens, D. W., Holland, C. W., Lamb (Jnr), C. W., and Moncrief, W. C. (IIIrd) (1988) Marketing's Role in Product and Service Quality, *Industrial Marketing Management*, 17, pp. 285–304, November.

Cullen, K. C. (1992) Management Cultures: East Meets West—The Nissan Experience, discussion paper for Quality of Service Co-ordination Group, North Yorkshire Police, June.

Haywood-Farmer, J. (1988) A Conceptual Model of Service Quality, *International Journal of Operations and Production Management*, 8, pp. 19–29.

Hirst, M. J. (1991) What do we mean by quality?, *Policing*, 7.

Howard, L. S. (1991) Police Liability Worries Seen Rising, *National Underwriter*, 95, p. 21, June.

Hudson, C. J. and Thompson, R. R. (1992) *Police and Public Working Together*, North Yorkshire Police, Force Strategy Group Paper.

Keogh, M. C. (1990) Performance Review—The Cambridgeshire Experience, *Management Services*, 34, pp. 20–25, February.

O'Connor, D. (1989) *Quality Bound*, Police Staff College Library, Bramshill, UK.

Parasuraman, A., Berry, L. L., and Zeithaml, V. A. (1991) Understanding Customer Expectations of Service, *Sloan Management Review*, 32, pp. 39–48, Spring.

Ram, R. A. C. (1991) *Flying Kites: An Examination of the Strategic Implications of BS 5750 for the Police Service*, Police Staff College Library, Bramshill, UK.

Rawson, B. (1990) The PS2000 Task Force on Services to the Public; the Chairman's Report, *Optimum (Canada)*, 21, pp. 14–20.

Richardson, J. (1991) *Quality Future*, Police Staff College, Library, Bramshill, UK.

Warcup, D. (1992) Abandoning tradition: The concept of Total Quality Management in the Police Service, *The Police Journal*, 65, pp. 56–61, January.

15
Supplier Development Strategy for Small and Medium Sized Companies: Cosalt Holiday Homes

INTRODUCTION

The aim of this chapter is to introduce the reader to supplier development strategy. Supplier development is of growing concern to managers genuinely interested in TQM and organisational viability. Large organisations have been able to implement this innovation relatively easily, by either buying-up their suppliers or bringing their economic power to bear to get things changed the way that they want them. But for small and medium sized enterprises such economic clout is not enjoyed and a wholly different approach needs to be adopted. This approach must be based on negotiation with suppliers.

A negotiation based approach to supplier development has been developed within Cosalt Holiday Homes over several years. I have been involved for the last two years. Cosalt is a multi-million pound turnover medium sized enterprise, that largely assembles holiday homes. The limited literature about supplier development has been consulted (reviewed later). Evidently much work remained to be done. The challenge was taken up. A strategy has been constructed. The strategy was worked out 'live' as part of the management process of Cosalt. Benefits accrued to date include a cut in expenditure of £750 K per year, greater understanding between supplier and purchaser leading to improved quality of supply and a more certain operating environment for all involved. This chapter documents the findings so far.

The content and structure of this case study is as follows. First a background to Cosalt's quality approach is given. The most important aims for working out a supplier development strategy are explained. A literature review is provided. Following this preparation, a full-blown account of Cosalt's supplier development programme as it stands today is given. Let us start by outlining the company's quality approach that supplier development has become an integral part of.

COSALT'S QUALITY PROGRAMME

Cosalt Holiday Homes a few years ago set itself a target to become a world-class manufacturing organisation. To help to achieve this the Directors chose to introduce a quality approach. Quality superseded productivity as the company's main thrust. Initially, QCCs were introduced in 1987 and have thrived since implementation. Satisfied with progress on this front the company was inspired to find out what other quality techniques were available.

A visit to Japan and to some of Japan's key successful manufacturing companies was made in 1989. The visit was a reconnaissance, to learn about some obviously successful quality strategies. The concept of Kaizen developed in Japan was considered to be particularly useful for the British context. It would impinge a little on UK worker culture, but did not demand radical overthrowing of traditional practices that other Japanese methods would call for. Kaizen was brought back to and implemented in Cosalt. Kaizen essentially means continuous improvement, seeking small improvements through the elimination of waste. These activities complement QCCs. Together, QCCs and Kaizen have proved to be very successful at Cosalt. A vision of a total quality approach began to emerge from their implementation. This led to the investigation of a much broader approach, BS 5750 (equivalent to ISO 9000). BS 5750 explicitly added the client to Cosalt's quality thinking.

The decision to go for BS 5750 was questioned by some of Cosalt's directors. Some doubted its value. One concern was that a lack of appreciation of the value of BS 5750 exists among Cosalt's clients. Another concern was more disconcerting, that some of Cosalt's suppliers who have been accredited with BS 5750 have given more than a few quality problems themselves, raising doubt about the standard's effectiveness (concurring with observations in the SWOT analysis at the end of Chapter 4). On balance, however, the Board of Directors felt that the standard was common sense and that it should not be blamed for the inadequate implementation of its clauses. BS 5750 was implemented. This harnessed even further the worth of QCCs and Kaizen, developing these to a company-wide approach. Looking even wider pointed to an, as yet, little dealt-with set of supplier-related issues. In fact, creating a focus on supplier development in Cosalt's total quality approach was inevitable given its own business context.

Cosalt Holiday Homes is essentially an assembly type factory where limited manufacturing is performed but the final product, be it a caravan holiday home or park home, is assembled only after purchasing a large number of components from outside suppliers. The real skill base of Cosalt's workforce lies in its ability to assemble components, although there is considerable skill and experience in cutting accurately the various timber-based materials. Success in achieving a good quality final product therefore depends to a large extent on competitively priced good quality supplies. This is essential because 70% of the selling price of a holiday home is attributable to purchased components. Cosalt's final quality and competitiveness is dependent on its supplier base.

Cosalt thus focused attention on its supplier base, whilst maintaining and improving achievements already in place. The company moved on to work out a supplier development strategy in addition to continuing its internal quality management programme through QCCs and Kaizen, and pursuing BS 5750.

RATIONALE BEHIND DEVELOPING THE SUPPLIER BASE

The main aim of developing a supplier base is to secure a competitive edge in terms of quality, design input and a more competitive cost structure. With Cosalt we wanted to build in a guarantee of stability of a minimum of six or, ideally, twelve months, to each of these three key areas. This is important because of the dependence that Cosalt has on its suppliers for quality, and hence viability. It is also important in the face of a changing business environment.

There are two main changes in the business environment that are of concern to Cosalt:

1 Technological and competitive pressures have resulted in more firms tending towards greater specialisation. The fact that few companies can maintain, in house, the complete range of expertise needed to keep pace with the latest advances in manufacturing processes, as well as products, coupled with increasing global competition, is forcing vendors to develop specialised capabilities.
2 The nature of competition is changing. International competition today is a combination of competition in its traditional form (product versus product) and an equally powerful (but less visible) form of competition involving company's skills in implementing and managing a total quality approach. Suppliers are a vital part of a total quality approach. The companies with the best suppliers, and that can make the most effective use of their supplier's capabilities, are likely to have a competitive advantage.

Cosalt's own position, being highly dependent on its supplier base for quality and viability, and the two business factors relating to technical advances and the changing nature of competition given above, are central issues. These issues underline the need for a supplier development strategy for Cosalt. Let us now review what has been written and practised in this area of quality management.

LITERATURE REVIEW: SUPPLIER DEVELOPMENT

Developing company–supplier relations is not straightforward. Dale and Lascelles in their studies of product quality improvement through supplier development found that supplier development requires a fundamental shift in the supplier–customer relationship. Companies should treat their suppliers as long-term business partners. Accordingly, the following five activities are key areas that have to be tackled:

1 To investigate the supplier base to ensure continuity of product against the standard required.
2 To improve communication and feedback, internally and between the business unit and the suppliers.
3 To eliminate supplier complacency.
4 To develop customer objectives and strategy for supplier development.
5 To develop and improve customer credibility.

The Philips' Group pursued a similar line of thought. They coined the phrase 'comakership' to describe the new approach. Comakership simply means working together towards a common goal. It is based on the principle that both parties can gain more through co-operation than by separately pursuing their own interests. Comakership means establishing a long-term business partnership with each supplier-based operation. It pushes a desire for both parties to continuously improve the product and to clearly understand their responsibilities.

The Philips' Group found, like Dale and Lascelles, that to develop comakership considerable changes in behaviour and attitudes were required from both customers and suppliers. Customers have to prepare to develop plans and procedures for working with suppliers and to allocate time and resources to this. Suppliers for their part must accept full responsibility for their products and not depend on their customer's inspectors. As a prerequisite of the new relationship, Philips found that it was necessary to establish a set of ground rules for working together. Cosalt had the same experience. Cosalt's ground rules are documented later in this chapter.

Masson undertook a comparative study of two electronic manufacturers. He argued that one company, that had developed a comakership approach, achieved a significantly better performance from suppliers than the other manufacturer who had not implemented comakership. The benefits of the comakership approach, from the manufacturer's point of view, were achievement of short lead times, lower stock levels, stable prices, faster implementation of design changes, more reliable delivery performance, and less schedule disruption.

Bevan in his studies, reports that one UK motor manufacturer faced with the threat of competition from Europe, the Far East and their competitors in America, came to the conclusion that the most serious threat came from Japan. (As witnessed earlier, Cosalt held a similar conception.) Among other things, it was noted that the relationship between Japanese motor manufacturers and their suppliers is entirely different from all others. Some of the main differences are summarised below:

1 There are fewer suppliers; which is congenial to a more manageable situation.
2 Working relationships are very close and promote 'problem solving'; issues are discussed openly and managed together. For example, the technical expertise of the suppliers is recognised and this is harnessed to help manufacturers with new designs and prototypes.
3 Suppliers were totally committed to their customers' objectives. They were able to identify improvements that their customers could make, as well as the buyer identifying changes required in the supplier's organisation.

Rank Xerox, TI Rayleigh and Lucas all adopted a comakership approach with their suppliers to improve quality and to adopt a Just-In-Time (JIT) philosophy. We will focus on the Lucas case for a while because it contains items that influenced the Cosalt approach reported later.

Lucas's efforts have mainly dealt with changing attitudes. They have identified and compared a set of traditional and new attitudes between customer and supplier. Businesses within the Lucas Group have adopted a model for supplier integration that targets achievement of the new attitudes. The model focuses on quality, cost and delivery in three areas:

1 There must be internal development in the business unit, to promote co-ordination and operation of the material supply process.
2 There must be improvement in attitude and relationships between the business units and its suppliers, as well as improved communications, both formal and informal.
3 Suppliers must develop to enable them to achieve high quality, low cost JIT objectives (e.g., by the adoption of good manufacturing systems engineering practices).

Lucas believe that change must take place in all three areas if a company is to achieve maximum competitor advantage from its supplier relationships. Lucas also state that their supplier integration programmes have four broad objectives. The objectives follow:

1 Zero defects.
2 JIT supply to manufacturing units.
3 Cost reduction for new materials.
4 Reduction in the added cost generated by the material supply system itself, in terms of staff and stock costs, capital equipment, computer services and transport.

A further essential ingredient to Lucas is their task force. They list seven points for success that have been established from their 60 task forces during a two-year period. The seven points follow:

1 Full commitment from senior business managers: whoever owns competitiveness is responsible for managing it.
2 Full-time team leader: experience has shown that multidisciplinary task forces must be professionally set up with a full-time leader who is trained in project management and systems engineering methodology. Failure to operate a professional, disciplined approach increases the likelihood of failure.
3 Full-time systems engineering input: a strong systems engineering input is essential to achieve innovation using systems methodologies.

4 Initial team training and team building: prior to the task force start up, local management and the team should be given training suited to the needs of the project, which will include systems engineering.
5 Clear and ambitious business targets: quantified task force targets are defined in key business ratio terms based on international market and product analyses.
6 High-visibility monthly reviews: formal reviews, chaired by the local factory manager or general manager to demonstrate action and progress.
7 Full involvement of business management and supervision in reviews: ways of managing business unit difficulties and needs embrace new job functions, new organisation structures and new information and control systems as well as elements of engineering and technology. The reviews are a forum for presenting proposals for change to management and super-vision across the site.

The task forces are essentially cross-functional groups with full-time representation from purchasing, procurement, quality and administration. They are supported by a full-time business systems engineer. Normal reporting and control procedures therefore had to change.

Traditional reporting relationships can result in fragmented responsibilities and a lack of overall accountability for ensuring total quality supply. With the alternative structure recommended by Lucas the supply module leader is given responsibility for all the elements of total quality supply and can, therefore, be genuinely held accountable for overall supply performance.

Lucas' approach followed several phases. They initially recognised that communication is a two-way process. Then 100 of their suppliers were selected for special attention. Each was considered to be key to the future success of the business. Two senior management contacts from each of the suppliers were invited to attend a half-day seminar. At this seminar the Lucas approach to supplier integration was presented and feedback noted and discussed. Cosalt have partially shaped their supplier development strategy on Lucas' approach. We will now consider another case, the Jaguar case.

During the early 1980s the production of Jaguar cars reached its lowest point as confidence and identity slowly ebbed from this most prestigious of car marques. A critical in-depth review of the business was carried out by the purchasing manager of Jaguar cars. Findings pointed to the necessity for Jaguar to address its internal controls, its dealer network and to enlist the support of its suppliers to improve overall quality of the vehicles.

The initial task was to identify the problem components from the warranty figures. Following this a supplier conference was held with the MDs and Chairpersons of the companies concerned to discuss the issues.

Multi-function task forces were set up involving the suppliers. Each had a specific role which clearly identified the supplier's responsibilities to quality. Poor suppliers were dropped. Components were resourced in the relentless quest for quality. A single source supplier strategy was implemented and care was taken to involve the supplier at the concept stage.

Jaguar claim that a single-source strategy was progressive and during the reduction of the supplier base quality improved, creating better value for money, whilst trust and stability were built into the relationships. With the mutual benefits of larger contracts, both Jaguar and its suppliers committed themselves to quality, acknowledging this as a merit of long-term commitment. Another feature of Jaguar's new approach was the introduction of a 'Supplier of the Year' award.

Now let us summarise our review. The main theoretical ideas draw our attention to three key issue areas, attitudes, communication and control. Each of these areas has a well-developed literature that has not been drawn upon in the comakership literature. In many less interesting cases, not reported extensively above, the practical emphasis has tended to be on vendor rating and appraisal systems. Furthermore, practical work has usually focused on large company models (e.g., Lucas, Nissan, Rank Xerox, Ford, IBM, Jaguar and TI Rayleigh). There is a notable paucity in efforts relating to small and medium sized companies such as Cosalt Holiday Homes. Overall, the theory and practice on supplier development, although putting across many common-sense ideas, was found to be insufficiently developed for our purposes. Cosalt therefore took up the challenge to develop its own strategy, taking as a start the lessons provided above.

THE GROUNDING OF A SUPPLIER DEVELOPMENT STRATEGY

Bevan emphasises our conclusions drawn in the review above. He postulates that the management of change with respect to comakership falls into two main areas:

1 *Changing attitudes* and gaining commitment from suppliers, staff and other people in the company who must be persuaded to adopt a new approach in their dealings with each other.
2 *Changing procedures and practices* which are historical (i.e., communication and control procedures like scheduling, source selection and contract terms and conditions).

Building on this, a supplier development programme has been suggested by Dale and Lascelles. A main principle that underlies their approach is to tackle the need for changing attitudes and procedures. Seven stages were advocated as follows:

1 Establish and articulate programme objectives.
2 Set priorities for action.
3 Identify key suppliers as potential long-term partners and make plans to reduce supplier base.
4 Assess the capability of suppliers to meet purchase requirements.
5 Engage in advanced quality planning with suppliers.
6 Formally recognise suppliers which achieve preferred status.
7 Develop an on-going quality improvement relationship with suppliers based on a free exchange of information.

Bevan, and Dale and Lascelles, provide what we consider to be the grounding of the Cosalt supplier development strategy. It was on the basis of these ideas that we launched our own programme of action research. Not surprisingly, as shown below, certain context dependent developments were necessary.

COSALT'S SUPPLIER DEVELOPMENT PROGRAMME

Programme Objectives and Principles

The first stage in Cosalt's supplier development programme was to set objectives and establish principles. These are summarised below:

1 The overall objective of Cosalt Holiday Homes is to buy at the lowest price, taking into account the lowest overall total cost to the company. This includes quality cost. Targets are to be set for each supplier that include quality and delivery performance objectives and take account of the whole supply chain through to customer warranty and after-sales.

2 The suppliers who best meet these objectives must be defined and sourcing strategies developed for families of products. Suppliers will need to have the capabilities to meet the quality and delivery performance criteria as well as make an active contribution towards reducing their own costs, passing on the benefits of lower prices.

3 A gradual move towards long-term contracts with a single-source supplier will be sought which should enable suppliers to implement investment and improvement programmes. In return suppliers should be in a better position to achieve accurate quality and delivery targets with year-over-year price reduction.

4 A material scheduling strategy must be provided to give suppliers greater stability.

5 A purchasing strategy must be defined to take into account the technical requirements of the supplier base. This must be done to achieve the objectives at the lowest overall cost to Cosalt.

Based on these objectives and principles, Cosalt's supplier development programme crystallised to three key stages. Each one of these requires skilful negotiation with suppliers. At least initially this skill must be held in Cosalt, needing to transfer over time to suppliers.

Stage I   *Narrowing the supplier base*—Identify key suppliers as potential long-term partners and establish plans to reduce the supplier base.

Stage II   *Advance quality planning*—Engage in advance quality planning with suppliers through a series of meetings chaired by the operational managers of both businesses.

Stage III *Total improvement strategy*—Develop an on-going quality improvement relationship with suppliers by introducing a co-development strategy for Cosalt's supplier base.

Now let us consider how far we have progressed to date.

Progress to Date

As mentioned earlier in the chapter, at the present moment the programme is concluding Stage I (i.e., the rationalisation of the supplier base). The supplier base has been reduced by about 35%. When rogue suppliers were located, Cosalt actively sought alternative suppliers to facilitate the necessary change in attitude. The general trend, however, is towards a reduction in the supplier base. Throughout Stage I some 85 supplier development meetings have been held, including factory visits, throughout the UK as well as visits to Germany and Belgium. Details of implementation of Stage I follow.

STAGE I, SUPPLIER DEVELOPMENT STRATEGY: NARROWING THE SUPPLIER BASE

The Methodology

The methodology developed and implemented at Cosalt can be considered to have seven steps. These are summarised below:

1 Ensure full commitment from Cosalt's management team.
2 Form a task force to evaluate the supplier base.
3 Evaluate the supplier base
   ● to identify rogues,

- to identify alternative suppliers,
- to determine types of supplier for families of product,
- to determine Cosalt's expenditure profile with the suppliers.
4 Invite all suppliers to preliminary presentations and discussions to state Cosalt's commitment to supplier development, and ascertain the supplier's reaction to this.
5 Prioritise suppliers on the basis of the evaluation in 3 and preliminary discussions in 4.
6 Visit prioritised suppliers (to achieve the following where relevant)
- for an in-depth evaluation and discussion,
- to explain the value of supplier development from the supplier's point of view,
- to pass on Cosalt's quality expertise,
- to receive from the supplier their quality expertise,
- to identify areas of improvement on both sides,
- to construct an operational and developmental programme to implement a supplier development strategy.
7 Repeat 6 until either the programme is agreed upon or the supplier is removed from the books.

Now let us see how this ideal set of things to achieve worked out in practice.

Implementation

The first step at Cosalt was to introduce the concept of comakership to the senior plant managers; covering purchasing, design, technical and production. Discussions took place to describe the aims and objectives of the supplier development philosophy to obtain full commitment from the management team. Once this had been achieved the next step was to form a task force consisting of a senior purchasing manager, a senior manufacturing manager, a technical manager with the General Works Director as the project leader (now the MD).

The task force set about the evaluation of the supplier base. Initially a SWOT analysis was undertaken. The evaluation showed two very broad classes of supplier:

1 The sole suppliers who tended to show supplier complacency, an indifferent attitude to product development and quality and whose attitude was that price increases could be simply passed on to their customers (as a right).
2 The vast majority of suppliers, who formed the basis of the traditional multi-sourcing of Cosalt in the traditional customer–supplier manner.

The suppliers in Class 1 were considered to be rogues. Alternative suppliers were sought. The suppliers in Class 2 were grouped by product. Cosalt's expenditure profile with them was set out. These evaluations contributed later to the narrowing of the supplier base.

The MDs and Sales Directors of each supplier were then invited to a presentation at Cosalt. This was given by the General Works Director with other task-force members present. In this presentation the following nine points were made:

1 Cosalt has a commitment to comakership and a genuine desire to develop suppliers as long-term business partners.
2 Single source suppliers were sought by Cosalt and the perceived benefits to both parties was explained.
3 Each supplier was asked to consider if they wanted to develop and grow with Cosalt along the comakership route and if they felt they had the ability to do so. Each supplier was also requested to propose a price advantage for Cosalt if it placed considerably more business to the favoured supplier.
   Price stability for six or twelve months was also required. It was made clear that Cosalt understood the supplier's need to maintain sensible margins.
4 Trust and integrity were considered to be the hallmarks of the new approach.
5 Quality is of prime importance.
6 Cosalt assured all the suppliers that full information with respect to Cosalt's budget volumes, sales and production programmes would be available to them and they would be fully involved at all important stages. Their expertise would be acknowledged and needed by Cosalt to obtain a competitive edge.

7 Cosalt's management would be prepared to help and to develop its supplier base by making available its own knowledge and experience (e.g., in Kaizen, QCCs and BS 5750) as well as wishing to receive help in terms of new ideas.
8 All suppliers would be expected to seek BS 5750 certification.
9 Each newly formed single source supplier would be evaluated by both parties after a trial period of either 6 or 12 months. The objective would be to award longer term contracts of, say, two then three years etc.

Following the above presentation and the evaluation already mentioned, a degree of prioritisation was undertaken. Arrangements were made for Cosalt's task force to visit the prioritised supplier's premises. This enabled a more in-depth evaluation to take place. The following characteristics of the suppliers were carefully analysed:

1 The attitudes and quality of the management team and its view of comakership.
2 The attitudes of the workforce.
3 The financial stability of the company.
4 The company's procedures and other systems.
5 The company's status with respect to BS 5750 and their quality approach, including their inspection procedures and view on responsibility for quality.

The process made clear to the suppliers that Cosalt is serious about developing its supplier base. It also pointed out what Cosalt's quality bottom line is. To meet these increasingly exacting standards, it was explained to suppliers that they would have to achieve certain things. The benefit of these would be realised by both companies. They included clearly defined strategic and operational objectives, competent management in-depth, a skilled and flexible workforce, and a culture that encourages involvement, teamwork and continuous improvement. The rewards for suppliers who achieve this was shown to be substantial.

Finally, in order to encourage achievement of the above objectives, Cosalt's suppliers were offered a structured programme of support. This is termed a 'Co-Development Strategy' and consists of two inter-related elements. First is a strategic planning programme tailored to the needs of Cosalt's suppliers. Suppliers were helped to achieve a number of things. They were helped to identify the future opportunities and threats faced by their company, and to establish clear future objectives in the form of a sound business strategy that can be communicated to and implemented by their employees. Second is an operational and development programme designed especially for Cosalt's suppliers. This is the construction of a programme capable of implementing and sustaining the business strategy.

The methodology and implementation, of course, set out to achieve ideals. These ideals are those of the Cosalt supplier development strategy. Ideals are strived for but never fully met. So let us now analyse how successful the programme has been to date, in terms of general findings, achievements and failures.

FINDINGS, ACHIEVEMENTS, FAILURES, AND IDEAS FOR FURTHER DEVELOPMENT

Findings

The findings may be listed as follows:

1　The same management principles should be applied to the supplier base and the internal organisation. Standards must be set and maintained. Credibility, respect, trust and involvement will pay dividends and the stability of longer term contracts will give confidence to suppliers and should enhance loyalty.
2　With some rogue companies only the surprise of competition forced a response. Competitive prices became a very important feature of Stage I. The arrogance and complacency among some suppliers was broken down by nurturing alternatives. The original supplier would have to win back the lost business.
3　The supplier base is so vital to a manufacturing company like Cosalt that considerable time must be devoted to this area on an on-going basis. A lack of attention in the past has clearly been to the detriment of Cosalt's business performance.

4 Cosalt has been charged too much for its components prior to this exercise and it is likely that many other small and medium sized enterprises are treated in the same way.

5 There is a wealth of experience and expertise among the supplier base that must not be ignored.

6 Without exception suppliers were very enthusiastic about comakership and wanted to take a very active part—even the rogue suppliers.

7 Very few suppliers had embarked upon supplier development and even then had made no great progress to date.

8 There is a growing awareness of the importance of quality, after-sales service, customer satisfaction, reduction in stock, JIT and lead-time reduction.

9 The general view of Cosalt, seen through the eyes of the supplier base, is that it is a very progressive, stable company.

10 University involvement through the Centre for Systems Studies was very well received. Cosalt and its suppliers had access to the University's experience and expertise.

11 Cosalt's purchasing power had a very limited effect on the size of some suppliers' turnover—a point made whenever this occurred.

Achievements

1 The most obvious achievement to date must be the financial savings. These are in the order of 5% of cost and for Cosalt that means a saving of some £750 K per year. These savings do not take into account the inflationary increases that would have taken place. Experience would suggest a further 3–5% has been saved in this way.

2 The realisation among the suppliers that a way forward to improve their future was on offer and, in their view, one which was based on a common-sense approach.

3 Cosalt's management team are very enthusiastic about comakership and their knowledge and expertise is being enhanced. There is also a growing confidence in the task force. There is a real sense of involvement and commitment to the company.

4 Comakership is involving all stratas of management from board level to first-line management. This level of participation helps to develop a cohesive corporate culture.

Failures

1 An early failure was over-eagerness to accept the lowest price on offer. It was all too easy to be seduced by this method, which takes no account of suitability of supplies. Some suppliers attempted 'to buy' business.
2 There are still areas within Cosalt where supplier development is not well received. This flaw must be eradicated if Cosalt is to achieve world class status.
3 Communications from the customer to the supplier is not good enough. Feedback is essential to optimise this vital area of business performance, but has proven very hard to maintain.
4 Gaining exact achievement of specification, quality and lead time is never possible. Suppliers that are not wholly owned as subsidiaries have conflicting requirements from different customers.

Ideas for Further Development

1 Vertical integration should be considered. In some areas it may be possible to eliminate the supplier and for Cosalt to produce the components itself. This will give control over specification, quality and reduced lead times. The vertical integration may well mean the purchase of a supplier or setting up a subsidiary company.
2 Stage II is Advance Quality Planning. It has already started. We will be concentrating on improving the following:
   - Quality in all its aspects
   - Communication and control
   - Reduction in lead times
   - Lower stock levels
   - Higher priority given to orders
   - Faster implementation of design changes.

3 Stage III is the Total Improvement Strategy. The Total
   Improvement Strategy as postulated by Lascelles and Burns
   is an in-company, action-learning programme. It is based on
   six one-day sessions, at one-month intervals, with a supplier's
   senior management team. The philosophy underlying it is the
   belief that a company's own management knows its own
   situation best and, therefore, is the only group capable of
   producing a realistic business strategy. This approach has the
   additional benefit of strengthening the common purpose of
   the management team and their commitment to implementing
   the business strategy.

   The first step of the Total Improvement Strategy is for the
   company's management team to develop a 'vision' of what
   they want the company to become in the next five to ten years.
   The programme then goes on to construct the functional
   strategies which enable the vision to be realised. This is an
   interactive process of negotiation, which recognises that each
   step of a strategic plan affects and is affected by the rest. The
   end objective of the programme is to construct a business
   strategy accompanied by an implementation programme and
   monitoring mechanism.

   This follow-on programme comprises a 'menu' of assistance, learning and related developmental activities. A vertical
   axis focuses on the main business needs of a company, whilst
   a horizontal axis focuses on a range of delivery mechanisms
   for meeting these needs. Given that no two businesses are
   alike, the menu approach allows a company to develop its
   own tailor-made operational and developmental programme
   by selecting the activities and delivery mechanisms which
   meet its needs in a manner and time scale that fit in with its
   business strategy.

The three main objectives of the operational and developmental
programme follow:

1 To allow a company to develop a programme of assistance,
   learning and progress which exactly matches its needs.
2 To build on a company's existing activities in these areas
   by shaping and adding to them rather than supplanting
   them.

3 For Cosalt to assist in constructing and facilitating the operational and developmental programmes' implementation. This needs co-ordination and a reshaping of the existing training and development activities of suppliers, and supplementing these with inputs from other tried and tested providers.

We will now conclude the case study.

CONCLUSION

Supplier development, or comakership, for small and medium sized companies is a most exciting and potent method for obtaining a competitive edge in terms of cost reduction, quality improvement and design advantages. The whole area of research has been very enjoyable and interesting for the management team at Cosalt. It has also provided staff with opportunities for development, to grow their confidence and expertise. Consequently a strong corporate culture has emerged.

Supplier development has the advantage of reaching many involved employees and companies through participation with the supplier base. Supplier development can, via negotiation as described in this chapter, tap into a vast reservoir of knowledge and experience. Despite there remaining a handful of failings, supplier development at Cosalt is seen as a huge success. Quality, viability, cost and corporate cohesion have all improved. Yet, much work remains to be done to implement Stages II and III successfully and these efforts will be reported in later editions of this book.

FURTHER READING

●This chapter was developed from the following article:

Flood, R. L. and Isaac, M. (1993) Supplier development strategy for small and medium sized companies: The case of Cosalt Holiday Homes, *International Journal of Quality and Reliability Management*, 10(6), in press.

● The main articles that influenced our supplier development strategy are:

Bevan, J. (1990) Comakership, *Management Development*, Vol. 27, No. 3, pp. 50–54.

Dale, B. (1988) An Assessment of the Practicalities and Problems of Implementing Comakership, unpublished notes. UMIST.

Dale, B. and Lascelles, D. M. (1988) Supplier Quality Management: Attitudes, Techniques and Systems, *Occasional Paper No. 8805* UMIST.

● Other articles used to construct the literature review are:

Anon (1985) *Comakership: Purchasing in Benelex*, Philips, NV, Eindhoven.

Bhote, K. (1987) *Supply Management*, New York, American Management Association.

Birch, D. (1990) Establishing Effective Supplier Partnerships to Fully Support the Goals of the Purchaser, unpublished notes. UMIST.

Feigenbaum, A. V. (1982) Quality and Business Growth Today, *Quality Progress*, 15(11), pp. 22–25.

Goddard, W. E. (1986) *Just-In-Time*, Vermont, Oliver Wright.

Harrison, M. (1986) Rayleigh Reveals Radical Survival Plans, *The Engineer*, 20 March, pp. 16–17.

Henderson, J. C. (1990) Plugging into Strategic Partnerships: The Critical IS Connection, *Sloan Management Review*, Spring.

Huckett, J. D. (1985) An Outline of the Quality Improvement, *International Journal of Quality and Reliability Management*, 2(2), pp. 5–14.

Johnson, R. H. and Weber, R. (1985) *Buying Quality*, New York, Watts.

Lascelles, D. M. and Burns, B. (1991) Total Improvement Strategy at Nissan, Internal UMIST document (unpublished).

Lyons, T. F., Krachenberg, R. and Henke, J. W. (Jr) (1990) Mixed Motive Marriages: What's Next For Buyer–Supplier Relations?, *Sloan Management Review*, Spring.

Mason, P. J. (1986) User–Vendor Relationships in the Scottish Electronics Industry, *International Journal of Quality and Reliability Management*, 3(2), pp. 51–55.

Stralkowski, C. M. and Billon, S. A. (1988) Partnering: A Strategic Approach To Productivity Improvement, *National Productivity Review*, Spring.

Stralkowski, C. M., Klemm, R. C. and Billon, S. A. (1988) Partnering Strategies: Guidelines for Successful Customer–Supplier Alliances, *National Productivity Review*, Spring.

White, I. and Wyatt, M. (1990) A Case Study: Lucas Industries' Approach to Supplier Integration, in B. G. Dale and J. J. Plunkett (eds) *Managing Quality*, Philip Alan, London.

Section III
EXERCISES AND GAMES

16
Exercises and Games

INTRODUCTION

Section I sorted out and developed an understanding of the main philosophies, principles and methods of quality management. A new understanding of TQM was developed. Section II underlined the main ideas put across in Section I and introduced some important additional material in four case studies detailing interventions using quality ideas. Now, in Section III, the lessons of the previous two sections are sealed through a number of exercises and games that get participants working on and used to employing quality ideas.

Naturally there will be limitations to what the reader can achieve in the following games and exercises, having only been supplied with limited briefs. Quite a bit can be accomplished however. The exercises and games will provoke thought and discussion, and will promote learning. The main aim of this chapter is to make it possible for participants to get a feel for the kinds of thing that need to be done when implementing quality ideas, and to sample the beneficial and problematic sorts of issues that might crop up.

STANDARD COTTONS

Introduction

In this game employing the general method for implementing TQM will be the primary focus. The method is introduced in

Chapter 9. One intervention using the method is documented in Chapter 12 and, to a lesser extent, in Chapter 14.

Your Task

Read through the background information given below and then do the following (*where necessary make your own assumptions*).

1   Develop an appreciation of the set of interacting issues that this organisation faces using the metaphors from TSI. Identify any key technical, cultural or political issues to be taken into consideration.

2   Assume that you have chosen to implement TQM. Set up the Executive Council. Identify who will have membership of it, pinpointing about 8+ people by specifying job positions. Act as if you are this Council.

3   Choose which structural or organisational representation of the company you are going to use to guide implementation of TQM.

4   Work out a mission for the organisation.

5   Work out the Council's view on; training needs, leadership, motivation, measurement and methods likely to be relevant for the next stages of implementation.

6   Set up a number of first level Quality Councils using the representation of the organisation chosen in 2 above. Make clear how they will communicate with each other and the Executive Council. Will there be a need for another level of councils?

7   For each first level council; set their mission, identify project areas, separate the projects into the vital few and useful many. Define in detail the vital few projects and then check out the consistency between projects.

8   Carry out a SWOT analysis along the following lines. Think critically about TQM as a method as such. Think critically about the output of your use of this method. How relevant do you think TQM is for this company?

9   Prepare and make a 5 to 10 minute presentation of your findings to other groups or individuals.

Background Information

Standard Cottons is a small subsidiary of a large multinational. The company enjoys a turnover of approximately US$600 million. It employs 2200 people with 1900 in production, 120 in administration and finance, 100 in sales and marketing, and 60 in human resources development. Production is split into three units, turning the raw resource into three items of clothing— blouses, skirts and dresses.

The subsidiary has performed adequately over the last 20 years despite the sometimes turbulent nature of the international economy. A change in economic thinking by the Government of the country where Standard Cottons is based has raised some concern however. Tariff protections are tumbling. Two years ago they stood at 35%. Currently they stand at 30% and will fall at 3% per annum until 15% is reached.

Head Office in the USA decided last year that all their subsidiaries would adopt and implement the Crosby approach (see Chapter 2 for details of this approach). The Human Resource Manager joined his equals from other countries at the Crosby College in Miami. He underwent intensive training and returned to preach the gospel to the workforce of Standard Cottons through his own courses.

Although participants of the course found the ideas in principle to be very simple, in practice they have struggled to implement them. In terms of management commitment, there was much confusion about what management was actually committed to. The Manufacturing Manager was new to the company. He was extremely keen and a quality enthusiast, believing that he could rapidly achieve positive change. He was a sincere and well-intentioned man but unfortunately caused much confusion. He mainly quoted Deming and Ishikawa, promoting continuous improvement whilst rubbishing the decreed company approach. He believed that Crosby was nothing more than a salesman.

To the Managing Director, quality was quality, meaning getting costs down by reducing waste of materials and people's time. He was not overly concerned whether the philosophy of Headquarters was followed or not, as long as quality improvements as he understood them were achieved. To this end he employed you as consultants, hoping to overcome the internal wrangling. He has heard that your approach assumes that Crosby, Deming and Ishikawa all complement each other. In this way the tensions could be resolved.

Apart from these cultural and political events, there were a number of major underlying assumptions that had not surfaced. Management had not acknowledged that benchmarking against the world's most efficient plants would be vital to Standard's future survival. They held on to productivity performance as their main philosophy. This was unfortunate because Standard did not have access to the same economies of scale available elsewhere in the world. It was assumed that everyone's job was safe. Headquarters, however, had a history of moving the work of an ineffective plant to some other location if they perceived it to be necessary.

The view of senior management was that quality could only be achieved through changes in procedures and attitudes, but not through restructuring. It was assumed that the quality process could be grafted on to the existing structure. There is now a growing fear that the quality process is not a miracle cure.

One of the main difficulties is that the company accepted and pushed the rhetoric of team-work idealism without implementing detailed action planning, accountability and control. The Manufacturing Manager, however, accused the Finance Manager of being caught up in the petty details of the here and now and not understanding the longer term implications of quality—that when fully implemented the quality process would drive costs down.

At Standard a customer focus and satisfying customer's needs was thoroughly discussed amongst the employees. Real strides forward in this respect were made. But a full inquiry into internal customer requirements has not been carried out. Some individuals continue to do their best by auditing and measuring their own performance. Other employees saw this as an attempt to cover themselves and pass on the blame.

A lot of effort has been put in to encourage employee participation. There has been some progress. Action team meetings were launched. The big surprise is that this has taken years rather than months of effort to realise success. There have also been some negative aspects to participation. What in effect happened was that some employees became overly curious about the role and activities of other departments and other people's jobs, limiting the time that they spent on tasks they were responsible for. Empowerment also created confusion at first because many supervisors did not have the skills nor confidence to run their own operations without guidance and control.

Complicating the issue was the difficulty of normal discipline control. Expectations had been raised and a few mischief makers capitalised on this when the expectations were not straight away met. They played on the suspicions of workers that, suddenly, management trusted them. Certain anomalies accentuated this, for example, the workers still had to clock-in whilst their supervisors did not, and were seemingly able to disappear at will.

Numerous corrective action teams had been established. They soon encountered difficulties. In particular co-operation and co-ordination between the groups was lacking. Tasks that they set themselves often repeated those of another team. Sometimes teams undertook actions that led to conflict and confusion. This left a legacy of frustration and disappointment. Where there was success there was usually more trouble as well. Disputes often broke out between teams, with the argument that only those people who carried favour with the bosses received recognition.

The three manufactured units already mentioned are produced completely separately. They use the same raw materials and have about an equivalent number of staff working on them. Recently there has been an upsurge in demand for skirts and blouses at the expense of dresses.

Sales and Marketing have learnt much about their competitor's methods of production. They are more advanced than Standard's methods. They are much more efficient. The strategy marketing has adopted to overcome this difficulty is to sell the idea that the best clothes are those manufactured using traditional methods. The Manufacturing Manager is not aware of the alternative methods.

Sales and Marketing have worked hard over the years to establish a reliable clientele and have made separate arrangements for terms of payment with them. Unaware of this, and concerned about cash flow difficulties that might arise as tariffs fall, the Finance Manager is just about to launch a new strict credit control system.

Currently the Human Resources Manager is working hard on a new set of courses, the Crosby way, hoping to revitalise his quality programme. He is planning to make these available in a few weeks time. He intends to make a big splash with the new courses and has kept his efforts quiet hoping to surprise and knock off-balance his main critics.

CYBER ENGINEERING

Introduction

IQAMSS were described and discussed at length in Chapter 4. They propose a set of clauses to be taken account of on the way toward achieving formal recognition as a quality orientated organisation. The aim of this game is to get a feel for the clauses in the face of a real company scenario. Participants will exercise their minds on the application of IQAMSS in the form of ISO 9000.

Your Task

Read through the background information given below and then do the following:

1   Develop an appreciation of the set of interacting issues that this organisation faces using the metaphors from TSI. Identify any key technical, cultural or political issues to be taken into consideration.
2   For each clause do three things;
    ● explain the meaning and relevance of the clause for the organisation in question,
    ● if necessary, work out an interpretation of the clause for the organisation in question,
    ● make any observation you think is valid concerning how this organisation might meet the requirements of the clause.
3   Produce an outline for the first manual, that documents the management statement on policy and objectives. This includes

the main aims, organisational structure, a definition of responsibilities and limits of authority, and naming the management representatives.

4 Produce an outline for the second manual, that documents how the quality system declared in 3 above is to be implemented.

5 Carry out a SWOT analysis along the following lines. Think critically about IQAMSS as a model as such. Think critically about the output of your use of this model. How relevant do you think IQAMSS are for this company?

6 Prepare and make a five to ten minute presentation of your findings to other groups or individuals.

Background Information

Cyber Engineering manufactures and sells control units for automatic regulation of air condition in factory workshops that suffer from poor air quality. The unit is made of light alloy. It is programmable through a keyboard and memory storage system.

The product was launched five years ago and unit sales and market share are shown in Table 16.1.

The unit retails at US$12 000. It has been used in a wide range of heavy and light industries such as steel, printing, chipboard, cottons, food processing and car assembly.

Reliability has not been acceptable and warranty claims on average absorb 5% of sales revenue, well above the expected level. Cyber Engineering offers a 12-month all-claims back-up service. Recently senior managers have become concerned about the effect that the guarantee is having on profits. They are close

Table 16.1 Product market share Cyber Engineering

Year	No. of units	Market share (%)
1994	600	24
1995	1200	27
1996	2600	36
1997	3400	30
1998	3900	28

to a decision that would reduce the value of the guarantee and hence protect profits.

The senior managers are upset that warranty costs are so high when very substantial amounts of money have been invested in the Quality Assurance Department. None of them are confident that the Quality Assurance Department can get to grips with the situation. Accentuating this feeling is the failure of the QCC programme. This was implemented three years ago. It fizzled out largely because the ideas generated by the workers were not taken seriously by management. Management, however, blame the quality group, or the workers, but will not accept responsibility themselves.

Profits, warranty costs, and quality costs are shown as a percentage of sales in Table 16.2. A recent estimate of total quality cost distribution is shown in Table 16.3.

Staff turnover is high, averaging 20% per annum over the last three years. Absenteeism is often as high as 10% or even 12%. Investment is low, falling from US$30 000 per person to US$15 000. Productivity has fallen from 12 units per person a year to only seven in the last year.

The units are manufactured using the following production process. Orders are received by the Sales Department. These are

Table 16.2 Warranty and quality costs as a percentage of sales Cyber Engineering

Year	Scrap and rework (%)	Warranty costs (%)	Quality department (%)
1994	2	2	8
1995	2	4	7
1996	3	5	5
1997	4	6	8
1998	5	8	9

Table 16.3 Distribution of total quality costs Cyber Engineering

Cost	%
Failure prevention	6
Appraisal and inspection	40
In plant failure (internal)	20
Field failure (external)	34

passed on to production. A Purchasing Manager determines the amount of alloy and components needed to manufacture at a rate equivalent to demand, and then orders them through the stores section. A lead time of two weeks is allowed for all orders. On arrival they are inspected using sampling techniques. Their acceptability is determined according to published certified quality standards.

Alloy sheets then go to the production line. They are cut and shaped. Scrap is disposed of. Pressers then shape the prepared sheets. The sheets are assembled using bolt guns. The shells are then cleaned and sprayed. They go for drying and then there are several stages where internal components are fitted. After inspection the units go to the warehouse ready for delivery.

There are three shifts operated keeping the manufacturing process going 24 hours a day for 6 days a week. The factory shuts down for 2 weeks in August and 2 weeks in December. Weekly

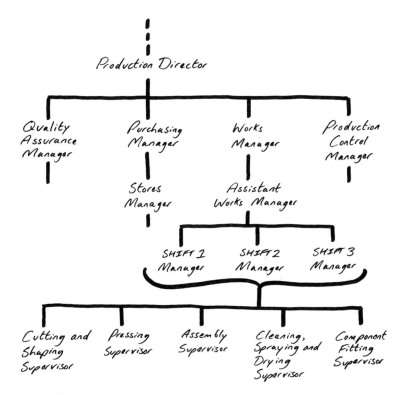

Figure 16.1 *Organisational chart—Cyber Engineering*

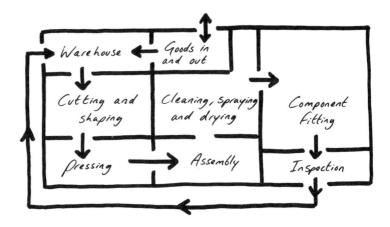

Figure 16.2   Factory layout—Cyber Engineering

maintenance is normally carried out on Sunday, whilst complete overhauls occur during shut downs.

The organisational chart is shown in Figure 16.1 and the factory layout in Figure 16.2. Senior management have decided to go for ISO 9000 and as consultants you have been brought in to steer Cyber Engineering through the process toward recognition.

AUTONOMOUS PARTS INC.

Introduction

TQM advocates participation and autonomy for members of an organisation. There are three interrelated concepts that come from the behavioural sciences that can be used within TQM to help to achieve participation and autonomy. The three concepts are vertical loading, task formation and job grouping. These were introduced in Chapter 7. The aim of this game is for participants to get some experience of employing them in an organisational context.

Your Task

Read through the background information given below and then do the following.

1 Suggest where responsibility can be loaded down, to the lowest level at which it can be managed. What advantages would be secured in doing this?
2 Are there any areas of fragmentation where tasks can be brought together to produce whole jobs? What advantages would be secured in doing this?
3 Are there any jobs that could be logically grouped? What advantages would be secured by doing this?
4 Carry out a SWOT analysis along the following lines. Think critically about the value of the three concepts as such. Think critically about the output of your use of the three concepts. How relevant do you think they are for this company?
5 Prepare and make a five to ten minute presentation of your findings to other groups or individuals.

Background Information

A plant in Skiffling manufactures pressurised tanks designed to hold liquid gas for use in a wide range of chemical manufacturing processes. Once the tanks have been completed at Skiffling they are supplied as a part to be assembled in a larger piece of equipment. Three sister plants are supplied, in Skidby, Cherry Burton and Withernsea. Skiffling produces four other products that are also dispatched to the three other plants. The geographical location of the four plants involved is shown in Figure 16.3.

There is a warehouse at Skiffling where all products are stored before dispatch. Apart from a manager, the warehouse has five clerks, each responsible for supplies of one particular product. The clerk responsible for delivery of pressurised tanks is currently distraught because of the high level of returned faulty product from Skidby, Cherry Burton and Withernsea. This is particularly worrying because deliveries from Skiffling are already well behind schedule. The reason is that management targets are not being met from the shop floor. On average there should be 20 units per hour manufactured to meet management targets and to satisfy demand.

The manufacturing process has a typical production line. Matching halves of the tank are passed to welders, who then

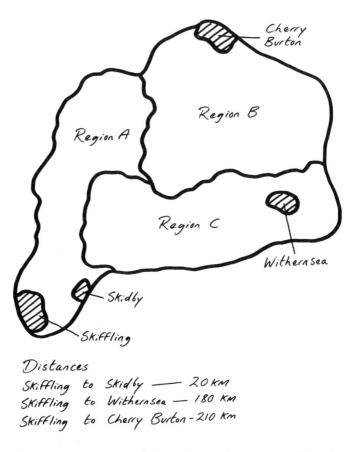

Cherry
Burton

Region B

Region A

Region C

Withernsea

Skidby

Skiffling

Distances
Skiffling to Skidby —— 20 KM
Skiffling to Withernsea — 180 KM
Skiffling to Cherry Burton - 210 Km

Figure 16.3 *Locations of four plants—Autonomous Parts Inc.*

weld them together at a rate of approximately 18 per hour (plus
two faulty ones). The whole tank moves on to the next group
of workers who solder on fittings. A third group undertakes
pressure testing and returns weak tanks to the welders. About
8% are found to be weak. Weak tanks then pass through the
solderers again so that all soldered fittings can be rechecked after
the further welding is complete. They are pressure tested again.

All tanks that pass the pressure test move on to be painted
and treated. The painters and treaters receive them at a rate of
16 to 17 per hour. They complain that their jobs are made difficult
when reworked tanks have to be dealt with. They are more messy
and often have to undergo lengthy preparation. At a rate of about
14 to 15 an hour, they are painted, treated, and passed on for

full inspection. Even at this stage a significant number of tanks are found to be unacceptable and returned to the appropriate point further back down the line. The store receives the product on average at about 14 an hour.

There are a few other relevant points. Workers do not know what the finished product is used for. There is much tension between the groups working on the line, each blaming the others for low output and poor quality. The staff are not properly trained.

FUNDAMENTAL CAUSES OF QUALITY FAILURE

Introduction

The failure to achieve quality in certain organisations and societies is often put down to fundamental causes. These causes are not found in the technical elements of organisations. As Ishikawa and Taguchi have shown, technical matters can relatively easily be identified and tackled. Fundamental causes are more deeply rooted then. They are rooted in socio-cultural socio-political characteristics of organisations and societies. Deming recognised this when he returned to North America and encountered strong resistance from the workforce, from both managers and the workers. He named five deadly diseases as the root cause of the resistance (see Chapter 2). It is such fundamental causes of quality failure that provide the interest in this management exercise.

Listed out below are 14 fundamental causes of quality failure. Another nine have been added to Deming's five deadly diseases. They have been extracted from the quality literature. In addition, the views of senior managers from many different nations and continents, representing an international outlook, have been gathered together and integrated into the list.

Your Task

Either individually or as a team, carefully work through the list provided below and pick out five most significant issues that are fundamental causes of quality failure in:

1 The organisation in which you work.
2 The society in which you live.

How strongly do the causes identified in 2 influence those chosen for 1? How can we go about tackling the fundamental causes that you came up with? What are the relevant methods and ideas from Section I of this book?

Select another region from the international economic scene and, once again, pick out significant issues that are fundamental causes of quality failure in that part of the world (e.g. North America, Europe, SE Asia, the Far East, Australasia, Latin America). Compare these to the list that you chose for your own society. How and why do they differ (if at all)? If you noted differences, what fundamental advantages and disadvantages can be identified for each region in comparison to the other?

Fundamental Causes

1 The organisation/society is regimented according to a bureaucratic structure that leads to a lack of dynamism and limits creativity.
2 The organisation/society is most obviously characterised as highly political and coercive and, as argued in Chapter 7, this strips quality ideas of their meaning and value when implemented.
3 There is a lack of constancy and purpose. The stability that is necessary for successful implementation of quality initiatives is therefore missing.
4 There is too much emphasis on short-term profits.
5 Evaluation of personnel and personal development is inadequate or carried out in a threatening rather than encouraging manner.
6 Management and/or employees are too mobile thus undermining efforts to establish a quality culture. This may be because crucial senior managers are head-hunted or that there is an employee market.
7 Management rely too heavily on data that can easily be served up in quantitative form using simple techniques such as graphs, bar charts, pie charts and so on. These do not

adequately look at direction of change and often seem to miss rate of change. Furthermore, less tangible but equally important qualitative factors are shunned, thus meaning that decision making is made without proper reflection on social, cultural and political issues.

8　There is a deep-rooted distinction felt in society between managers and workers, us and them. This leads to a lack of willingness to co-operate and work together.

9　People are inward looking and egotistical. There is too much emphasis on individualism.

10　There is a lack of emphasis on personal development through training and education, be it post-experience or academic.

11　Short-term thinking and targets dominate. Response to and preparation for threats and opportunities is reduced to crisis management.

12　Too many senior managers and administrators know very little about management and organisation theory, and the management and systems sciences. They are not qualified to do their job.

13　Emphasis is placed on solving problems rather than managing issues. Management is therefore sporadic rather than continuous.

14　Management relies on a limited number of over-simplistic tools and techniques, and operates without a method to help them understand each one's strengths and weaknesses.

DEPARTMENTAL OR ORGANISATIONAL MINDEDNESS?

Introduction

Standard management models and much of management practice fail to take account of the value of systems thinking. This book has put the record straight by underlining the value of systems thinking to quality management and by pointing out limitations inherent in the alternative fragmentary approach. For quality management, however, systems thinking raises all kinds of issues. This exercise focuses on just one, the conflict between being organisationally or departmentally minded.

Managers normally hold responsibility for departments (or distinct areas of an organisation). Running a unit successfully leads to personal recognition and improved career prospects. TQM, however, places an emphasis on the whole, on the organisation rather than concentrating on departments. But contributions to the whole are often less visible. There is the worry that time invested on organisational matters, therefore, will bring less reward. It may be better to concentrate efforts on improving things in one's own sphere of responsibility. In this way TQM can give rise to conflict between personal goals (running a department well and being rewarded for it) and organisational goals (taking a total quality approach). This is particularly pertinent where the reward system in an organisation recognises success only at a departmental level, say.

The aim of this exercise is to highlight and generate debate about tension introduced when seeking to change the career culture, switching to some degree from departmental to organisational mindedness.

Your Task

It is first thing on Monday morning. Over the weekend you attended a seminar on TQM and were very impressed. You hope to use some of the ideas in your own job. You are the manager of an accounts department and have just arrived at work. On your desk is an in-tray that contains a whole variety of jobs to be done by your department. There is not enough time for you to do them all, as usual, so the first thing that must be done is to go through the bundle of tasks and prioritise them. You have five choices:

1 To leave the job until another day.
2 To delegate the job to a junior member of staff to handle on their own.
3 To delegate the job to your personal assistant, following a briefing, and allow for further consultation on the matter if necessary.
4 To do the job yourself tackling only the main issues involved.
5 To do the job yourself thoroughly.

The jobs are listed below. A guestimate of the amount of time in minutes involved in doing 1 to 5 is recorded alongside each job in the list. A dash means that in this case that option cannot be selected. Now, go through the jobs and decide on your prioritisation. Select either 1, 2, 3, 4 or 5 for each job. Record this on a sheet of paper. Work either individually or in teams. It is better if there are at least two teams so that their prioritisations can be compared. Carry out this analysis before moving on to the next section.

Your working day starts at 9.00 hours and finishes at 17.00 hours, a total of 480 minutes without a lunch break. You could work up to 1.5 hours late adding another 90 minutes, although this means cancelling a dinner appointment with Ivor Grouse, your boss, scheduled at 18.00 hours. Grouse is firmly in the old school of thought. He likes to see managers keeping their departments shipshape and to follow the well-established bureaucratic lines of authority. The purpose of the dinner appointment with him is to discuss how well your department has performed. It is part of your review for the next round of promotions.

	Selection				
Job	1	2	3	4	5
(a) Ivor Grouse wants a summary of your department's performance covering the last 6 months for tonight's meeting.	0	20	30	95	120
(b) A bought ledger clerk has been persistently late for work and has extended lunch breaks despite warnings. You have according to the company's rules to give a final warning by the end of today.	—	—	—	30	30
(c) The Sales Director has requested management information on sales figures against publicity expenditure for the six geographical regions that your company operates in, to assess the success of different types of campaign in each region.	0	10	30	60	120

(*continued*)		Selection			
Job	1	2	3	4	5
(d) The credit control clerk needs to discuss with you some of the more serious outstanding payments.	—	—	15	30	45
(e) There is a meeting today with the Senior Personnel Officer and representatives from each department to discuss the introduction of a new training module called 'Systems Thinking for Managers'.	0	10	20	60	60
(f) The local newspaper wanted an interview with you by telephone for comments on the rumours that your company is in financial trouble, with the threat that up to 50 jobs will be axed. The Managing Director is keen for you to dispose of these rumours.	0	—	10	20	30
(g) There is some general mail that needs attending to.	0	10	30	70	90
(h) A client has turned up to complain about persistent errors in invoices to his company.	0	20	30	35	45
(i) You need to have a meeting with one of the sales clerks to discuss computerisation that is currently under way.	0	—	15	50	60
(j) A long-standing colleague of yours is retiring this week and has invited you and a number of others to a farewell lunch-time drink. The company will be presenting her with an award and photographs will be taken to publish in the next Newsletter. This is part of the company's strategy to bind employees in the organisation.	0	—	10	60	60

(*continued*)		Selection				
Job		1	2	3	4	5
(k)	A visit to one of the company's suppliers has been arranged this afternoon as part of a supplier development strategy. You have been asked to attend to provide financial advice.	0	15	30	90	90
(l)	You have been asked to write an article for the company Newsletter on TQM following attendance of the seminar at the weekend.	0	15	30	90	120
(m)	The need for task formation in your department is urgent. A meeting with all staff is scheduled for today.	0	—	20	75	90
(n)	An interim report is to be given by the company's auditors to representatives of all departments. The aim is to raise a few concerns that have company-wide implications and to debate how these can best be tackled.	0	10	30	90	90
(o)	Last week's accounting reconciliation was several thousands out. The supervisor responsible, who joined last week, needs advice on how to proceed.	0	10	20	75	90

Analysis For Discussion

The jobs set out above are focused either on your department (D) or the organisation (O). This is shown below:

(a)	D	(f)	O	(k)	O
(b)	D	(g)	D	(l)	O
(c)	O	(h)	D	(m)	D
(d)	D	(i)	D	(n)	O
(e)	O	(j)	O	(o)	D

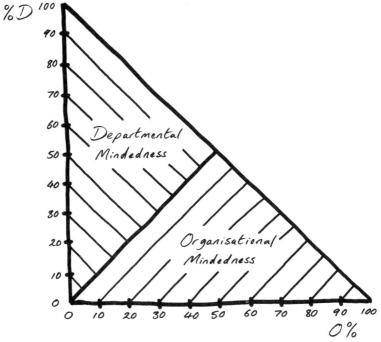

Figure 16.4   *Departmental or organisational mindedness rating chart*

Calculate how many minutes you chose to spend on departmental matters and how many on organisational ones. The total amount of time needed to do either the departmental or organisational jobs thoroughly is 570 minutes. Calculate the percentage of D that you covered by dividing the number of working minutes allocated to D by 570 and then multiplying by 100. Repeat this for O. Plot the results of these calculations on a graph like that in Figure 16.4 and then discuss the results. (Note: this is nothing more than a fun exercise designed to provoke thought and debate. It does not claim in any way to provide an accurate measure of organisational or departmental mindedness.)

Do you appear on the organisationally minded side or on the departmentally minded one? How does this compare with other groups who carried out the same exercise alongside you? What were the main factors that influenced your decisions? What do you think are the main issues for implementing TQM, with respect to a dilemma of this sort, which generates tensions for managers? How can these issues and tensions be managed?

STRUCTURE AND ORGANISATION

Introduction

As we saw in Chapter 7, many different models have been drawn up and promoted as effective ways of structuring or organising businesses, firms and other organisations. One of the earliest proposals came in the form of a bureaucracy, a hierarchical organisational tree. This has had its influence and still dominates modern-day management. Much more recently a revolutionary new model has been put forward called the Viable System Model (VSM). It has been argued that the VSM is highly relevant to modern-day management. In Chapter 7 complementary relationship to quality management was demonstrated. In this exercise you are asked to explore the two models and make up your own mind about the relevance and appropriateness of them to an organisation that you are familiar with.

Your Task

Draw up a simple representation of your organisation, or any other one that you have knowledge about, using a traditional hierarchical organisational tree. Make sure that you show the quality department or function on this diagram if one exists. If there is not one then insert it where you think that it should/could be. Explore whether you think the representation constructed is adequate as a tool for thought. (Hint: what fundamentally does this structure tell us about the organisation and how quality has been, or would be, implemented using it.) Now draw a simple Viable System Model of the same organisation. Where is the quality function located? Is this representation an adequate tool for thought? How do the two representations that you have constructed compare in the context of the organisation and business context that you have selected to analyse? Are there other circumstances where you might come to different conclusions than those you have just drawn?

FINDING VARIABILITY

Introduction

A main goal for quality management is to locate variability and eradicate it. TQM recognises that variability may be detected either quantitatively or qualitatively. For example, control charts help analysis of quantitative data whereas fishbone analysis aids investigation of qualitative issues. In this exercise we will be focusing on the basics of quantitative analysis that were discussed in Chapter 9. The task is to undertake a simple analysis of a small sample of data. The aim is to get participants looking for variability such as, too much variation from the centre, a shift away from the centre, and/or a trend away from the centre.

Your Task

Either individually or as a team, calculate the centre, range, and standard deviation of the data given in Table 16.4. Draw a control chart to aid your analysis. Interpret the chart. Draw conclusions about variability, shifts and trends away from the centre. The data is a tabulation of batch sample averages taken from three machines in a manufacturing process. Assume 25.00 to be the ideal measure, with ±0.20 the agreed limits (i.e. between 24.80 and 25.20).

DOES EMPOWERMENT WORK?

Introduction

Much emphasis was placed in Section I of this book on five principles from behavioural science. Three of these were the focus of the Autonomous Parts Inc. game in this chapter. Two in particular make their point on empowerment. These are vertical loading and task formulation. These have a special significance for the philosophy of quality management as has already been argued in Chapter 8. The acid test, of course, is whether the philosophy and principles can be translated to practice. The aim

Table 16.4 Batch sample averages from three machines

Batch	Machine A	Machine B	Machine C
1	25.08	24.93	25.00
2	24.85	25.00	24.96
3	25.00	24.96	25.08
4	25.02	25.08	25.02
5	25.15	24.85	25.01
6	24.93	25.01	25.02
7	24.96	25.02	25.15
8	24.63	25.07	25.07
9	25.08	25.15	25.15
10	24.95	24.95	24.85
11	25.38	25.01	24.97
12	25.01	25.04	24.78
13	24.77	24.80	24.76
14	25.56	24.85	24.75
15	24.92	24.98	24.86
16	24.85	24.91	24.95
17	25.49	24.81	24.95
18	24.61	24.95	24.89
19	24.98	24.83	24.73
20	25.41	24.98	24.79

of this exercise is to critically analyse a cover story from the magazine *USA TODAY*, suggesting that tapping workers' experiences and giving them responsibility and autonomy lies behind the quality revolution in one of US Steel's works.

Your Task

Read the following cover story and then debate the following questions with other participants in pairs or groups. What were the main difficulties Gary Works faced? What were the key developments behind Gary Works' revival? Why did they occur? Under what circumstances could they be repeated?

Cover Story

'US Steel learns from experience', by James R. Healey, *USA TODAY*, 11 April, 1992. Reproduced by permission of LA Times Intl.

Gary, Ind.—The situation was bleak as a foggy afternoon on nearby Lake Michigan.

US Steel's Gary Works was all but banished from General Motors supplier rolls. Ford Motor was threatening the same. "Find a new way of doing your business", was the blunt mandate from Ford's Pete Urchek in a 1987 ultimatum to Gary Works.

Not only was the steel bad, it arrived late. "And they told us we were arrogant", recalls Robert Pheanis, a manager. Gary Works—the biggest mill in the biggest steel company—was alienating customers and roiling with labour problems. It was also losing more than US$100 million a year. The heart of Big Steel was about to stop beating.

Revival came from a small team of gritty union hard-hats in the dreary 6-mile-long steel mill. Plant Manager John Goodwin—operating outside US Steel's corporate culture, if not quite breaking its rules—had improved other plants by unleashing hourly workers. Why not here? First one, then another—eventually five steelworkers were freed from mill jobs to visit automotive customers' plants and see problems for themselves.

Goodwin and other Managers stayed on the sidelines. The union crew was generally free to change how steel was made, stored and shipped so that 50-ton rolls and quarter-ton sheets arrived at customers' plants in better shape.

They demanded rubber pads on flatbed trucks to cushion the steel. They created plastic rings to protect the rolls from crane damage. They persuaded workers who package and load each roll or stack to take responsibility for its condition by signing a tag attached to the shipment.

The result: Automotive customers, who buy almost half of Gary Works' steel, now reject just 0.6%, down from an industry worst 2.6% in 1987.

"When you hear right from the customers that you made a difference, that's the deal", says Jeff Grunden, co-ordinator and pioneer member of the quality team.

Gary Works' trip from unwanted to almost indispensable won its problem solving team the RIT/USA Today Quality Cup for manufacturing.

"I can't tell you how excited I am", says Quality Cup judge Thomas Johnson, quality management professor at Portland State University's business school. "Its Gary, Ind. It's US Steel. It's not Nagoya, Japan".

It's important to keep the victory in perspective. Big Steel lost US$2.5 billion last year, second only to a record loss of US$4.1 billion in 1986. US Steel's portion of the red ink: US$507 million last year. It won't break out Gary Works' results. The market is tough enough this year that steel makers haven't enforced a 3% price hike planned for

April 1. They also lost a hedge against foreign steel when important restraints expired last week.

Gary Works—which accounts for 60% of US Steel's shipments—"is a bright spot in a dim industry", says Quality Cup judge Mark Gavoor, quality trainer at Colgate-Palmolive.

Gary Works' quality improvement program differs from many because it was created from, and continues to be built on, the experience and intuition of hourly workers battling to save their plant, their jobs, their way of life. It did not flow from force-fed quality improvement classes or text books. But neither is it a by-guess and by-gosh effort. In the best tradition of statistical process control, computers measure every variation and tolerance at the plant so workers know when something is too hot, too thick, or too slow and where the problem is. Ford, which nearly flunked the plant in 1987, last year gave it the Q1 award as a high quality supplier. "I'm amazed at what these guys have done. It's a breakthrough", says Ron Wallace, Manager of Ford's nearby Chicago Heights stamping plant, where sheets of Gary steel are formed into doors and fenders in huge presses. "We'd have instances of breakages where we'd get the Managers, the engineers, the metallurgists working on it. Then the (Gary Works and Ford) hourly guys would come in and get their heads together, and the problem would go away", he says.

The problem solving team of hourly workers was the brainchild of Gary Works quality Manager George Lukes and plant Manager Goodwin. They came to Gary in 1987 to a plant just coming off a six-month strike. Morale was so bad and so much money was being lost that Gary Works was considered US Steel's equivalent of Siberia. Goodwin and Lukes fixed some manufacturing bottlenecks to speed production, a gesture of fantastic optimism at the time. Then, Goodwin brought in a parade of unhappy customers to convince the 7,850 plant workers that business as usual would mean no more business. Then, hourly worker Bill Barath, now retired, was pulled from his galvanising job applying anti-corrosion coating at the end of the Gary steel line and was sent to Ford's Chicago Heights plant to eyeball the steel.

He found a galvaniser's nightmare: flaking zinc. Steel he so carefully coated at Gary was shedding its anti-corrosion skin like a snake when Ford formed it into fenders and doors.

Barath knew instantly: too much zinc build-up on the edges of the steel. The rods that trim it off at the mill were out of whack. Barath took that intelligence back to the mill, and an amazing thing happened under the new Management. The problem got fixed. Right now. No tangled bureaucracy, no scapegoating. Word spread, and other auto plants demanded Gary Works' liaisons. Even GM came around and has increased Gary Works purchases fivefold since 1987.

"These are line workers in the steel industry, supplying the auto industry. I can't think of two more battered industries. They've really pushed this idea of empowerment down where it belongs", says Gavoor. "That's the spirit of American industry that's coming back, and people don't know".

CONSOLIDATION

Introduction

You have now completed this book. It is time to critically assess your own view on TQM. The aim of this exercise is to establish what you have learnt about TQM and what your current opinion is concerning its general applicability as the management philosophy for the third millennium.

Your Task

Set aside about 1 hour in a quiet place. Ensure you have a pad of paper and a pen, but nothing else. Spend about 20 minutes writing down in note form the key features of TQM, those that you would wish to get across in a short presentation. Spend about 20 more minutes noting down your opinion about the strengths and weaknesses of each key feature. Finally, answer to yourself the question—'Is TQM the management philosophy for the third millennium?'

FURTHER READING

● In this chapter a number of exercises and games have been presented. They focus on the contents of this book. This strengthens the book and helps to raise awareness of difficult issues that will need to be managed when implementing quality ideas. Implementing quality management does, however, demand a thorough programme of development for all members of the organisation. Many consulting companies are eager to sell this training. I recommend detailed reference be made to the literature on training and development before any training programme is bought-in or started. This will make it more likely that an adequate programme is embarked upon. The following texts are recommended:

Robinson, K. R. (1988) *Handbook of Training Management*, Kogan Page, London.
Stewart, J. (1991) *Managing Change Through Training and Development*, Kogan Page, London.
Thomas, B. (1992) *Total Quality Training*, McGraw-Hill, New York.

Index